AF540927

THE LAST DANCE OF RATIONALITY

THE LAST DANCE OF RATIONALITY

Making Sense of an Unravelling World Order

ROHIT PRASAD

First published in 2023 by Hachette India
(Registered name: Hachette Book Publishing India Pvt. Ltd)
An Hachette UK company
www.hachetteindia.com

1

ISBN 978-93-5731-275-2

For sale in the Indian subcontinent only

Hachette Book Publishing India Pvt. Ltd
4th & 5th Floors, Corporate Centre,
Plot No. 94, Sector 44, Gurugram 122003, India

Typeset in Dante MT Std 11/14.5
by R. Ajith Kumar, New Delhi

Printed and bound in India
by Manipal Technologies Limited

To Soham, Chaitanya and Sonali,
harbingers of a new age in my life.

CONTENTS

INTRODUCTION

With the US bitterly divided, an autocratic China unabashedly ascendant, and illiberal democracies the new flavour of governance, global politics has never been more unsettling, disorienting or uncomfortable.

With the planet facing a climate crisis, food systems exhibiting increasing fragility, and displacement of human settlements becoming a perennial reality, the human interface with nature has never been more unstable, unsustainable or unsteady.

With the Russian invasion of Ukraine arriving close on the heels of a global pandemic, cultural warriors asserting the imperative to recognize 72 genders[1] while conservatives double down on family values, the metaverse altering the nature of our physical realities* even as cryptocurrency threatens to uproot the foundations of our monetary systems, the world has never been more confusing, complex, or uncertain.

If you've ever caught yourself wondering, 'What's going on? How did we get here? Where might we be headed?', this book has some answers for you.

It characterizes present day events as a 'great unravelling'

---

* See Chapter 6.

in which our economic, political, social, technological, ecological and geopolitical systems are being refashioned into new configurations. The seismic changes reveal that the fundamental premises that have powered our world for over 350 years – reason, empirical observation, and individuality – have run their course and are in the process of being supplanted by new cognitive foundations.

The Great Unravelling

Despite remarkable progress across all dimensions – economic, political, social and technological* – our world is characterized by intense dualities of various kinds. The following are some of the noteworthy schisms that come to mind.

As of 2020, 56% of the world population lives in urban areas, up from only 34% in 1960.[2] The number of children dying before reaching the age of one fell from 15% in 1950 to 2.6% in 2022.[3] Global prosperity has never been more widespread,[4] with China and India emerging as drivers of global growth over the last several decades. And yet, inequality within countries[5] has become a major threat to the social fabric. Further, with global debt to GDP ratio rising to an unsustainable 350% of global GDP, the world is on the brink of a debt crisis.[6]

On the political front, it is heartening that in the twenty first century, the number of democracies has overtaken the number of autocracies.[7] But, with the world's pre-eminent democracy facing sizeable threats to its political system, and with the rise

* For a more comprehensive list of the achievements of our civilization, please see *Enlightenment Now: The Case for Reason, Science, Humanism and Progress* (London: Penguin UK, 2018) by Steven Pinker.

of electoral autocracies, i.e., democracies characterized by authoritarian regimes, the very model of democracy is under attack.

A wave of economic development in emerging economies has brought millions out of poverty. However, the hollowing out of the middle class across the world is depriving societies of the essential glue of social cohesion, exposing all sections of society to the risk of disorderly social transitions.

In a world built on the foundations laid by dazzling technological progress, continued innovation holds out the promise of being a panacea for all these problems. However, it poses even more thorny challenges as developments in artificial intelligence technologies have brought us within striking distance of creating algorithms that could seriously undermine human agency and put millions out of work.

With rapid developments in green energy technologies, it seems possible that the world could transition away from carbon-based energy systems dating back to the eighteenth century.[8] And yet, it is unlikely that the transition will take place at the pace needed to avert the ecological crisis that poses an existential threat to the human race.

Finally, the old geopolitics is giving way to a new alignment of powers that threatens the interconnected economic systems which have powered the greatest phase of economic growth the world has ever seen. This process is destabilizing not just the powers that are becoming less powerful, but also the newly emerging centres of gravity.

This book asserts that the multihued unravellings represent the last dance of 'the ideology of rationality', a worldview that evolved through a long arc of history that spans the European

Renaissance of the 1500s, the scientific and political revolutions of the 1600s and 1700s, and the waves of Industrial Revolutions that started in the mid-1700s.

The Ideology of Rationality

Starting from the mid-1500s, the radical social transformation referred to as the 'Enlightenment' sought to loosen the grip of three forces over human beings – organized religion, monarchy, and material want, which in its most extreme form took the shape of complete subjugation to the forces of nature. It replaced the received wisdom of scripture, the divine right of monarchs, and the tyranny of nature, often seen as an instrument of divine retribution, by a human-centred vision that presented the faculties of reason and observation as the new lodestars for human beings.

Over the years, a narrow interpretation of the faculty of reason, emphasizing the use of the mathematical principles of logic and probability in decision-making, was held up as the ideal.[9] The human being was conceived of as a 'tabula rasa', an empty slate, who could perfect himself* to express such universal faculties. The role of inborn qualities was discounted, and a universalist conception of the rational individual was perpetuated. In this book, the word 'rationality' refers to this prevalent interpretation of reason.

The emergence of reason and empiricism led to tremendous progress in science and technology, the constant regeneration of which became the 'bread of life' of the new world. The

---

* The enlightenment tended to be very male-centric.

dominance of science meant that decision-making across all realms of human activity – spiritual, temporal, commercial, social and personal – became infused with the ethic of rationality.

The institution of the market emerged as a natural mechanism to organize the activities of a growth-driven society. Over time, the reach of markets expanded, going beyond material objects of human consumption to include a wide array of emotional and spiritual requirements. Thus, the ideology of rationality became associated with the increasing 'marketization of life'.

Traditional cultures accorded a place of reverence to nature. However, the worldview driven by rationality failed to assign any value to natural bounty, or when it did so, was unable to recognize the deep interconnections between human beings and nature. Hence, the ideology of rationality became associated with an increasingly exploitative relation between human beings and nature.

With organized religion and the divinely anointed monarch fading away, sovereignty came to rest in the people at large. This gave birth to democracy.

The power of the people was meant to rein in the power of markets, and vice versa. However, an important building block of the cognitive superstructure of rationality is the conviction that the pursuit of self-interest in the context of markets leads to efficient outcomes. Adam Smith, a Scottish philosopher considered to be the father of modern economics, wrote in 1776: 'It is not from the benevolence of the butcher, the brewer, or the baker that we expect our dinner, but from their regard to their own interest... '[10] The fictional stock trader Gordon Gekko memorably said in the 1987 Hollywood blockbuster *Wall Street*, 'Greed, for lack of a better word, is good'. Thus, the ideology of rationality seemed to condone selfishness as a value consistent with the public good and tended to load the dice in favour of markets.

Many influential schools of economic theory proposed the redistribution of wealth as a way to ensure both efficiency and equity. But the sanctity of private property was a foundational premise of the philosophy and politics of Enlightenment. Naturally, the norm of equity fell by the way side.

The devaluation of ethics was another result of the Enlightenment worldview. Material progress replaced ethical norms, flowing from scriptural authority or the inner voice of conscience, as the proof of a life well lived. Consequently, the undermining of democratic institutions by a corrupt handshake between politicians and business leaders became an inevitable feature of societies driven by Enlightenment ideals.

While the philosophers of rationality emphasized the inalienable rights of an individual, societies powered by the ideology of rationality were rather contemptuous of the rights of non-Enlightenment cultures. Enlightenment values were spread with the zeal that had earlier been reserved for religion, with as little regard for the beliefs and values of other societies. Thus, the Enlightenment became militarized, as strong states backed by formidable arsenals attempted to spread the credo of the new age.

In sum, the ideology of rationality envisioned a predominance of logical reasoning in all spheres of individual life and brought every aspect of human affairs into the ambit of self-interested calculation through the operation of markets. It emphasized efficiency over ethics or equity and discounted the embeddedness of human beings in the natural world.

Simultaneously, it undermined the rights and beliefs of cultures other than its own, using a strong state backed by military might to spread its influence across the world.

The Imprints of Rationality in our Present Age

The consequences of the ideology of rationality as manifested in the world today can be understood by using a triad of concepts: structural duality, entanglement and complicity.

Structural Duality

The worldview of rationality led to the most dazzling phase of human material progress in recorded history. It was a progress fuelled by an extraordinary burst of creativity in science and social organization, but also by a rapacious exploitation of non-Enlightenment cultures and societies. In 1750, per capita industrialization levels were similar in the UK and India-Pakistan-Bangladesh, with the US lagging far behind.[11] By 1913, thanks to merciless economic and political exploitation, per capita industrialization levels in the UK were more than 50 times those in India-Pakistan-Bangladesh.[12] Meanwhile, the world had witnessed the first and second Industrial Revolutions powered by the steam engine and electricity, respectively.

As the list of the multiple types of unravelling mentioned earlier shows, the simultaneous occurrence of dazzling light and enveloping darkness remains a feature of the rationality-driven world to this day. In this book, this phenomenon is referred to not merely as a 'duality', a word which would be sufficient to indicate a coexistence of opposites. It is referred to as a *structural duality,* a phenomenon in which the extremes of the good and the bad are inevitable outcomes of the underlying processes.

Many refer to the persistent view that the 2020 US election was stolen,[13] or the increasing levels of wealth inequality, as avoidable irrationalities that can be separated from the great achievements of the Age of Rationality. They refer to the increasing prevalence of such phenomena as unfortunate manifestations of an Age of Unreason.* In contrast, this book characterizes the current time as the pinnacle of the Age of Rationality.

As the case studies covered in the book show, each unravelment bears the signature of the fundamental beliefs of this age – faith in free markets, breakdown of traditional community structures and customs, pride of place accorded to technology, primacy accorded to capitalism over democracy, and eagerness to impose a rational worldview on other cultures.

For instance, the crisis of democracy in the US is shown to be the result of unprecedented opening up of global labour markets that moved jobs to emerging economies, the abandonment of the working class by the government without the possibility of their being aided by community support systems, the facilitation of extremely fragmented echo chambers of opinion through technology, the justification of the highly divisive communication style of President Trump by his electoral success, and the attempts to bring China into the fold of the global democratic order helmed by the US.

---

* See for instance the remarks of the finance minister of Tamil Nadu, India, in a debate in the Oxford Union. It can be accessed at https://www.youtube.com/watch?v=U1r9v0soSaI. Similar sentiments are expressed by Harvard Professor Steve Pinker in his book *Rationality: What It Is, Why It Seems Scarce, Why It Matters* (London: Penguin, 2022).

Academic disciplines such as game theory have extensively explored the possibilities of the ideology of rationality leading to sub-optimal outcomes.[14] They have conceived of situations in which the pursuit of self-interest leads to high individual gains but generates losses that are distributed across the population with consequences that are catastrophic. An example of such a context is high industrial pollution.

Thus, both lived history and academic thinking show us that the ideology of rationality is perfectly consistent with the kinds of dualities we witness today. Indeed, these dualities are not aberrations of our current pattern of development, but rather an inherent structural outcome.

The unsustainability of these deep structural dualities is the strongest driver of the epochal shifts that are underway in our world.

Entanglement

In most crises, the wealthy and the privileged are able to use their power and position to remain unscathed. However, our moment in history is unique in the sense that escape is no longer possible, even for the upper crust.

The word *entanglement* means 'a complicated or compromising relationship or situation.'[15] I use this word to refer to the phenomenon of negative outcomes accruing to classes of people, enterprises, cities or countries that may be regarded as dominant or privileged in the prevailing order.

The loss of life among rich and poor during the COVID-19 pandemic is the most obvious testimony to the phenomenon of entanglement. But, as this book shows, entanglement is the thread running through phenomena as disparate as the US debacle in Afghanistan, the rise of Trump, the rapid adoption of cryptocurrency, the emergence of China as a geopolitical power, the divorce of Jeff Bezos, ecological disasters in the urban capitals of the world, and the global challenge mounted by governments against the overweening power of Big Tech.

This is not to say that inequalities do not exist or that different social groups possess similar abilities to respond to the emerging threats. Indeed, the development patterns of our times have been brutal on the masses. What's novel is that the processes of globalization, urbanization, democracy, technological progress and data proliferation have also started becoming inimical for entities that have gained the most from them, exhibiting new dynamics as they cross certain thresholds of scale or scope.

The book highlights these dynamics by delineating the channels through which seemingly insurmountable power structures crumble and fall – how protégé turns provocateur, concessions forced upon oppressors ('safety valves') become 'escape hatches' for liberation, technological development turns the tables on established power centres, and internecine warfare among the elites lays waste to carefully guarded citadels of privilege. And yes, as events in Afghanistan demonstrated, armed rebellions also play a role.

The phenomenon of entanglement is the surest indicator of the systemic unsustainability of the present pattern of development. In this book we will see that *entanglement* is a consequence of the *structural duality* that characterizes our age.

Complicity

The irony is that the *structural duality* is a result of a series of conscious choices made by those in the upper echelons of power keeping their best interests in mind. These 'rational' decisions have resulted in a slew of unintended consequences that collectively represent a repudiation of their will. In other words, not only are the elites entangled by the *structural duality*, but they have been actively involved in creating the conditions of their own entanglement.

In this book, the word used to describe their role is *complicity*. Complicity is defined as 'the fact or condition of being involved with others in an activity that is unlawful or morally wrong.'[16] The geo-political overreach of the US after the fall of the Soviet Union, or the incestuous links between elite scientists in virology research and academic journals, revealed in the aftermath of the pandemic, are instances of complicity. However, in our context, the word is not always used to connote illegal or immoral behaviour, although many instances of such actions are cited. Most commonly, I use it to refer to the self-serving belief in and operationalization of the ideology of rationality – the credo of the pursuit of self-interest, where 'self' is defined in narrow individualistic terms and 'interest' is limited to material interests without considering the emotional needs of a human being. A vast intellectual architecture has been put in place to argue that such an individualistic pursuit is consistent with, and in fact necessary for, the attainment of the public good.

The complicity of the elite in their own entanglement is the surest pointer that the cognitive foundations and incentive structures of the present pattern of development have long passed their usefulness. Indeed, the triad of structural duality, entanglement and complicity indicate that we are experiencing a collective action failure similar to the fabled prisoners' dilemma in game theory, in which the individual pursuit of self-interest leads to suboptimal outcomes for all concerned.

While the great unravelling appears to have suddenly come upon us, the present moment has actually been in the making for a long time. It has been fashioned by a set of interlocking narratives spanning disparate geographies, realms of human activity and serendipities.

Hence, we are led to examine our histories. These are not remote accounts of a distant past, but urgent narratives of recent times that illuminate our present as nothing else can. The book presents these histories through disparate case studies including the COVID-19 pandemic, the US debacle in Afghanistan, the rise of Trump, the appeal of Putin, the rapid adoption of cryptocurrency, the emergence of China as a geopolitical power, and the erosion of human relationships in the wake of sex-tech.

The Age of Meta-reason

The playwright Arthur Miller once wrote: 'An era can be said to end when its basic illusions are exhausted.'[17] This book argues that our multihued unravelments indicate that an era is ending because its basic illusions have outlived their purpose.

What will take its place? What happens in the long term, after the immediate changes resolve themselves? Is the Age of Rationality going to be followed by a regression into blind faith and superstition?

This book argues that we are at the dawn of the age of meta-reason, a worldview that acknowledges the immense potential of reason but also recognizes its absolute limits in mapping the immeasurable subjectivity of human existence. A fragment of this view had already been expressed by a philosopher regarded as part of the Enlightenment, the sceptic Immanuel Kant, who, in his three-volume work *Critique of Pure Reason*, had identified the 'transcendental' as a realm that reason was powerless to comprehend.[18] Beyond the transcendental, one must add ethics and social structure as two additional realms where reason has its limits, although it certainly has a role to play as a tool to gain knowledge even in these spheres.

The vacuum left by rationality will be filled by a variety of claimants ranging from the ridiculous to the sublime. These include superstition and blind faith on the one hand, and intuition, awareness and consciousness on the other. There will be a new humility towards knowledge systems not based in mainstream Enlightenment thought and, in parallel, attempts to explore the underlying logic of such systems. Traditional medicine would be a prime example of such a system. In the process, both quacks and charlatans, and seers and savants will gain ascendancy.

When one is talking of a transitioning age, what is important is not one's fancies about what needs to happen, but the appreciation that powerful forces bringing the new world into being have already been set into motion. As readers will see, my prognostications are based on a series of developments in the sciences and the humanities, including cognitive neuroscience, quantum science, and postmodern thought, on the emergence of new centres of economic power that are characterized by strong elements of non-Enlightenment thought, and on the new existential imperatives facing the human race, including the possibility of being displaced from the top of the food chain by algorithms.

The Age of Rationality gave primacy to the individual within a global world collective. The Age of Meta-reason is giving birth to a new collectivism which comprises small tribes of individuals, each of whom belongs to multiple such groups. These tribes extend across national borders, thus according to nations the status of just another tribe, albeit an especially powerful one. While the rules of the previous world order were based on the principle of efficiency, the new rules will focus on sustainability and identity.

In sum, this book examines an age characterized by a deep structural duality leading to the entanglement of the elites, an entanglement in which they are complicit on account of the key role they have played in generating the duality. The perpetuation of the worldview of rationality is the main element of their complicity. This confluence of factors suggests we are in the midst of an ongoing epochal shift, the last dance of rationality, which will give birth to the Age of Meta-reason, an age characterized by heightened clarity and confusion in equal measure.

Structure of the Book

The book is divided into two sections. The first section presents a narration of the relevant developments of the past seventy-five years up until the pandemic and the invasion of Ukraine.

It is organized as a series of case studies. The second section synthesizes the findings and presents some scenarios for the emerging epoch.

It is in the nature of the enterprise attempted in this book that the topics covered will represent a small subset of those that could or should have been covered, and that much will remain unsaid. One hopes, however, that the collection of cases is sufficient to clearly elucidate and establish the central theses of the book.

At the end, a small personal note. My first book, *Start-up Sutra* was suffused with optimism about the digital world coming into being through the power of human initiative. My second, *Blood Red River*, was a rather dark exploration about the ravages of extractive industries on communities living in mining zones. At the end of the two books I was left with a nagging sense of a lack of closure. What did I believe in – the promise of entrepreneurship or the destruction wrought by human greed? And then there was the rather reductive question, frequently asked even by well-wishers: 'So what's your solution to the darkness and the light?' It was a question I struggled to answer.

The writing of this book brought a kind of resolution. The extreme forms of both human ingenuity and greed are manifestations of the same overarching worldview, the ideology of rationality, an ideology that has enabled startling levels of progress, but is now collapsing under the weight of its own contradictions. This book is a depiction of these dissonances.

And for those with the questions about solutions, may I overturn the words of a rather influential thinker of the 19th century by saying: 'The philosophers have tried to refashion the world in various ways. However, given its complexity, the point, is to first be sure you have comprehended it.'*

* The philosophers have only *interpreted* the world, in various ways. The point, however, is to *change* it.
– Karl Marx, *Eleven Theses on Feuerbach*

SECTION 1

1

THE USA: A UNION DIVIDED

The last 30 years have seen the USA rise to the zenith of its power and become the world's unipolar hegemon. This ascent is the finest achievement of the age of rationality. However, ironically, all through this process it has been eaten from within by two sectors of the economy that are considered the most evolved manifestations of market-led innovation – finance and Big Technology. Together, these two sectors have left the US a nation divided, with its democracy facing threats not seen since the American Civil War that lasted from 1861–65.

As you go through the account of this falling apart, notice how banks, driven by the promise of financial engineering and the pressures of democracy, have broken free of the traditional standards of responsible lending, how the consumption levels of households have decoupled from incomes based on global trade and unregulated loan markets, how businesses have broken free from the profit imperative, thanks to the backing of successful entrepreneurs – the evangelists of the new age, and how governments have shaken off the burden of facilitating better long-term economic outcomes for the working class through a combination of unfettered credit and diversionary access to technology. In sum, society is anchored only by the chimerical dream of technological progress, a hyper-advanced operationalization of the ideology of rationality.

On 6 January 2021, after a rally of close to 1,00,000 people, a group of 2,000 protestors, incited by the 45th President of the United States, Donald Trump, attacked the US Capitol, the building where the US Congress sits. Trump was trying to overturn the results of presidential elections held in November 2019 where he had been defeated by the candidate of the Democratic Party, Joe Biden. He and his Republican Party colleagues had been repeatedly asserting that the election was rigged. A slew of court cases and investigations carried out by states, including some run by Republican governments, found no basis to the allegations.

Nevertheless, Trump continued to assert that the election had been 'stolen'.[1] As a result, the Trump supporter base was in a highly inflamed state on 6 January, the day the Congress met to certify the results.

The Make America Great Again (MAGA) movement had planned a million strong march to the Capitol building. The march was preceded by a rally on The Ellipse, a 52-acre park located close to the White House. The rally was addressed by Donald Trump, his lawyer Rudy Giuliani, Republican Senator Josh Hawley, and Trump's National Security Advisor, Michael Flynn.

Trump addressed the crowd: 'We're going to walk down to the Capitol and we're going to cheer on our brave senators and Congressmen and women.'[2] He exhorted his supporters 'to fight'. 'We will never give up, we will never concede,' he declared. After listening to such rhetoric for about 50 minutes, some flag-waving supporters began moving towards the Capitol Hill which became the scene of unprecedented mayhem.

The protesters forced their way through police barricades and strode into the building, entering the lawmakers' chambers. Under the circumstances, the certification process had to be summarily stopped. Vice President Mike Pence and members of the Congress were evacuated to a makeshift chamber where they remained for close to six hours before they reconvened to complete the counting of the electoral votes. One civilian was shot dead. A police officer lost his life.

Given the symbolism of the Capitol building, it was not cement and stone walls that had been breached. It was the ramparts of liberty that had fallen.

One might have thought that the outrageousness of the act would have triggered a reasoned response that put a stop to actions that had already put American democracy in peril. And that, finally, there would be a widespread acceptance of the election results.

But nothing of the sort happened. Trump continued to peddle his lies. The Republican Party, by and large, continued to support him, and the majority of Republican supporters continued to believe that the election was compromised.

Given these trends, it is quite likely that a large mass of voters will view the next presidential election as suspect. The world's flagship democracy is not in a pretty place, to say the least. And the nation, as a whole, is not just divided but highly polarized with very little middle ground to speak of. This chapter is a telling of how the US arrived at this impasse.

The Rise of High Finance and the Splintering of the American Dream

Many who formed part of the mob at the Capitol were among those famously referred to as 'the deplorables' by the 2016 Democratic presidential candidate, Hillary Clinton. Donald Trump had stormed to power as the 45th president of the United States on the back of their disaffection. They were the Trump voters – people who seem to be the very antithesis of the Silicon Valley elites and the Wall Street titans. Except that both technology-entrepreneurs as well as financial whiz kids owe their meteoric rise in no small measure to them. And they, in turn, have drawn their fuel from the actions of the elites.

Let's see how.

Outsourcing

The story starts in the 1980s with a marriage made in heaven – between the Chinese Communist Party under Deng Xiaoping and the US multinational corporations (MNCs).

The world had somehow gone past the tumultuous decade of the seventies when rising prices of crude oil and growing tensions in the Middle East halted the two decades of the golden age of capitalism following World War II (WWII). The Information and Communications Technology (ICT) revolution was on its way. The growing ease of communication meant that production processes could be unbundled and distributed across the globe to take advantage of cheap labour.

The country that gained the most from this development was China. By then, it had made a definite shift away from the doctrinaire communism of Mao to the pragmatism of Deng who created enclaves of economic freedom even as he maintained the political power of the Communist Party.[3] With a well-fed and literate population, China had a labour force ready to contribute to world markets. In 1972, Nixon had fashioned a détente between China and the USA to create a schism in the erstwhile monolithic Communist Bloc headed by the Soviet Union. In 1980, the US had accorded China the status of Most Favoured Nation (MFN) with respect to bilateral trade relations.[4]

The US MNC made the most of the opening up of China. It had already emerged as a force to reckon with in the two decades following WWII. However, its activities had remained limited to the advanced countries. From the 1980s, MNCs began to expand their sphere of operation to the emerging economies.[5] The untapped economies of China, India, Brazil, and Eastern Europe represented undreamt of possibilities. As Jack Welch, the iconic CEO of General Electric (GE) once said: 'If GE's strategy of investment in China is wrong, it represents a loss of a billion dollars, perhaps a couple of billion dollars. If it is right, it is the future of this company for the next century.'

Over the next three decades, the gross domestic product (GDP) per capita of the Chinese economy would grow at close to 9% per year, a miracle for a country of its size and history of anaemic growth.[6] A significant aspect of China's economic boom was the scale and strategic importance of production activities of newly opened branches of US MNCs, producing for the Chinese market, or using the Chinese economy to produce finished goods for nearby markets. The flip side of this development was that production that could have taken place within the US moved to China.

Indeed, the increasing power of China was intimately interconnected with the declining fortunes of the American working class. Besides the large-scale outsourcing of manufacturing jobs to China (and later to other emerging economies), the increasing proportion of white-collar jobs in the workforce, the rise of automation, and the increasing heft of corporations are believed to be the main causes of the decline in the power of the American worker. The number of workers enrolled in unions declined by more than 10% from 1980 to 1990, reaching levels even lower than those of the 1950s.[7]

According to a 2017 National Bureau of Economic Research (NBER) Working Paper,[8] the lifetime income of the American worker has been in decline since the 1970s. The median 'real wage', i.e., wage adjusted for inflation, fell continuously, although the real income of women and of workers in higher income percentiles increased. In the 1970s, household earnings increased due to the increasing participation of women in the workforce, but this effect ceased to operate in the 1990s.

Further, American workers at the bottom of the pyramid were losing out to immigrants from Asia and Latin America, who took over some of the low-skilled jobs. This effect was especially pronounced in certain regions such as Florida and evoked a heightened emotional reaction due to the phenomenon of illegal immigration.[9]

Meanwhile, the American corporation grew not just in terms of expansion to new geographies but also in terms of market dominance within the US market.

The breakup of the telecom giant American Telephone and Telegraph Company (AT&T) in 1982 marked the end of an aggressive phase of antitrust enforcement. The new regulatory approach was inspired by University of Chicago's ideological position that bigger is better, or at least, it need not be worse. Between 1982 and 2012, industry concentration, as measured by an index called the Herfindahl-Hirschman Index (HHI), increased by 416% in retail, by 135% in finance, by 47% in services, and by 37% in utilities. From 1996 to 2016, according to a report by Credit Suisse, the number of companies on the stock market fell by half.[10] Today the US has only four major airlines, four major telecommunication carriers, three major drug stores, and just two major beer manufacturers.[11]*

How was such a long-lasting decline in the economic fortunes of such a large number of people alongside increasing prosperity for a relatively tiny elite possible in a well-functioning democracy? Are such outcomes not usually associated with authoritarian regimes such as Russia, China, and Saudi Arabia?

Rise of the Liberal Consensus

In the US and UK, the Keynesian consensus that emphasized the key role of government spending and welfare state had been shattered by the period of stagflation of the 1970s, i.e., a phase when the US economy saw a combination of high inflation and stagnant growth.[12] Its successor, the 'rational expectations' school helmed by Nobel Prize winner Robert Lucas asserted that workers, as rational beings, would anticipate the higher prices that would result from any expansionary policy by the

* For a slightly technical discussion of increasing market concentration, see 'Are US Industries Becoming More Concentrated' by Gustavo Grullon, Yelena Larkin and Roni Michaely published in *Review of Finance*, Volume 23, Issue 4, 697–743, July 2019.

treasury or central bank. In response, they would negotiate for higher wages. As a result, the national income would remain unchanged, but prices would rise. Hence, any government or central bank intervention, far from being beneficial, would be counterproductive. In any case, the unfettered workings of markets would eliminate any involuntary unemployment. Thus, policy intervention was both unnecessary and harmful. In other words, the need for the welfare state was merely a figment of imagination of those wedded to unsound ideas or driven by vested interests. This policy stance is referred to as the 'liberal consensus'.

This ideology found able flag bearers in the charismatic US President, Ronald Reagan and UK's Prime Minister, 'Iron Lady' Margaret Thatcher. Thatcher asserted, 'There is no such thing as society: there are individual men and women, and there are families,'[13] meaning thereby that the state bore limited responsibility even for the basic needs of the citizenry at large. Across the Atlantic, Ronald Reagan declared in his 1984 political campaign, 'It's morning again in America,'[14] suggesting that Americans were back to work after the crippling recession of the 1970s. Unfortunately, that morning had little place for the American worker as American jobs were headed eastward.

By the end of Reagan's term, the liberal consensus had acquired so much heft, that the Democrat Bill Clinton fought and won the 1992 election as a 'new democrat', a political persona that adopted a position similar to market-friendly Republicans while differing on social issues like abortion and gun control.

However, the working class could not be mollified by ideology alone. They needed access to material goods and services as well, if not via their own income, then via the extension of credit. Thus, the political elite and the surging financial services industry found common cause in subprime lending, i.e., lending to households with sub-standard credit ratings, principally to help them buy homes. The rate of growth of household debt picked up pace in the mid-1990s reaching a high of 100% of the GDP in 2008. The foundation of this acceleration of household indebtedness was laid by a savings glut in a faraway country and by the mobilization of those savings to finance consumer lending in the US.

The Flow of Chinese Savings to the US

One of the persistent puzzles of the Chinese growth story is the high level of savings by households, corporations, and the government. The level of savings has ranged between 34–53% of the GDP over the past four decades.[15] In other words, on an average, the Chinese have been saving 34–53% of their annual incomes! In contrast, saving rates in other emerging economies such as Brazil, India, and Russia have hovered between 20% to 35%.

The unusually high savings rate has been attributed to a number of causes – suppression of wages and interest costs by an authoritarian government to keep corporate profits high, increased efficiencies following privatization resulting in high business surpluses, high tax rates, and so on. Many commentators have also emphasized the link between high savings and high levels of inequality in China. As per this thesis, the high savings rates are a result of the concentration of income and wealth in the hands of a few which creates a high propensity to save.

The relative importance of the different factors need not concern us here. For our purposes, there are two relevant points. First, a large amount of surplus savings remained in the economy despite high levels of domestic investment. This is referred to as a 'savings glut'. Second, these surplus savings were roughly equal to the export surpluses, and became available to finance the consumption of deficit households in the US. Here's how.

The surplus dollars of Chinese exporters (China's exports minus imports) would normally be converted into Chinese currency at a foreign exchange bank. This process would drive up the cost of Chinese currency vis-à-vis the dollar and hurt Chinese exports. However, instead of letting dollars be converted on the market, the People's Bank of China (PBC) printed domestic currency and used it to buy the dollars from the Chinese exporter at the existing yuan-dollar exchange rate. This prevented an appreciation in the value of the yuan. The PBC then invested a sizeable proportion of the dollars in the most reliable investment instrument in the world – US treasury securities, the loan instruments issued by the US government. This ensured a high flow of savings into the US economy, thus keeping interest rates in the US low and incentivizing borrowing by US households which in turn enabled them to buy consumer goods, durables, and homes. We can think of it this way – the Chinese government kept the Chinese worker in a fairly impecunious state so that the American worker, also impoverished relative to their wealthy US compatriots,* could borrow money cheaply, acquire material possessions (including

* Although not impoverished in relation to the Chinese worker.

homes and Chinese imports) and thereby, not feel the pinch of the worsening labour market conditions.

But there was much more to the increase in household debt in the US than the inflow of Chinese savings – the brave new world of financial engineering and a bipartisan consensus. Starting from the 1970s, cutting across party lines, Republican and Democratic governments passed legislation, set up institutions, and eased regulation for the financial-services industry to achieve relaxed credit standards for consumer lending.

Bipartisan Agenda on Home Ownership

Home ownership has always been an integral part of the American dream. The agendas of both Republican and Democratic governments have facilitated the provision of cheap credit for American home buyers. For instance, in 1933, the landmark Glass-Steagall Act passed after the Great Depression especially incentivized banks that gave loans to home buyers.

Conditions in the primary mortgage market in which originators of home loans extend credit to home buyers were eased by creating a vibrant secondary market for mortgages, meaning that banks originating the home loans could easily sell the mortgages to other entities. Two government backed institutions, Fannie Mae and Freddie Mac, were created in 1938 and 1970 respectively to buy home mortgages from home loan originators. They provided finance to banks for onward lending to home buyers or bought the portfolio of home loans already originated by banks. This increased the liquidity available to banks and helped them to lend more. On account of their government backing, Fannie Mae and Freddie Mac were able to raise money from bond markets at significantly lower rates of interest. They were also allowed to 'securitize' the mortgages they acquired, i.e., they could combine mortgages to create new assets with reduced risk. These assets were sold to investors at healthy premiums, thus further increasing their ability to buy mortgages from banks (how this happened will be explained in detail in a later section).

In the primary mortgage market, a series of amendments in the Community Reinvestment Act (CRA), 1977, served to push loans to subprime borrowers, i.e., borrowers with less than standard credit ratings. The CRA was originally put in place in 1977 to prevent the practice of 'redlining' under which banks would not extend credit to any household in low-income neighbourhoods even if it had received a good credit appraisal. The aim was to ensure that credit-worthy borrowers did not suffer on account of living in low-income neighbourhoods.

In the first decade of its existence, the CRA operated in a hands-off way and didn't have much of an effect. Then, in 1989, Republican President George H.W. Bush signed into law the Financial Institutions Reform Recovery and Enforcement Act (FIRREA) which required regulators to issue public performance evaluations of banks. Such public scrutiny resulted in additional pressure on banks to issue more loans to low-income borrowers, which often entailed relaxing the lending standards. Shortly thereafter, to address bank fears that the low-income lending would cause unacceptable levels of risk in the banking system, Fannie Mae and Freddie Mac pushed harder to buy mortgages from home loan originators. They were betting that securitization would allow them to create value from sub-standard loan assets.* This was the beginning of subprime lending.

In 1995, Democratic President Bill Clinton rewrote the CRA, putting added pressure on institutions such as Freddie Mac and Fannie Mae to lend in low-income neighbourhoods. This came a year after the signing of the North American Free Trade Agreement (NAFTA) that cost the US close to 4,00,000 manufacturing jobs.[16] Thus, the easing of lending standards went hand in hand with worsening income prospects.

The push for laxity in lending standards was not merely a preoccupation of politicians interested in securing their votes while also keeping powerful monied interests happy. The central bank, usually the custodian of sound macroeconomic sensibilities, had got into the act as well. In 1998, Fed Governor Laurence H. Meyer addressed a conference of bankers on the CRA where he praised low or no down payments and up to 100% loan-to-value ratios on home loans.[17]

In late 2000, the Clinton administration asserted that at 67.2%, the home ownership rate was the highest ever recorded, with almost nine million more home owners than in 1993, partly on account of its funding of insurance schemes for subprime mortgages.[18] The Republican President George W. Bush, Clinton's successor, made a strong push for expanding home ownership among minority groups. The initiative furthered his ambition to expand the appeal of the Republican party among those groups as well as keep his biggest donors happy. He asked

---

* The first mortgage-backed securities were created in 1970 at the Government National Mortgage Association (Ginnie Mae) by packaging securitized mortgage loans. Fannie Mae and Freddie Mac were quick to follow suit in the nationwide push to foster homeownership.

for a mortgage policy that required no low-to-no documents and the elimination of down payments, 'We certainly don't want there to be a fine print preventing people from owning their home,' he said in a speech in 2002.[19] In this manner, the tango between presidents cutting across party lines successfully decoupled home ownership from the broad-based growth of incomes.

The series of steps to relax lending standards only took off in the 2000s because in the 1990s investors and speculators were preoccupied with the internet bubble. They weren't fascinated by mortgage-backed securities emanating from home loans just yet. Further, in the wake of the dot-com bust, a shrinking consumer asset base created a demand for loans collateralized by home-equity. Households switched from expensive credit card debt to cheap home mortgages.

A NBER study of the CRA[20] between 1999 to 2009 showed that in the period preceding the inspection by the Fed, lending was elevated on average by about 5% every quarter and loans in these quarters defaulted about 15% more often. In other words, the CRA actually inflated lending quantities and reduced lending standards.

This, then, was the blueprint of how the world's largest democracy continued to function with increasing inequality. The key factors were the rise of a liberal consensus regarding the efficacy of markets, the flow of Chinese savings into the US that created a low-interest-rate environment, the bipartisan consensus on aggressive household lending especially for home purchases, and the conviction that financial engineering could enable lending to low-income households without an unacceptable increase in risk.

The bewildering value chain of financial engineering embroiled households from around the world in its net. We will cover the regulatory relaxations that facilitated the system in Chapter 3. Here, a scenario of how it affected households, not just in the US but over the world, will be presented. The extent of the spread of the system will convey why the level of outrage was so high after the system came crashing down in 2008, with no apparent downsides for those at the helm.

Financial Engineering and the American Dream

Let's take the case of Joe Blow, a hard-working long-distance lorry driver from Connecticut who has put his savings into Century International, a small 'thrift' that originates loans to home buyers. Century gives a home loan to Melinda, an owner of a family farm on which she wants to build a homestead. Melinda is a subprime borrower, i.e., she does not have much of a credit history. But Century does not have to bother about collection. It sells Melinda's loan (and those of others like her) to Bank of America. So now Melinda owes money to BofA.

The BofA bundles such loans and creates assets whose ratings are higher than those of any of the underlying loans. The technique involves more than just diversifying the risk across a bunch of loans with differing risk profiles. It involves creating asset classes with different priorities for payment.

To show how this works, let's make a simplifying assumption that BofA bundles together 100 loans with identical risk profiles. By virtue of owning the hundred loans, BofA is entitled to a certain stream of income from the repayment of those loans. It can create new assets by defining priorities with regard to the claims on this income stream.

Let's say, the topmost asset class is defined as one which will pay its holder their entire dues if any 10 of the hundred repay. The second-in-priority asset class is defined as one which will pay its holders their entire dues if any 20 of the 100 repay. If only 16 repay, the holders of the top asset class will receive their entire dues, while the holders of the second asset class will receive 60% of their entire dues. In this way a series of asset classes can be created all the way up to the asset class which pays in entirety only if all 100 borrowers repay.

If recovery rates on subprime loans are 80–90%, the holder of the top two asset classes can be certain they will receive the entirety of their claims. So, these assets are very valuable, triple A in quality. On the other hand, the asset class that is lowermost in priority is worth very little, if anything at all.

The BofA sells such assets to investment banks like JPMorgan while holding on to some, often lower in priority, itself. Thus, a large part of the loans moves off their books on to the books of investment banks. Now 'Melinda plus' (the cohort of borrowers in the bundle of 100 loans) owes money to BofA as well as the investment banks who bought the newly engineered assets from BofA.

The investment bank holds on to a large number of assets and sells the rest to investors around the globe including pension funds, insurance companies, and family offices. Now the dues of 'Melinda plus' are owed to pension funds, insurance companies, and family offices around the globe* as well.

---

* An interesting sidelight of the system was that many insurance companies that had invested in mortgage-backed securities also sold policies protecting the value of mortgage-backed securities to banks and other institutions. Thus, they were both investors and insurers. It was like a fire insurance company taking out insurance policies on a house it partly owns.

Let's extend the example to include the Macrons, a middle-class family in France, that had been investing their hard-earned savings in a pension fund for their retirement. The Siegels in Germany had bought an insurance policy for similar reasons. Thus, the fate of these households depended on the repayment made by 'Melinda plus', at least to an extent that the assets were sold to pension funds and insurance companies. One would think that since the fates of these ordinary households was linked with the ability of powerful investment banks who also held assets with similar priorities to collect their share of earnings from 'Melinda plus', all would be well.

But there was a catch. The health of investment banks did not depend on their ability to collect from people like Melinda. They had already made their money by 'flipping' the assets, i.e., selling them forward to pension funds and insurance companies, at higher prices. And their rates of return were astronomical because they had high leverage ratios, i.e., most of their investment was financed by funds borrowed from banks. For instance, at the time of its bankruptcy, Lehman Brothers had a leverage ratio of 30:1.[21] So, if Lehman bought an asset for $31, $30 was coming from banks and bank depositors. If an insurance company bought the asset for $33 in two months, Lehman made $2 on their equity investment of $1, a 100% return in two months! So, the repayment of dues became incidental.

Why did the prices of these assets rise? As house prices rose, people like Melinda (remember her, the original recipient of the home loan) were able to use the higher house prices (referred to as 'home equity') to borrow money to repay their previous loans. So, while before the price rise, one may have expected 20% of borrowers to default, the price rise resulted in lowering the expectation of default based on the ability to raise new loans to repay the old loan. This resulted in an increase in the prices of the assets, especially those lower down in the priority order.

But financial returns are not made by waiting till home prices rise in order to buy assets. They go to those who buy assets *in anticipation* of future increases in home prices. Hence, buyers of assets were making bets that home prices would continue to increase, thereby allowing asset classes with lower priorities to avoid default.

Since home prices can't rise forever, this bet became increasingly risky.

A steady rise in world fuel prices during 2003–07 (caused in large part by rising demand from emerging economies such as China) reduced real incomes and the ability of borrowers like Melinda to pay their debt service obligations. In 2006, the Fed started raising interest rates in response to the housing bubble. These developments raised doubts about the possibility of continued rise in home prices.

Up to that point, the price of mortgage-backed securities and homes had enjoyed a mutually reinforcing effect. An expectation of a rise in home prices increased the price of mortgage-backed securities. Conversely, an increase in the price of mortgage-backed securities also resulted in a greater amount of home loans, thus shoring up home prices.

The risk with such mutually reinforcing forces is that they act powerfully in the reverse direction as well. So, it was no surprise that when conditions started worsening, the housing market as well as the market for mortgage-backed securities came crashing down even faster than they had risen. A vicious cycle of falling home and asset prices was triggered.

This led to panic as financial derivatives were perceived to have become unviable. As the value of these assets declined, the financial condition of a variety of investors including pension funds, insurance companies, and investment banks became precarious. This led to the panic selling of derivative securities, leading to further decrease in their prices. As the health of investors like JPMorgan worsened, the condition of banks like BofA became fragile. The superstructure of financial derivatives built upon deregulation unravelled and collapsed.

Consequently, the small originators of home loans such as Century International to whom Joe Blow, the original protagonist in our story, had lent his hard-earned savings, started becoming insolvent, as they could no longer find banks to whom they could sell their subprime loans. Thus, people like Joe found their deposits increasingly difficult to access.

Countries across the globe including Canada, France, Germany, Japan, Switzerland, and the UK, that were exposed to the derivatives faced economic stress. In the US alone, the crisis led to the loss of 8.6 million jobs.[22]

After the system crashed, the Fed stepped in to buy the mortgage-backed securities, and the Treasury injected close to $475 billion into rescuing distressed institutions and home owners under the Troubled Asset Relief Program (TARP).[23] This included the banks and financial institutions primarily responsible for the crisis such as Citigroup, JPMorgan Chase & Co., Bank of America, Morgan Stanley, and Goldman Sachs Group Inc. Fannie Mae and Freddie Mac needed a bailout of $187 billion of US taxpayer money.[24]

The justification for the bailout was that the institutions were 'too big to fail', that allowing them to fail would bring down the entire macroeconomy, and hence, it would be like cutting your nose to spite your face. Though much of the money has been paid back through a restoration of growth patterns of the financial sector that remain largely unchanged after 2008, the fact is that the fundamental rule of capitalism that failure should have its consequences seems to have been given the go-by.

A year after the onset of the crisis, financial executives were back to a business-as-usual scenario. In 2009, the year after the financial sector was bailed out by taxpayer money, employees at Wall Street financial firms earned more than $20 billion in bonuses.[25] The only casualties seemed to be the millions whose homes had been lost. In 2008 alone, homes with at least one foreclosure filing tripled from 7,17,522 in 2006 (0.6% of all housing units) to 2,330,483 (1.8% of all housing units).[26]

But, after a tiny blip, for the executives of Wall Street, it was just another day in paradise.

The Ascendancy of Big Tech and the Schisms in American Society

The innovations devised by the financial elite averted the political fallout of income inequality for a while. But the 2008 financial crisis showed that the financial fix could not last forever. In fact, when the entire ecosystem of relaxed lending standards finally came undone, it created financial distress of a magnitude that made the inequity of the underlying trajectory of development all too clear.

Naturally, the financial crisis and its aftermath grabbed the attention of the world. But, in parallel, there was a political hailstorm brewing in the crucible of technology.

The Third Industrial Revolution

The development of digital telecommunications and computing started in the 1960s and became a part of mainstream life by the 1980s. It has been described as the third industrial revolution after the development of the steam engine and electricity.[27] There were three main dimensions of the technological developments: personal computing, mobile telephony, and the internet. These dimensions converged over the 1990s and 2000s as the handheld device became a phone, computer, and internet terminal – all rolled into one.

The value generated by the internet for end users included the ability to easily access and share content, create and connect with communities, and buy and sell goods and services at a global level. It was the content-creation and community-building potential that became political game changers. The warp speed with which they became commonplace in everyday living played a decisive role in their impact.

The Human-Assisted Acceleration of Technological Development

In just over a decade and a half, by 2010, the internet and the mobile phone were all but ubiquitous in the US. Over 75% of Americans had access to the internet[28] and the number of mobile subscriptions per 100 inhabitants stood at 92.[29] The percentage of American households with a personal computer at home was also 75%.[30] The smartphone penetration rate crossed 50% in 2014.[31] The number of monthly active users of Facebook in US and Canada combined crossed 200 million in 2014,[32] over 60% of the population.

The digital world was developing at an awe-inspiring pace. This development, apparently emerging from a perfect storm of scientific development, entrepreneurship, and financing had an air of inexorability about it. However, institutional structures in the financial services industry and the pattern of income distribution that had emerged after the 1980s had, in fact, a lot to do with the speed of the unfolding events.

The internet is characterized by network economies, the phenomenon of benefits to users increasing with the addition of new subscribers. For instance, a social network such as Facebook becomes more valuable for each user with an increase in the number of users, on account of the increasing number of people that can be reached. Therefore, competition on the internet resembles winner-take-all contests, with each firm trying to achieve a critical mass of subscribers in the earliest possible time. In other words, the Holy Grail of an internet firm is 'eye balls', the number of people on their site and the amount of time they spent there.

It seems inevitable, given the inherent nature of the competitive dynamics, that many firms would choose to lose money for long periods of time in order to acquire critical mass at the soonest. And that is what seems to have happened. For instance, the poster boy of e-commerce, Amazon, racked up losses for its first six years of operation. This phenomenon was specially marked during the 1999 dot-com boom where startup companies would flaunt not just their losses but their revenue-free state as a badge of honour.

But social networks and e-commerce platforms were not the first examples of industries with network externalities. The plain old telephone service also became more valuable for each subscriber with every additional connection. Thus, it can also be said to exhibit the property of network externalities, albeit at a lower scale and a lower level of positive spillover effects across industries.* Similarly, the traditional video industry also exhibited this property – the triumph of VHS over Beta resulted from an earlier attainment of critical mass, not a superior technology.[33] Then why did the business model of telephone companies or video cassette recorder companies never get decoupled from earnings in the way the businesses of internet companies did?

The 20-year dream run of corporate America had created an enormous amount of wealth, driven mainly by sharp spikes in the market value of corporations and of residential housing.[34] Not only was there a dramatic increase in the total amount of wealth, but a sharp increase in wealth inequality. This inequality was not driven by differences in the economic performance of the top and bottom 20% of the population, but by differences between the top 20% and the middle 60%, as well as stark contrasts *within* the top 20%. Starting from 1979, while the incomes of the top 1% more than tripled, the incomes of the next 19% increased by only 91%, i.e., by less than double. There was a remarkable difference even within the top 0.1%, with the top 0.01% doing far better than the next

* For instance, the synergies between the fixed-line phone and traditional retail were far lower than those between mobile telephony and e-commerce.

0.09%.[35] Thus, by the 1990s, the US possessed a small cohort of extremely wealthy people surrounded by a stagnant middle class and a bottom 20% whose gains were negligible in relative terms.

These people wanted to give back to society, stay in touch with new developments, and provide mentorship as technology boomed with a new generation of entrepreneurs at the helm. And, of course, they wanted to continue to multiply their wealth. Hence, vast sums of private wealth were channelled through angel networks and private equity firms to enterprises in the so called 'new economy'. This kind of wealth was not available in the days of the plain-old telephone service.

Proponents of these developments characterized this inflow as 'patient capital' that did not require firms to show profits or even revenues in the near term, but aimed to make big returns by cashing out on the one out of 10 companies that would make it big. This was capital prepared to wait. This view of events casts the investor as a 'saint of the secular world', a sailor patiently steering society toward the high seas.

However, often, this capital did not have to exercise too much hermetic patience. As the liberal consensus led to a relaxation of the rules put into place after the Great Depression to curb speculative investment, the stock market boomed. The National Association of Securities Dealers Automated Quotations (NASDAQ) stock market index that is based on a portfolio of technology stocks rose from 2517 in August 1998 to 7315 in March 2000, an almost three-fold increase in just 19 months.[36] There was a spate of Initial Public Offerings (IPOs) of technology companies with valuations far beyond those warranted by fundamentals. In November 2015, Facebook crossed $300 billion in market capitalization, overtaking the 123-year-old GE after only 11 years of existence.

Early-stage investors cashed out from these IPOs if they had not already cashed out in the funding rounds (usually three to four in number) that preceded the IPO. The vast amount of wealth accruing to tech entrepreneurs and companies generated a fresh flow of capital for digital startups, thus creating a self-perpetuating cycle.

The Fed chose to ignore these developments. Alan Greenspan, the Fed Governor, argued that as long as asset price bubbles did not unduly affect the price of goods and services, i.e., there was low inflation, the central bank did not need to intervene. In taking such a stance, Greenspan implicitly condoned risky practices, such as buying stocks on the margin (borrowing to buy stocks and repaying by using the increase in stock prices), that had led to the stock market crash of 1929 that heralded the Great Depression.

The dot-com crash of 2000 led to a momentary fall in stock prices. However, the market index resumed its upward climb in August 2002 following a series of facilitative monetary policy measures under the new Fed Governor, Ben Bernanke. Similarly, the fall of stock market prices in the aftermath of the Great Financial Crisis was only momentary. The NASDAQ index increased from 1,781 in February 2009 to 15,940 in November 2021, an almost nine-fold increase.

Thus, high levels of inequality and speculation from the angel investment stage to the IPO and beyond, facilitated by decisions of successive governors of the Fed, made large amounts of capital available to technology companies. The conditions were different in the decades that saw the growth of telephony or the video industry. Had telephone companies shown the revenue models and paths to profitability exhibited by the internet companies, they would soon have been shown the door by their financiers.

As a result, internet companies, unlike their predecessors in network industries, could adopt subscriber-acquisition strategies that were divorced from the spending capability of the subscriber. Even the cost of connectivity was rapidly dropping as infrastructure companies such as Cisco switched to valuations rather than profits as the metric of success.

The health of internet companies was also enhanced by competition regulators turning a Nelson's eye towards vertical mergers that allowed dominant firms in one industry, for instance internet search, to establish advantageous positions in complementary industries like the online travel brokerage service. In contrast, in 1982, AT&T had been broken up to prevent it from using its monopoly in the local phone market to establish a similar vice-like grip on the long-distance telephony market, thus promoting fair conditions for new entrants in that space.[37]

After firms had achieved a measure of success, ads constituted the major source of their resources. Using their vertically integrated structures and the possibilities of data mining provided by the internet, they developed highly sophisticated algorithms to target ads to users based on their behaviour patterns. By converting the everyday actions, expressions, and communications of consumers into predictions regarding whether site users would click on or buy things, firms were able to maximize ad revenues with questionable consequences for user privacy.

Consequently, people were able to access search engines, social networks, and a vast array of websites free of charge. From the user point of view, the great thing about all this 'freedom' was that, for a time, consumption levels with respect to the internet became decoupled from incomes. Whether or not the internet served the core needs of its users is a different question. For the time being, it was enough that it diverted, distracted, and entertained.

To summarize, in the early years of the new century, banks broke free from the traditional standards of responsible lending, consumption levels of households became decoupled from incomes, businesses were unshackled from profits, and governments were liberated from the burden of facilitating better long-term economic outcomes for the working class. Society and economy became untethered from any anchor save for the dream of technological progress.

Social Media and Trump

As social media sites acquired critical mass, they became a boon for entrepreneurs, innovative thinkers, and long-lost friends. If TV had afforded everyone 15 minutes of fame, Facebook gave people unlimited 'FaceTime'.

However, these sites also became havens for conspiracy theories, racist rants, nativist nattering, and psychological catharsis as people gravitated to insular cliques or 'echo chambers' that amplified biases and reinforced oddball, even extreme, worldviews, rather than exercising a moderating influence through the operation of social norms.

It is true that prior avatars of social media had also followed a familiar path – talk radio, cable news, and blogs were all once media-commanding integrated markets that over time broke up into increasingly niche segments.[38] However, they did not fragment the population at the speed of internet media sites on account of their much slower rates of diffusion. Further, internet sites were able to use algorithms to direct content precisely aligned to the user's past patterns of behaviour, thus creating sharper levels of polarization.

The 2008 presidential election had given the US its first African–American President. While Obama emerged as a symbol of hope that America could finally move beyond its deep racial divides, the reality was that for many the election represented an unacceptable secession of power to the Black community. His election became a lightning rod channelling ancient animosity into newly minted hatred.

A slow burning fault line was also emerging from the inexorable demographic shift of the US from a white to a non-white majority since 1950. In 2020, non-Hispanic white people, were still the majority race in the US, representing 59.7% of the population. Studies show that by 2045, this number will drop below 50%, making whites a minority.[39]

The multiple transitions – economic, political, and demographic, made rich fodder for online polarization.

Idiosyncratic outpourings are best expressed within the controlled environments of family, therapy, or circles of friends. When articulated in the context of the social media networks, they became smouldering embers waiting for a rabble rouser, a demagogue to set them ablaze.

What happened next had an air of inevitability about it. A businessman, formerly a bit player on the political landscape, began to acquire increasing heft. His name was Donald Trump.

The coming together of Trump and social networks was a marriage made in hell – or heaven, depending upon your point of view. A master manipulator of the human psyche, the real estate mogul from New York had an unerring instinct for igniting the meaner instincts of people, a scant regard for fact, and the firm conviction that his personal fortunes and the public good were perfectly congruent. In other words, he had all the qualities a rabble-rousing demagogue needed.

In 1949, in his introduction to *Prophets of Deceit*, Max Horkheimer noted 'demagogy makes its appearance whenever a democratic society is threatened with internal destruction [...] its function has always been [...] to lead the masses towards goals that run counter to their basic interests'.[40] And the demagogues that Horkheimer discussed did not even have access to Twitter.

In Twitter, Trump had a channel that would allow him to mainline 140-character stimulants to a public deprived of economic prospects, hungering for a home to call their own, and haunted by the nagging doubt that they had been left behind. Twitter gave Trump access to a public convinced that it needed to 'take back America', from the gaggle of illegal immigrant communities from far off places including India, China, and Lebanon. And from a Black President who allegedly was a 'Communist', a 'Muslim', an 'Arab', and not even born in the USA.*

* The 'birther' controversy movement, of which Trump was a prominent promoter, falsely alleged that Obama was not born in the US and therefore not eligible to run for office.

In Twitter, Trump had a tool that would allow his acolytes to amplify his throwaway pronouncements and diffuse them widely through an action as simple as pressing a 'like' button. In Twitter, Facebook, and Instagram, he had found his keys to the kingdom.

According to communications expert Panayota Gounari, the 140-character limit format of Twitter promotes a lean, anti-intellectual, decontextualized discourse in which fiction and fact, fact and opinion, opinion and reality, all meld to create a situation where all that counts is the identity of the person issuing the tweets. All that matters is whether the tweet comes from People Like Us (PLU) [41]. And Trump with his ability to apparently 'tell it like it is', to make a virtue of lack of civility, to model rage against the way things were, and present a one-point solution – himself – uncluttered with anything but the most rudimentary ideas ('build a wall'), was certainly PLU.

From 14 June 2014 to 3 November 2016, election day, he issued approximately 17,000 tweets, almost 19 a day.[42] He invoked racism, sexism, nativism, xenophobia, the China bogey, and the mistrust of politicians. He railed against Big Tech, promised to bring back jobs, and build a border wall to hold back the swarms of illegal migrants from Mexico. He insisted everything was broken, and that only he could fix the mess. Here are some of his tweets:

> 13 May 2015: TRAIN WRECK just the beginning. Our roads, airports, tunnels, bridges, electric grid – all falling apart. I can fix for 20% of pols<*sic*>, & better.[43]

> 29 May 2015: Wow, the economy is really bad! GROSS DOMESTIC PRODUCT down 0.7% in 1st. quarter - and getting worse. I TOLD YOU SO! Only I can fix.[44]

> 28 December 2015: Many of the great jobs that the people of our country want are long gone, shipped to other countries. We now are part time, sad! I WILL FIX!.[45]

None of the pundits thought he had a chance to win. But he did. Convincingly. And as he was taking the oath as the President of the United States, talk show hosts ranted, management consultants railed, and Ivy League educated women sought therapy. Little did they realize how surely their own success, based on a heady cocktail of inflowing savings from a dictatorial China, financial deregulation, technological progress, and political expediency had paved the way for his ascendancy.

Polarization

By the end of Trump's tenure, the polarities that he had exploited, and done so much to deepen, had only worsened. He continued to play on the fears of his support base while adopting policies that would only increase their economic woes, such as curtailing the benefits of President Obama's health insurance plan.

The Annenberg School for Communication and Journalism at University of Southern California has developed a polarization index based on data analysis of social media posts across a wide variety of contentious issues. Its analysis starting late 2020 shows that major disputes over voting integrity drove high levels of polarization in the final months of Trump's tenure, a period marked by unprecedented civil unrest.[46]

However, polarization levels nine months into the presidency of Joe Biden remain at roughly the same level as they were on account of increases in schisms related to immigration, policing policy, racial equity, and COVID-19 vaccines. The issues of gun legislation, abortion, climate change, and minimum wage saw a drop in polarization. Meanwhile, immigration has been the most polarized issue quarter over quarter, and it remains the most polarized issue in the index.

Some of the social media posts by Judicial Watch, 'a conservative foundation, that fights for accountability and integrity in law, politics and government…because no one is above the law!'[47] on immigration include the following sensational, provocative updates: 'Homeless Shelter Cleared to House Illegal Aliens, Dozens Infected with COVID-19'[48] and 'Gangbanger Awarded Asylum at 13 Under Obama Program Guilty of Machete Murder'.[49]

By 5 January 2022, according to a Axios–Momentive poll,[50] more than 40% of Americans still believed that Joe Biden 'stole' the 2020 presidential election, despite no evidence of widespread voter fraud. Of the 2,700 adults surveyed, 57% – about half the Republicans and 70% Democrats – thought that events similar to the Capitol attack were likely to recur. Moreover, 37% said they had lost faith in American democracy (48% Republicans and 28% Democrats), while 10% had never had faith in the system. Only 49% said they had faith.[51]

The task of building a more perfect union in the US has always been filled with moments of transcendence followed by demoralizing setbacks. It took close to 100 years from the Great Abolitionist War waged by Lincoln to pass the Civil Rights Act of 1964 that outlawed discrimination based on race (and other identity markers such as religion). Today, the union once more faces a titanic test, one made especially challenging by the unprecedented concert of the tech and financial elite.

Over the last 75 years, with all its ups and downs, the US has been a beacon of democracy. One watches the latest developments with hope but also with no small measure of trepidation.

2

CHINA: AN UNCERTAIN GLORY

USA, the new hegemon of the post-colonial liberal world order, attempted to use economic rather than militaristic methods to assimilate China into its fold. The assumption was that market-led economic progress would automatically weaken the power of the Communist Party of China. The emergence of China as a great economic power rivalling the USA along with the reinforced power of its authoritarian government is, obviously, evidence of the failure of the US approach. This chapter outlines how and why the US plans went awry. It also identifies the fault lines that threaten China's current growth path.

The Rise of Huawei

It would be fair to say that China is quickly replacing Russia as the country Americans most love to hate. The levels of suspicion and enmity are probably reaching the levels last seen during the Cold War with the Soviet Union. The times when Pixar released the blockbuster film *Kung Fu Panda* based on the adventures of a lovable Chinese panda in the ancient dragon kingdom seem like distant history, although the first film in the series was released less than two decades ago.

And yet, it is easy to forget that the two nations represent two of the principal protagonists in the wave of globalization that lifted millions out of poverty in China, established the US as the preeminent global power, and brought a breathtaking array of goods within the reach of the American middle class. How did we go from a partnership that seemed to epitomize the choicest promises of globalization to reach the present impasse? And, if we forget the angst of the US for a moment, can China be adjudged to have attained an unbreachable utopia in its own right?

The inflection points can be well understood by tracing the mercurial trajectory of Huawei, a telecom equipment manufacturer that surpassed Ericsson, a 150-year-old company, to become the world's largest telecom vendor in 2013, within only 35 years of its existence. By emerging as a high technology powerhouse from what was seen as a 'developing' country, it upended established behemoths and rewrote the rules of the game.

In the early 1980s, China made a definitive move away from its past. The doctrinaire communism of Mao was followed by the expedience of Deng who created enclaves of economic freedom even as he maintained the political power of the Communist Party.[1]

While the Chinese population had achieved reasonable life expectancy and literacy, the economy had been stagnant for many years. In 1978, the number of telephone subscribers was only two million, a measly 0.38% of the population.[2] Clearly, building communications infrastructure was a strategic imperative. But there were no telecom equipment manufacturers in the country. Opening up the markets to international vendors was the only way to achieve a higher diffusion rate. And Deng did not hesitate to bite the bullet.

In the 1980s, the telecom market in China was dominated by AT&T from the United States (whose network division was later spun out as Lucent Technologies), Alcatel from France, Ericsson from Sweden, Siemens from Germany, Northern Telecom (later Nortel) from Canada, and Nokia from Finland. There were also close to 400 Chinese telecom companies, both state-owned enterprises (SOEs) and private companies. One of them was Huawei.

The Early Days

Huawei began as a private trading company under Ren Zhengfei, a former engineer of the People's Liberation Army of China.* Ren's father had been the principal at a local college in Zhenning County. He had fallen into the bad books of the Communist Party of China (CPC) during the Cultural Revolution, when 'capitalist forces' were being purged. As a result, the family grew up in abject penury. All doors were closed to Ren and his siblings till the downfall of the 'Gang of Four' in 1976 brought an end to their exile. Ren was 32 years old then. He joined

---

* Many details on Huawei have been sourced from Tian Tao and Wu Chunbo, *The Huawei Story* (New Delhi: SAGE Publications India, 2014).

the People's Liberation Army (PLA) as a non-member of the CPC, but finally managed to upgrade himself to the status of a party member. After he was discharged from the army during a phase of downsizing, he became the manager of an electronics company, where he claims to have been 'cheated', without offering further details.[3] With few options in hand, he started Huawei.

In the early days, Huawei was a trader of switching equipment, a so-called 'dirty-dealing reseller' that would buy Private Branch Exchange (PBX; systems that allow enterprises to connect calls to employees without having to provide a separate external line for each individual) from Hong Kong and send them to county level post offices, small towns, and mines. At that time, private enterprises were definitely far below SOEs in the pecking order in China and were even looked at with the measure of suspicion. Consequently, they lacked capital, human resources, and brand value. But they benefited from not having to follow the arduous bureaucratic procedures imposed on SOEs. They were also free to choose their location of operation, and many, including Huawei, gravitated to Shenzen, an emerging hub of entrepreneurial activity.

While trading was a profitable venture, the runaway success of international equipment vendors in China convinced Ren that the real money was to be made in the equipment business. In 1991, Huawei decided to concentrate all its capital and human resources into developing its own PBX product. To this end, the company moved 50 research and development (R&D) personnel into a separate three-storey building. After almost a year of incessant work, they finally cracked it. As the company's bank balance had hit rock bottom by this time, success came not a moment too soon.

When China opened its markets to foreign equipment vendors, it had described its policy as one that was 'exchanging the market for technology'.[4] This was a polite way of asserting that when the government gave firms from overseas access to the vast Chinese market, the privilege came with the rider that Chinese firms would have the unrestricted right to the intellectual property of the international firms! Up until China became a member of the World Trade Organization (WTO) in 2001, such intellectual property rights (IPR) violations were rampant. Doubtless, Huawei gained from this unfettered access. However, in its defence, it could be said that of all the telecom firms who were granted this indulgence only Zhong Xing Telecommunication Equipment Company Limited (ZTE) and Huawei emerged victorious. And ZTE was a state-owned enterprise favoured by the Chinese government.

In 1994, Huawei launched its own telephone switching system. Next, it started developing technology for the second generation of mobile communications, also called 2G. Since international firms dominated markets in dense urban areas, Huawei had to focus on remote hinterlands that were characterized by small clumps of human habitation set in between mountains, fields, and water bodies. Huawei perfected a frugal network architecture that was suitable for such terrain and captured a sizeable share of this business.

Huawei's early products were characterized by low quality but excellent service levels. Defects were common but customers remained satisfied due to the high level of responsiveness of the maintenance engineers. This customer centricity became a hallmark of everything Huawei was to do.

After success with 2G technology, Huawei invested ¥6

billion (about $750 million) into third generation, or 3G, technology. However, due to China's delay in issuing licenses, the 3G business had no income for close to three years and was at breaking point. Eventually, respite came from unexpected quarters. A small telecom operator in the Netherlands, Telfort, decided to buy Huawei equipment when they were promised that it would address their main pain point – patchy indoor coverage. Huawei was able to refashion the 2G architecture used in remote habitations in China to provide indoor 3G coverage in the Dutch market! This allowed it to break through the habitual distrust European customers harboured towards Chinese companies whose low prices induced a perception of low quality.

Entry into the World Trade Organization

Competition in the Chinese communications market in the 1990s created a template for competition in Chinese industries as a whole. By the 1990s, China had sufficiently developed its internal markets, and its domestic firms were ready to compete on the world stage. They were prepared to fulfil the obligations (including the intellectual property obligations, with some leniency!) and partake of the benefits of being a part of the global trading system through membership of the WTO.

As with Huawei's 3G business, Europe lent its heft to China's cause. The Maastricht Treaty of 1994 had created a common market in Europe. The European Union (EU) emerged as a large trading bloc that was willing and able to view China through the economic lens without the interference of political considerations.[5]

The US on the other hand had continually vacillated between 'strategic containment' of China – designed to curb its economic growth till political reforms to the Communist system were wrested – and 'engagement' under which economic relations were encouraged to the utmost in the belief that economic integration would eventually lead to political transformation.

But China's transformation was by far not the only consideration promoting a policy of engagement. In 1971, President Nixon had initiated a détente with China to take advantage of Sino–Soviet differences and create a schism in the Communist bloc. Engagement was also necessary for establishing a counterpoint to the increasing economic power of Japan and the East Asian tigers, as well as to create a model of economic transformation other Communist countries could follow. Equally significant was the fact that engagement with China played a key role in the rise of the American MNC as a dominant force in world affairs. As mentioned in Chapter 1, a significant portion of China's economic boom comprised production activities undertaken by newly opened branches of multinational companies that were either catering to the Chinese and East Asian markets or exporting intermediate goods to other branches of the same firm (intra-firm trade) or to other firms in the same industry.

Between 1980 and 2013, MNCs prospered as they gained access to vast markets around the world, even as the costs of borrowing as well as the price of labour, equipment, and technology went down. They also gained from the emergence of regulatory and tax havens that allowed them to incorporate in 'friendly' jurisdictions despite having operations elsewhere. The largest companies in the world grew their net profits from $2 trillion in 1980 to $7.2 trillion by 2013 – a shift that increased the contribution of corporate profits from 7.6% to almost 10% of global GDP.[6] Similarly, after tax profits of US firms also went up from 4.5% of GDP in 1970 to 8.4% in 2021.[7] Engagement with China was a key element of creating a global playing field for MNCs.

With regard to the negotiations over China's accession to the WTO, there were a few sticking points. The US was concerned about human rights abuses in China. These concerns had become heightened in the wake of the Tiananmen Square massacre of 1989 when student-led demonstrations against the authoritarianism of the Chinese Communist Party were brutally repressed. The US was also insistent that China needed to become more sensitive with regard to IPR and copyright protection, grant market access to US firms by reducing tariff barriers, and allow US banking and insurance companies to operate in China. Meanwhile, the breakup of the Soviet Union had reduced China's strategic leverage as a counterpoint to the Communist bloc.

Protracted negotiations between the US and China allowed a deal to be struck. This only became possible because in 1992 China agreed to get rid of most of its import restrictions, overhaul the import substitution regulations, and gradually reduce tariffs in order to contain its growing trade surpluses with the US. It also committed to making improvements in its IPR conduct and law enforcement as well as increase the transparency of its trade system. The two sides also found middle ground on the US's support of Taiwan, a stance that China steadfastly opposed in line with its 'one China' policy.[8,*]

In 1980, the US had granted China conditional MFN status with regard to trade. After the Tiananmen Square crackdown, a number of conditionalities got attached to this status. Partly as a result of EU pressure, in 1994, the Democratic administration of Bill Clinton delinked China's conditional MFN status from human rights considerations. When Republican President George W. Bush made the MFN status permanent in 2001, the deal was done. China entered the WTO in December 2001, and took its place on the high table of nations.

As the Chinese economy had picked up speed, its stewards had far sightedly moved to secure supplies of natural resources through partnerships with resource-rich countries in Africa and Latin America. In the 1990s, this led to the birth of the stereotypical Chinese MNCs, a public sector enterprise focused on securing access to minerals, metals, and other natural resources.

A handful of high-tech Chinese companies such as Huawei had gained from such forays by securing contracts to build out telecom networks in far flung parts of the globe. But with the accession to the WTO, these firms had unfettered access to world markets. Soon enough, Huawei products made their way throughout Europe, and further into Japan, Latin America, and North America. By 2010, 70% of Huawei's sales came from international markets.[9] By mid-2023, its networks had reached 150 countries and one third of the global population.[10] This embodies a key feature of Huawei's business strategy – rapid

---

* This middle ground, of course, seems to have receded, given the growing geopolitical tensions between the US and China.

expansion of scale resulting in reduced per unit costs and high profitability despite low prices.

The East Asian crisis of the latter half of the 1990s in which countries such as Thailand, Indonesia, Malaysia, and South Korea saw a crippling drop in capital inflows of more than 100 billion dollars in the first year of the crisis had resulted in a shift in the doctrinaire position of the IMF that postulated emerging markets should maintain fixed exchange rates.[11] It became more acceptable for such economies to use undervalued exchange rates to promote exports. China was the country that gained the most from this relaxation. As dollars poured in to purchase Chinese goods and productive assets, the nation's Central Bank stepped in to buy them, creating an artificial demand for dollars while also keeping the value of the Chinese currency low. This further cemented the competitive advantage of Chinese exporters including Huawei. A safety valve opened in the aftermath of the East Asian crisis had helped to fashion an escape hatch for China!

With the accession of China to the WTO, international companies became acutely aware of the competitive threat posed by Huawei. In 2003, Cisco, the global communications giant, took the company to court for IPR infringement. Litigation took place in a district court in Texas, known for quick judgements and severe penalties in IP cases. A number of media outlets branded Huawei as a 'technology thief'.

The suit ended with a mutual settlement under which Huawei accepted a number of changes including changing portions of its source code in some of its products, and discontinuing sales of certain products.[12] Both parties welcomed the final settlement. This was among the first of many such accusations levelled against Huawei, including the allegation that it was using its networks to spy for the Chinese government. Ironically, Huawei remained on the scanner since its very inception, but for different reasons at different points in time – at first as a private company in a newly transitioning Communist economy, and then as a Chinese company making inroads into strategic Western markets.

The IPR case with Cisco was an important milestone in Huawei's evolution. In the course of taking on the legal challenge, Huawei developed an entirely new core competency – of navigating the global system of IPR. It began a series of R&D partnerships with universities and other research institutions. In 2008, the World Intellectual Property Organization (WIPO) announced that Huawei had become the first Chinese company to top the list of patent applications – it had filed a massive 1,737 applications that year.[13] Huawei also began a systematic process of paying royalties to its technology partners. Since 2010, more than 80% of its royalty payments have been made to Qualcomm. It is estimated that the royalty paid to Qualcomm up to 2016 amounts to $1 billion.[14]

Learning from the Masters

A group of Huawei's senior executives led by Ren Zhengfei had visited US in 1997. Their itinerary included stops at several iconic American companies including IBM, Bell Labs, and Hewlett Packard. On Christmas Eve, they locked themselves up in a modest hotel in Silicon Valley for three days and churned out a document of more than hundred pages outlining the various lessons that could be learnt from American technology giants. Soon after, Huawei implemented the process-based management approach that it assimilated from IBM. Ren once said: 'We must study advanced things in the United States, if we ever intend to surpass our American counterparts... we should not give up the opportunity to learn from America out of distaste for a few individuals within its government.'[15]

In fact, Ren has repeatedly expressed his admiration for American tech pioneers. Speaking of Steve Jobs, the co-founder of Apple, he told CNBC, 'Mr. Jobs was great not because he created Apple, but because he created an era, the mobile internet era. Saying that he was great is an understatement. I think he was super-great.'[16] In a very real sense, Ren can be regarded as the most outstanding protégé of the American tech entrepreneurs.

However, this does not mean that Huawei does not incorporate elements of Chinese culture into its management philosophy. For instance, in order to avoid complacency and inject 'rooster blood' (believed by the Chinese to charge the body with vitality), it stages frequent 'mass resignation' events. In October 2007, 7,000 employees 'voluntarily' resigned and applied for re-employment on a short-term contract of one-three years.[17] Huawei also incorporates Confucian elements such the golden mean and 'peaceful coexistence' into its philosophy. On one occasion, it desisted from bidding on a contract which, if it had won, would significantly reduce the footprint of Alcatel, a French mobile phone and telecommunications equipment manufacturer that traces its roots back to the late 1800s and is considered an integral element of France's technology history, in its home ground.

In fact, by drawing from practices around the world, and infusing his own native wisdom into them, Ren has fashioned a unique management philosophy and succeeded in ingraining that philosophy in the everyday choices of the thousands of Huawei employees. At the heart of his credo is customer-centricity.

Huawei's Customer Centricity and the Stock Market

It is but obvious that creating the world's largest telecommunications company from scratch in a developing economy would have required a level of dedication bordering on fanaticism. Stories of Huawei executives returning to war-ravaged countries to fulfil customer requirements (including post-Gaddafi Libya and Mumbai, India, after the 2008 terror attack on the Taj Hotel) are legion. But dedication is probably not the first quality that Huawei would itself single out as its key differentiator. That place belongs to customer-centricity – being hyper-responsive to 'visible or invisible' customer needs.

Again, this seems like a business cliché. After all, doesn't every successful company put the customer first? But Ren goes beyond to emphasize the private ownership of Huawei as a necessary structural feature that allows the company to remain single-mindedly focused on customer needs. He could not have expressed his belief more starkly than when he said, 'If we do not go public, we might someday take over the world.'[18]

To better understand Ren's point of view, let us look at stock price trends of two iconic American brands – Motorola, recently acquired by Google, and Lucent Technologies, now no longer in existence. From September 1998 to March 2000, over a period of roughly 15 months, the stock price of Motorola increased more than fourfold from $49.5 to $205.[19] Similarly, from March 2020 to November 2021, over a period of 20 months, the Motorola stock price almost doubled from $135 to $247.[20] In a similar vein, after breaking off from its parent AT&T in October 1996, the Lucent Technologies stock price saw runaway growth. In April 1998 it overtook its former parent in market value and, at its peak, was worth $258 billion.[21]

As per the Huawei worldview, these phases of hyper growth create a level of sudden abundance that corrupt individuals and take away from the team's 'collective fighting spirit'. They reduce the control of the core management over the company and diffuse its focus from long term goals to short term targets. For instance, Huawei did not earn a return on its investment in 3G technologies for a long time. Yet it was able to stick to its long-term vision and ultimately earn sizeable returns. This, Ren believes, would not have been possible had Huawei been a publicly listed company.

Indeed, a technology company enjoying a bull run on the stock market can fall prey to the temptation of becoming technology-obsessed rather than customer centric. In the absence of any other fundamental drivers, it can be tempted to justify its inflated stock price by its technology attainments. With a sizeable war chest, it may attempt to sustain the stock momentum by even more futuristic investments in research. In the process, it runs the risk of taking its eyes off customer needs.

Instead of public listing, Huawei adopts the model of employee ownership, with the founder himself holding only

1.14% shares.[22] Partly, this was an outcome of Ren's conviction that his most critical assets (apart from customers) are his people and that their incentives need to be completely aligned with the company. But this distributed shareholding also reflects the historical backdrop of the 1980s when capital was almost a dirty word in China. The recent fate of publicly listed Chinese tech companies in which founders had a much larger share holding, demonstrates the wisdom of Ren's approach.*

The Fall of Evergrande

The story so far paints the picture of a path-breaking company in a surging Chinese economy. Both the company and the economy went from strength to strength, even as deep fault lines emerged in the economy and polity of the US. However, that picture is only half complete.

In December 2021, news emerged that Evergrande, a poster child of China's real estate boom, with far flung interests in electric cars and bottled water, had defaulted on its debt obligations. At one time, Xu Jiayin, the founder who owns about 60% of the company, was the third richest person in China with his wealth estimated at $49 billion.[23] Xu's exploits as a self-made billionaire were legion. His cult figure in the public eye was amplified by his ownership of the highly successful Guangzhou Evergrande football club.

But by 2023, Evergrande's total debt amounted to hundreds of billions of dollars, and Xu Jiayin's personal wealth was down to $3 billion.[24] Reports suggested that Evergrande represented

* For more on these tech companies, read Chapter 6.

only the tip of China's debt problem which extended across the infrastructure sector and even had ramifications outside its borders.[25]

In Chapter 1 we saw how the expansion of the US economy was founded on the flimsy foundation of increased household indebtedness. But in a global economy, the borders of countries can be porous with respect to debt crises. Let's see how the debt-fuelled growth of the US transposed itself into a debt crisis in China.

In 2007, the net exports of China constituted 9% of the GDP[26] with exports to the US constituting 19.1% of its total exports.[27] US households were borrowing and spending not just because credit was freely available but because Chinese imports were easy on the pocket. Then came the global financial crisis, and, by 2011, the net exports of China had fallen to 2.4% of the GDP.* In order to continue to grow at double digit rates, the Chinese economy needed to substitute rapidly shrinking export markets.

Since consumption demand is relatively hard to change overnight, expanding investment further was the only possible solution for avoiding a slump. But investment in China was already very high at close to 40% of the GDP. Nevertheless, gross investment did in fact increase from 38% of the GDP in 2007 to 44% in 2011[28] – financed by a dramatic rise in corporate debt.

Spurred on by the Chinese government, companies were borrowing at a breakneck pace to make investments. Martin

---

* Author's calculation from export and import figures available at https://www.macrotrends.net/countries/CHN/china/exports and https://www.macrotrends.net/countries/CHN/china/imports.

Wolfe, the respected China watcher, cited a report by the Institute of International Finance (IIF) that stated that gross debt rose from 171% to 295% of GDP between the fourth quarter of 2008 and the third quarter of 2017.[29]

But while state-run banks can boost credit at a single instruction from the government, ramping up genuine investment opportunities at this rapid rate is hard. The returns on investment started reducing. While the Chinese economy was able to grow at 14% on the base of 39% of investment in 2008,[30] in 2017 an investment of 42% of GDP yielded a growth rate of only 7%,[31] i.e., half the rate of growth despite a slightly increased investment rate.

The rush for infrastructural investment led to the creation of 'ghost towns', and an increasing percentage of debt given to Chinese companies started going bad. The collapse of Evergrande and other real-estate firms depicted the fragility of this pattern of growth. Given that real estate has contributed 26% to the Chinese economy since 2018 and is a major source of income for local governments, this is a major cause of concern.[32]

But the Chinese government was not relying on domestic investment alone to shore up the GDP. In 2013, the Chinese government launched the ambitious Belt and Road Initiative (BRI), a trillion-dollar project, which aims to recreate the infrastructure of the Great Silk Road from the East to the West. It is a massive project that aims to cement China's status as a global leader. But it is also expected to help reorient the Chinese economy. The project aims to create demand for Chinese products and services from foreign governments that build up their infrastructure using credit extended by Chinese banks. But this strategy of replacing export demand has its own limitations, with foreign governments such as Sri Lanka and Pakistan finding it difficult to service their debt obligations, and facing a domestic backlash on account of a perceived loss of sovereignty.

In sum, the Global Financial Crisis made it imperative for China to find new engines of growth. The quest to find such growth drivers created a corporate debt crisis within China. Further, the attempt to use the BRI to replace export demand threatened the political sovereignty of China's partners and created debt crises in their economies.

The economic challenges of 'rebalancing' the Chinese economy had important repercussions for China's politics as well, both domestic and international.

Protégé Turns Arch Rival

A constant factor throughout the growth of the Chinese economy has been the unquestioned authority of the Communist Party of China. The sustained spell of economic growth was a critical source of legitimacy that allowed the party to justify its vice-like grip on Chinese society. However, with economic growth facing structural challenges, and with greater prosperity leading to a demand for greater freedoms, the party needs other sources of legitimacy to retain its absolute power.

In domestic politics, the party has sought to mobilize support through an invocation of the communist ideology, an avowed aim to rein in high inequality levels through a program of 'common prosperity', a war against corruption in high places, not excluding the high echelons of the party, and increasing restraints imposed on the leaders of Big Tech companies. The draconian lockdown to tackle COVID-19 can also be partly interpreted as an attempt to achieve greater control under the pretext of a health crisis.

The increasing centralization of power is embodied in the personality of Xi Jinping, the 'paramount leader' of China since 2012. Much like Ren, the CEO of Huawei, Xi's family had faced tremendous hardship when his father fell foul of the authorities during the cultural revolution. He managed to gain an entry into the CPC after several failed attempts and steadily made his way up the ranks. He became the general secretary of the CPC and chairman of the Central Military Commission (CMC) in 2012, and in 2013, took office as the president of the People's Republic of China (PRC). Many observers consider Xi the most powerful Chinese leader since Mao Zedong, especially since he managed to end the two-term limit in 2018 and continued on for a third term as president.

The rapid private sector fuelled economic growth of China had led to a period of ideological ambivalence about Marxist-Leninist-Maoist doctrines. Xi has brought back ideological certitude in the communist ideology. He has declared that 'only socialism can save China' and socialism with Chinese characteristics is the 'only correct path to realize national rejuvenation, and that socialism will eventually triumph over capitalism on the global stage'.[33]

Thus, the US policy of engagement far from bringing about ideological alignment seems to have created a China even more at variance with the ideal of the 'free world'.

But the provocations do not stop at divergent domestic ideologies. Today, China makes no bones about its desire to play the role of a great power. To some extent, the desire for greater geopolitical assertion is a natural result of economic growth achieved on such a large scale and over such a long period of time. But it also serves the dual purpose of unifying the nation and legitimizing the hegemony of the CPC in an environment of flailing economic growth.

As mentioned above, the BRI serves both a financial and geopolitical purpose. Besides the BRI, there are increased efforts to create a homogeneous political system across Hong Kong, Tibet, Xinchiang, and Taiwan and aggressive posturing across international borders in the South China Sea and in India.

In sum, the economic challenges of the US got transferred to China. This led to greater insecurity of the CPC, and Xi Jinping emerged as the man of the moment who chose to tide over the crisis by a revival of Marxist-Leninist-Maoist ideology, a greater centralization of domestic power, and a muscular assertion of Chinese interests in the international sphere.

This in turn lead to further economic reprisals against China as the US erected tariff barriers and clamped down on Chinese investment. These reprisals increased the economic challenges of China, exacerbating the problem that the government had set out to solve in the first place. It appears as if a vicious cycle has been set into motion.

The 'Huawei ban' was just one of various actions taken by the US and its allies to try to contain China. More than any other measure, it reveals the full nature of the entanglement of China and the US and the difficulties both face in decoupling from each other.

Implications of the Huawei Ban

In May 2019, the American government released a note outlining principles that could form the basis for the disqualification of foreign businesses, followed by the release of an 'entities list' that explicitly mentioned Huawei.[34]

The souring of the relationship between Huawei and the US runs on two parallel tracks – the first is the increasing tension between China and the US. The second track relates to the competitive threat posed by Huawei to the dominance of Western technology companies.

At first it was believed that the ban would only affect the networking equipment business of Huawei. Since Huawei networks do not have a major presence in the US, this would not be worrisome to them. However, Huawei had been making rapid strides in the market for smartphones as well. In 2016 it claimed that it would rise to become the number one smartphone manufacturer of the world by 2021. By 2019, it was in second position and the promise seemed within reach.

But there was one catch. The attractiveness of Huawei phones integrally depended upon the suite of Google apps such as Chrome, Gmail, YouTube, Google Drive, and Google Play Store. Further, while Android, the Google-developed operating system on which Huawei phones run, is open source, i.e., anyone is free to use it for their own purposes, many of its integral features that users rely on are actually owned by Google – they aren't a part of 'pure' Android. For instance, running Google Maps requires the development of certain interfaces not included in pure Android.

But the story does not merely end at the usual trope of 'Chinese hardware, US software', i.e., a Chinese hardware company crippled by lack of access to US software. There's another plot twist. The Kirin processors used in Huawei's smartphones and tablets are designed in-house, but they are produced by a Taiwanese company called Taiwan Semiconductor Manufacturing Company Limited (TSMC). With frosty relations between China and Taiwan due to the former's 'one country' policy, a critical element of Huawei's supply chain became vulnerable.

While at first, TSMC assured Huawei that the production of Kirin chipsets would remain unaffected, later it went back on its statement. It was probably trying to avoid losing out on its business with US companies. Thus, Huawei was caught in a double bind – affected both at the hardware level and at the software level by the US ban. But the risks extended to the US companies as well on account of the steps that Huawei took to cope with its radically transformed competitive environment.

In response to the setbacks, Huawei developed its own operating system, Harmony OS, and app store, and sold off the Honor sub-brand smart phones.[35] While the loss of Google applications cost them dearly in most markets, its travails led to it becoming even more widely accepted in the home market of China. On account of runaway growth in China, for a brief period in 2020, it surpassed Samsung and became the top smartphone manufacturer in the world.

The prospect of Huawei's operating system gaining momentum represents a competitive threat for firms such as Google that rely upon the software developed by them to establish a powerful hold on other parts of the internet market. This is a threat posed not just in the Chinese market but worldwide.

Conclusion

The story of the entanglement of the US vis-à-vis China rests on the planks of the self-interest of the American MNC, the fading fortunes of the American worker, the ability of China to wrest maximum advantage from the presence of foreign companies to outdo its mentors, and sheer luck. It can be summarized by an old Chinese proverb: 'Throwing your fists like mad will kill the kungfu master.'[36]

But the entanglement extends to China as well. Today, the nation is attempting to overcome economic and geopolitical uncertainty with greater political centralization, enhanced ideological mooring, and overt global assertiveness. Given the many contradictions inherent in such a policy, how far it will succeed remains an open question.

3

FINANCIAL FAULT LINES

This chapter explores how the Federal Reserve acquired the power to print trillions of dollars to navigate itself out of trouble created by its own past policies. Its compulsions and extravagances highlight the risks stemming from firstly, the agenda of creating a global currency to facilitate an integrated global economic system (a key objective flowing from the ideals of the Age of Rationality), secondly, the use of financial aid to establish spheres of influence in Europe, and lastly, making financial regulation subservient to the business goals of financial conglomerates.

The 'exorbitant privilege' of the Fed has led to an attempt by techno-utopians to create cryptocurrency, a monetary system that is free of the intermediary role of any central bank. The failures of the cryptocurrency system show the pitfalls awaiting disruptions that, however noble their intentions might be, are driven by the same underlying ethic of the Age of Rationality – the ethic that asserts that greed is good.

The Federal Reserve Captures the Commanding Heights of Global Finance

In May 2021, a cryptocurrency called Solana was trading at $32.82. In five months, it was trading at $208.67, almost seven times its original value. In June 2022, it returned to the value it had in May 2021.[1] Critics of cryptocurrency pointed to this and other such examples to argue that the crypto market was at best a casino, a gambling den, where innocent investors were being gamed by powerful interests with the power to rig the market.

But, since the 1980s, on occasion, the global financial system too has resembled a casino rigged in favour of the rich and powerful.

1944–71: The Exorbitant Privilege of the United States

Let us pick up the story in 1971. It has been 25 years since the Allied powers came together in Bretton Woods, a bucolic town in New Hampshire, USA, to design the post-war international monetary system. The Bretton Woods conference aimed to create a global economic architecture that would prevent a recurrence of the financial instability of the interwar period.[2]

An international trading and financial system needs a currency or a commodity that can function as a reliable medium of transactions. A freely floating exchange rate regime under which countries have the freedom to change the price of their currencies was regarded as a significant cause of the interwar instability. Hence, there was a feeling that in the post-WWII world the value of currencies should be pegged to a physical object such as gold so that if countries mismanaged their international transactions, they did not have the option of manipulating their exchange rates to get out of trouble. Instead, they ran the risk of depleting their gold reserves. This was the system of the 'gold standard' that was in place before World War I (WWI).

At Bretton Woods, the United States, which controlled two-thirds of the world's gold, insisted that unlike the classical gold standard which was based only on gold, the post-WWII system should be based on both gold and the US dollar. The exchange rates of countries were pegged to the dollar, and the price of gold was fixed at $35 per ounce.[3] For all practical purposes, the system was based on the dollar. The motivations of the US for taking this stance will be clear shortly.

In the first couple of decades of the Bretton Woods system, the US gave generous grants for the reconstruction of war-torn European countries. Hence, it ran deficits in its overall balance of payments even though it enjoyed surpluses in its balance of trade (roughly, exports minus imports). Its grants were viewed as an economic necessity as they put money in the hands of countries which demanded goods from the economies relatively unaffected by the war, thus bolstering global growth. The grants also served to cement the Western alliance in the face of the Communist Bloc.*

However, by 1971, the US was beginning to run deficits in

* The generosity of the US toward fallen enemies after WWII is in contrast with the relative indifference to Russian concerns after the dissolution of the Soviet Union (see Chapter 4). The political necessity of pre-empting further expansion of Communist influence is, thus, a likely factor for the different attitudes exhibited.

its balance of trade on account of its increased dependence on crude oil imports and geopolitical instabilities in the Middle East. It had also been waging a financially crippling war in Vietnam. Both capital account deficits of the kind the US ran in the decades immediately following WWII and trade deficits of the kind it started running in the 1960s, put dollars in the hands of participants in the global economic system and therefore served a useful purpose in making the system run. However, as far as some countries were concerned, the US trade deficits represented an economic compulsion, not efforts to shore up the global financial architecture, or fortify the world against Communism.

When other countries ran trade deficits, they had to work hard to move into surplus territory for fear of creditors demanding payments in gold or global investors losing confidence and withdrawing their capital. The USA, on the other hand, seemed to have the singular ability to run trade deficits with impunity as the US dollar was as good as gold for creditor countries. Valery d'Eistang, French Foreign Minister under President Charles de Gaulle, referred to this asymmetric ability of the US as an 'exorbitant privilege'.[4]

The patience of US allies started growing thin. France threatened to convert its surplus dollars into gold at the Bretton Woods rate of $35 an ounce and sell the gold thus obtained at the higher rates available on the market. This would have been a powerful signal of the growing mistrust in the global financial architecture anchored by the US and could have led to the unravelling of the entire system.

In response, on 15 August 1971, President Nixon applied the 'Nixon Shock', summarily closing the 'gold window' and suspending the official conversion of dollar into gold. However, this did not end the age of the 'exorbitant privilege' of the US. It only marked a new phase of its manifestation. In this new era, the privilege of the US was exercised not by the US Treasury but by the Federal Reserve Bank and by financial services firms freed by the Fed from regulations of the era of the Great Depression.

1971–2008: Regulatory Complicity in Creating Unsustainable Risk

The Nixon Shock ushered in the age of fiat money, as money ceased to be backed by any real commodity, even in notional terms. It made trust in the government of the day the sole basis of the acceptance of the currency. The US dollar became the de facto gold standard of international currencies, first within the capitalist world, and later, after the fall of the Soviet Union, in the world at large. The US Federal Reserve acquired the status of the central bank of the world, seemingly enjoying the power to print money at will, with a rise in domestic inflation, i.e., inflation in the US, being the only restraining factor.

In the domestic sphere, with the decline of the Keynesian consensus, the role of the Finance Ministry (i.e., the Treasury) in smoothening business cycles became diminished.* The Fed became the key player in the macroeconomic management of the US economy. A key feature of this age was the expansion of the financial services industry from 4% of the US GDP in 1980 to 8% in 2007.[5]

Till the late 1970s, the US banking system was primarily

* See section 'The Rise of the Liberal Consensus' in Chapter 1.

based upon the Glass–Steagall Act that had been put in place in 1933 in response to the Great Depression. Banks were designed to be conservative custodians of the process of transmitting hard earned savings of households into viable lending. They were prohibited from carrying out investment banking activities or earning more than 10% of their income from selling securities.*

Investment banks help companies raise capital from private investors, bond markets, or the stock market. Without a sizeable investment, they earn significant commissions on the millions of dollars raised. Hence, the business of investment banking tended to be far more lucrative than that of traditional banking. Why then were banks not allowed to carry on investment banking activities?

If a bank was allowed to raise money from third parties for one of its own borrowers, it might have an incentive to suppress certain facts to successfully raise money. It may even lower credit appraisal standards, since it has the power to shore up a borrower's financial position by artificially inflating its prospects in the supplementary markets for funds. By separating commercial and investment banking, such conflicts of interest can be prevented. Such a separation also ensures that banks do not use depositors' money for risky proprietary trading, a process in which investment banks use their resources, including borrowed resources, to invest in financial markets.

Banks were also allowed only limited participation in securitization activities. As a part of securitization, a bank bundles together loans (or equities) and offers investors different levels of priorities on the underlying income streams.

* These mainly comprise corporate stocks, bonds, or derivative assets based on underlying stocks or bonds.

This allows the banks to package low quality loans in a way that makes them attractive to third party investors. Therefore, securitization enables a reduction of credit rating standards in the primary loan market. When carried to an extreme, it results in an increased risk for the financial sector. The Great Depression had hammered home the point that it was crucial to create an ecosystem in which borrowers were subject to stringent credit appraisal processes. The Glass–Steagall Act took the stance that excessive securitization was inimical to this objective.

However, by the 1990s, the architecture of the Glass–Steagall Act began to unravel. Commercial banks began to aspire for a share of the business of investment banks. They felt that since they were taking a risk by lending to corporate America, they should get a share of the lucrative commission-based business that investment banks were addressing without even taking risks. In the dawning age of the liberal consensus* in which the benefits of free markets were far more emphasized than their drawbacks, the separation of functions between commercial and investment banks began to seem like an unnecessary fetter. The benefits of an integrated view of the borrowing company across lending and fund-raising activities began to acquire prominence in regulatory thinking. The magic pill of 'governance' seemed to solve the problem of conflict of interest: commercial and investment banking functions would operate at arm's length within the same umbrella structure, but organizational structures, processes, and incentives would be put into place to ensure that the drivers of the investment banking arm did not distort the loan approval process of the commercial banking

* See Chapter 1.

arm and vice versa. Banks such as JPMorgan, Citibank and Chase Manhattan were at the forefront of the trend of commercial banks encroaching upon the territory of investment banks.

Meanwhile, the drive to enable home ownership led to increasing securitization of home loans. In 1970, mortgage-backed securities were created at the Government National Mortgage Association (popularly referred to as 'Ginnie Mae') by packaging together securitized mortgage loans. With advances in financial engineering, regulators began to believe that securitization, rather than increasing risk by promoting lax lending standards, would increase efficiency and reduce risk in the system as it allowed banks to make money from bad loans. Hence, banks were allowed to engage in securitization to a greater degree.

Increasing levels of securitization made less conservative lending practices acceptable. The Alternative Mortgage Transactions Parity Act of 1982 did away with restrictions against classes of mortgage loans with exotic features, for instance, adjustable-rate mortgages. These carried low 'teaser' rates during the first few years which were reset at much higher levels later. With strictures against such loan instruments having been removed, they became commonplace.

The Savings and Loan Crisis of 1987, a direct result of deregulation of lending practices for real estate, marked only a minor pause in the march of deregulation. In 1998, Citigroup formed the world's largest financial services conglomerate by merging a commercial bank with an insurance company that owned an investment bank. Then came the Gramm-Leach-Bliley Act in 1999 which axed all the rules that prohibited any one institution from acting as any combination of an investment bank, a commercial bank, and an insurance company. It also made a host of other concessions, signing into law what was already a ground reality. The Glass–Steagall Act was history.

The scenario became even more laissez faire in the 2000s. Home loan companies started targeting lower-income, higher-risk borrowers with poor credit ratings as they enabled higher value addition through appropriately designed securities. Banks were allowed to give 'liar's loans', i.e., home loans on which the credit appraisal was based on unverified self-certified data provided by the borrower. Further, a borrower's credit limit would increase with the value of the home which they had bought. Thus, a borrower could make the higher interest payments due at later stages of an adjustable-rate home loan by further borrowing based on rising housing prices. Moreover, by taking out a loan to buy a home, the buyer could expect to take out further loans to buy electronics, white goods, etc., based on the rising value of the home.

Many subprime loans involved banks making loans to borrowers in order to help them to avoid defaulting on their existing home loans. The bet that the banks and investors were making was that the subsequent financial engineering as well as the rise in the value of the homes that formed the collateral would be sufficient to take care of their interests.

If securitization was meant to enable the bank to adopt less conservative lending standards, at the very least, it was important to ensure that the transfer of loans out of the banking system was subject to the discipline of a well-functioning market in securities. Maintaining a level of regulatory oversight on this secondary market was also necessary.

However, neither precaution was undertaken. The Gramm-Leach-Bliley Act had no mandate for a market-based mechanism for derivatives. Such instruments were usually sold through over-the-counter processes, often from one unit of a financial conglomerate to another. In addition, the Commodity Futures Trading Commission could not regulate most over-the-counter derivative contracts because of the explicit exemption made in the Commodity Futures Modernization Act, 2000. Finally, under the Gramm-Leach-Bliley Act there were no provisions to regulate large investment bank holding companies. Thus, a large 'shadow banking sector' sprang up in the penumbra of the gaze of regulatory authorities and bereft of the discipline of the market.[6] Estimates of the size of the assets controlled by this sector in 29 jurisdictions including G20 countries in 2018 ranged from $45 trillion to $100 trillion,[7,8] 13-30% of total financial system assets.*

The advantage of such activities was that assets could be customized to the needs of the investors. In the words of Alan Greenspan, Governor of the Federal Reserve Bank between 1987 and 2006, and high priest of the age of deregulation, 'These instruments [derivatives] enhance the ability to differentiate risk and allocate it to those investors most able and willing to take it... [they] enable entrepreneurs to finely allocate real capital facilities to produce those goods and services most valued by consumers, a process that has undoubtedly improved national productivity growth and standards of living.'[9]

But the downside was that dangerous levels of risk in the shadow banking system went unheeded. The vaunted 'increase

---

* The share of the shadow banking sector fell during COVID-19 when supportive government and central bank stances supported the real economy, including through an injection of liquidity into the traditional banking system.

in the standards of living' came to an abrupt and calamitous halt in 2008. In retrospect, it was perhaps prophetic that Greenspan, the guiding light of perhaps the largest destruction of economic value in human history, was nicknamed 'The Undertaker' by his mentor, the philosopher and novelist, Ayn Rand.[10]

The 2008 financial crisis was not the first episode of instability that arose as a result of financial deregulation. There had been many before, but they had mostly originated outside the US. Understanding the nature of those crises allows us to appreciate the new nature of the US's exorbitant privilege after the Nixon Shock.

The Washington Consensus and the Shenanigans of Speculative Financial Capital

All central banks, not just the US Fed, had seemingly been empowered by the Nixon shock. The world at large moved into a phase of fiat money – money that was legal tender solely by the command of the government and the central bank.

However, the real power of central bankers in countries other than the US, especially emerging economies, was circumscribed by a new cognitive paradigm – the Washington Consensus – the intellectual successor to the Keynesian worldview that had formed the basis of the Bretton Woods agreement. The Washington Consensus was a set of ten directives that embodied the core principles apparently agreed upon by the leading economies of the world, most prominently the US, and by anchor institutions such as the International Monetary Fund (IMF) for the creation of a global economic system.

The formulation was initially associated with the English economist John Williamson. The original objective of Williamson was to create a global level playing field for trade and foreign direct investment (but not for the movement of global financial capital) in order to promote broad-based economic development. The prescriptions included rationalizing tariffs to open up economies to foreign trade, eliminating government subsidies for export promotion and import substitution, liberalizing inward foreign direct investment, promoting competitive forces in domestic industry, and enabling market-determined exchange rates.

As per Williamson's original vision, the speculative movement of financial capital was to be heavily regulated as it came with unacceptable risks. However, by the late 1980s, growth in mature economies had begun to taper off, and new geographies such as China, India, and Brazil started emerging as vibrant nodes of economic activity. They became attractive targets for global capital, not merely to set up production facilities, but also for financial investment in debt, equity, and real estate.

Financial capital's quest for returns that were higher than those provided in mature economies resulted in a reading of Williamson's manifesto that he himself would emphatically oppose.[11] At the ideological centre-stage of the new paradigm was the efficient market hypothesis that asserted that asset prices by and large reflected fundamental value. Therefore, as per this view, stock markets and other financial markets were not susceptible to frequent boom-bust cycles on account of speculative activity. This meant that global movements of financial capital did not need to be frowned upon. Rather, they needed to be facilitated. Consequently, creating conditions for the free movement of global financial capital became a central mandate of institutions such as the IMF.

A key feature of an environment favourable for global financial flows was a fixed exchange rate regime which protects investors from a possible depreciation of the currency of a target country. Such a depreciation, were it to take place, would reduce investor returns at the time of exit when they convert their assets back into dollars. A fixed rate also ensures that an appreciation of the currency would not reduce the attractiveness of investments in terms of their dollar costs. Note, this was a departure from Williamson's emphasis on market-driven exchange rates.

But while global financial investment was meant to stimulate growth, it often had the opposite effect. Many countries that became hotspots for financial investment found themselves facing recessions a few years down the line. The process worked as follows: global finance, in search of supernormal returns, would attempt to *anticipate* winners and losers among countries, and invest early in order to maximize returns, i.e., they would invest before clear signs of vibrant economic activity were visible for all to see. Central banks in target destinations prevented their exchange rates from appreciating by mopping up incoming dollars at the fixed exchange rate in return for the local currency. This led to an increase in the money supply and bank credit in their economies and created inflationary pressures. The surge in liquidity also resulted in speculative investment in real estate and stock markets creating asset bubbles that stoked inflation without necessarily increasing the productive potential of the country. As a result, at some point, an economy that had once shown some signs of promise began to look increasingly fragile. Meanwhile, the US would have accessed a rich source of savings as central banks used their acquired forex reserves to invest in safe assets like US Treasury bonds.

Over time, one or more of the following phenomena would emerge in the target economies: loans would start going bad, or steep stock market corrections would take place, or the government would find itself unable to service debt, or the real estate market would crash. Such mounting instabilities would make a flight of capital imminent. Again, important players within global capital would attempt to anticipate the flight, hoping to avoid its full impact on their investment. Their attempted early exits would be in the nature of self-fulfilling prophecies, bringing about the downfall of the economy, although the captains of global finance might still make hefty returns.

Note, target countries were forced to maintain exchange rates at levels that were based on speculative inflows of capital for the purchase of financial assets and real estate. There was not necessarily an accompanying increase in the demand for the country's goods and services in the international market. Hence, from the perspective of international trade in goods and services, the currencies were overvalued to begin with and became even more so, as the target economies became beset with instabilities following financial inflows.

Historically, depreciating currencies to make exports competitive had been an integral part of the growth miracles in East Asia. It would also work well for China. Not being able to depreciate or at least correctly value the currency with respect to the actual competitive position in international trade took away an important lever of growth from the hands of the country.

If one were to be cynical, one might surmise that captains of global capital played the game of dressing up a country to look good, entering early, and exiting before the music stopped. Their returns were independent of the real performance of the target economy. The steps outlined above formed the songbook of the collapse of the East Asian economies in the mid-1990s, although investors such as George Sorros made a killing in the process.* China escaped this fate by maintaining tight controls on global financial investment.

This, then, was the new face of the exorbitant privilege of the US. Excess savings of emerging economies flowed to the US through the purchase of low-interest-yielding US Treasury securities by the central banks of those countries.† These savings cycled back to many of the same economies in the form of high-return-bearing financial capital. This led to high returns for US financial services firms, but frequent financial volatility across the globe. From the 1980s to 2007, the Savings and Loan Crisis and the 'dot-com' bust‡ were the only major financial flashpoints for the US. However, financial crises of various flavours occurred in Russia, Mexico, Argentina, Japan, Chile, Thailand, Indonesia, Malaysia and Taiwan in this time.

---

* Between 1979 and 2011, using his wealth, Sorros has donated more than $11 billion to various philanthropic causes, mainly focused on promoting democracy and free markets around the world. Sourced from 'Philanthropy vs. Tyranny: Inside the Open Society Foundations' Biggest Battle Yet' by David Callahan, 17 August 2017.

† See chapter 'The Rise of High Finance'.

‡ Described later in this chapter.

External instability could potentially have impacted the US economy as well if borrowers in foreign countries who owed money to entities in the US had defaulted on payments or as investments turned sour. And yet, till the financial crisis of 2008, the mainstream view was that the Fed had solved the puzzle of macroeconomic management that had beguiled economists since the Great Depression – bringing about healthy and sustained GDP growth with low levels of inflation. How did that come to be?

The Great Moderation or a Grand Churning?

The period starting from the mid-1980s until 2007 has been called the Great Moderation on account of low rates of inflation and a reduction in the volatility of business cycle fluctuations in developed nations. Inflation was controlled on account of the reduction of real wages, cheap imports, and the development of efficient global supply chains. Crude oil prices fell till the 2000s after which they started to rise on the back of a global commodities boom. Interest rates were low on account of the transfer of savings from emerging economies to the US. The economy grew at a steady rate on an already high base.

However, as shown in the previous section, the Great Moderation was a period of grand churning in financial markets across the globe. The financial instability created huge amounts of uncertainty, volatility, and unrest in the affected economies. This unrest could well have circled back to the US on account of the interconnectedness of the global economic system. Financial distress overseas could have resulted in financial stress in the USA. Further, the US economy was also vulnerable to domestic risks stemming from financial speculation and the unrestrained pursuit of opportunities generated by new technologies.

The Fed tackled all these threats through infusions of liquidity into the economy, often through a reduction in interest rates. These interventions would re-infuse energy into the business investment landscape or energize consumer spending and help to tide over the crisis. But ultimately, the injection of liquidity would flow in the direction of financial markets, local or global. And soon enough, there would be another bubble on the way. This pattern of macroeconomic management led Raghuram Rajan, the future governor of central bank of India, to quote the adage: 'When America sneezes, the world catches a cold.'*

For instance, the housing boom of the 2000s and the 2008 crisis were engineered by the Fed's attempts – including interest rate reductions, and relaxations of home loan lending standards – to navigate out of a previous boom-crisis episode related to the dot-com era.

In the late 1990s, with the rising popularity of the Internet, there was a massive wave of speculation around 'new economy'. It was a time when 'everyone and their grandmom' was setting up a dot-com company, and extravagant 'launch parties' were a daily affair. All the old rules of doing business – aim for profits, or at least maximize revenues, or at the very least make a realistic financial plan – were thrown out of the window. Hundreds of new dot-com companies achieved multi-

---

* Quoted by International Monetary Fund, @IMFNews. The original phrase was, 'When France sneezes, the world catches a cold.' Please see Elizabeth Nicholas, 'Where Does the Phrase "When America Sneezes, the World Catches Cold" Originate?', Culture Trip, 22 April 2018.

million-dollar valuations in early rounds of funding. And many multiplied that valuation several hundred times when they went public. The NASDAQ Composite Index, home to most of these technology and dot-com company stocks, that stood under the 500 mark at the beginning of 1990 soared to a peak of over 5,000 in March 2000. However, it crashed shortly thereafter. By October 2002, it had plunged by 80% and triggered a recession in the US.[12]

The dot-com rollercoaster itself was a result of the reduction of interest rates and liberalized lending practices after the Mexico peso crisis of 1995. There had been a previous reduction of rates after the Savings and Loan Crisis of the 1980s when a crash in real estate prices led to many thrifts going bust.

The wave of liquidity injected into the US economy after the dot-com bust flowed overseas to create inflationary pressures and asset market bubbles in emerging economies. Thus, the great moderation was far from a great smoothening of the business cycle in two major respects. First, repeated cycles of monetary easing seemed to avert immediate crises but only pushed the can further down the road ultimately leading to the Great Financial Recession of 2008. Second, much of the economic volatility got exported outside the US.

It is noteworthy that a reduction in interest rates hurts those who deposit their money in banks. When assessing their returns, in addition to interest rates, depositors also need to factor the effect of an increase in prices wiping out their buying power in the future. The depositors in US experienced low average real rates of return, i.e., the interest rate minus the rate of inflation, with high variability, on account of the generally low and highly variable interest rates. Their real returns often were lower than

1%, and are currently in the negative territory. This does not speak of a Fed that promotes a sense of monetary stability in the general populace.

After 2008

By the time of the 2008 financial crisis, the hands of the Fed were tied because interest rates were already so low that any further decreases would result in breaching the 'zero lower bound' on interest rates. This played an important role in the choice of the Fed's strategy in the aftermath of the Global Financial Crisis.

As before, the Fed chose to inject liquidity. When the Fed injects liquidity, it does so by buying government securities from banks and other financial institutions. The purchase of securities increases their price. Given that these securities are associated with a fixed income stream, for example $1 a year, the increase in price amounts to a reduction in the interest rate.* The reduction in the interest rate on government securities leads to a cascading fall in the entire structure of interest rates in the economy, and a resulting increase in the demand for loans. Thus, a wave of lending is triggered by an initial injection of liquidity by the central bank.

---

* Government Securities are associated with a face value, for example $200, along with a fixed annual income stream, for instance $10. In our example, the implied interest rate is 5%. However, depending on the demand and supply of such securities, their market price could be different from $200 – greater in the event of excess demand and lower in the event of excess supply. When the market price increases, the implied interest rate falls, and when the market price decreases, the implied interest rate rises. For instance, the implied interest rate corresponding to a market price of $210 is 4.76%.

But, after the 2008 financial crisis, the Fed did not trigger liquidity by announcing a lower interest rate or buying government securities. Instead, it bought mortgage-backed securities from banks. This option was chosen for two reasons: first, the demand for such securities in the market had crashed. Therefore, the actions of the Fed cleaned the books of banks and established a floor price for mortgage-backed securities which helped investment banks and other institutions that carried mortgage-backed securities on their balance sheets. Second, it was the only option in a scenario where interest rates on government securities were so low, they could not go lower.

When the COVID-19 crisis hit in 2020, once more the risk of a financial collapse loomed. And once more, with key interest rates hovering between 0% to 0.25%, the Fed had lost its ability to influence the economy by reducing interest rates. Yet again, the Fed had to resort to the purchase of mortgage-backed securities to bail out the economy.

Trillions of dollars were poured into the economy in this way. As of September 2021, the total money supply circulating in the US economy was about $21 trillion. Of this, close to $5.5 trillion, i.e., almost 30%, came into the economy after January 2021.[13] The move was seen as necessary to douse the fires raging through the economy. But people began to ask why those fires were repeatedly ignited in the first place, and why those primarily responsible faced such limited repercussions.

Of course, the allegation that the US enjoyed an exorbitant privilege was only one side of the picture. Since the US was the anchor economy of the global system, there was a heightened demand for the dollar. This inflated the price of the currency and reduced the competitiveness of US exports, resulting in an increased risk of trade deficits. Thus, the privilege came with costs. It was a crown of thorns, not just a silver spoon.

But the issue here is one of unwise trade-offs. The dollar's dominant position in the basket of currencies adversely affected the US's balance of trade. However, the same strength was used to create a global playing field for its financial services firms, granting them an 'exorbitant [financial] privilege'. Instead, the US, and the world at large, would have benefitted from the US voluntarily circumscribing the power of the dollar by keeping it pegged to gold as envisaged in the Bretton Woods system. This would have resulted in a more limited degree of influence of the dollar as a reserve currency, higher trade competitiveness, and lower financial muscle. Overall, a more stable system would have emerged.

In sum, the period following the Nixon Shock resulted in a steep increase in the power of the Fed and the global financial elite, a power that by no means was always used responsibly. There were four main kinds of complicity involved. First, large financial institutions were bailed out despite playing a key role in causing various crises. This was the 'moral hazard problem'. Second, by suppressing interest rates, middle class depositors were made scapegoats to privilege the aspirations of financial investors. Third, external instability became a necessary cost of internal stability. Lastly, a large shadow banking sector was allowed to flourish, and it compromised the Fed's ability to control the economy.

Those who gained the most from the system faced the fewest consequences for failure. Meanwhile, those who lost out, faced repeated shocks from financial volatility. By 2008, the conditions were ripe for an insurrection. And, indeed, it arrived, engineered by a group of people who go by the name of 'techno-utopians'.

Cryptocurrency Unsettles an Exorbitant Privilege

The rising power of the Fed was accompanied by a rising wave of criticism of its overweening influence. The most radical of the critiques came from the Austrian school of economists. The Austrian school, founded by luminaries such as Ludwig von Mises, a rare Jewish member of the Austrian nobility, and Friedrich Hayek, his Nobel Prize-winning protégé, has a deep scepticism with regard to the ability of governments to serve the public good. Its criticism extends to the monopoly of central banks over the custodianship of the monetary system.

The Austrians believe that monetary systems controlled by central banks are prone to inflation, which they regard as extremely harmful for economic wellbeing. In his much talked about work *The Denationalization of Money*,[14] the first edition of which came out in 1976, Hayek recommends free markets in banking comprising multiple private banks competing with each other. Each bank would issue its own currencies, and the public would choose the currency with which to transact or enter into contracts. An exchange rate between currencies would emerge from the operation of market forces.[15]

With fashions in monetary architectures swinging in the opposite direction from WWII till the 1970s, the Austrian school seemed to have had little impact. However, in the 1990s and 2000s their visions found resonance in the efforts of the tribe of 'techno-utopians'. Techno-utopians believe that technological progress is the panacea for the evils befalling humankind. They bristle at government control of any kind.[16]

'We were beginning the revolution against the central banks on the beach in Anguilla,' recalls Peter Thiel, co-founder of PayPal, a pioneering digital payments company, speaking of a meeting of 200 tech pioneers in February 2000.[17] Also present at the event were the founders of e-gold, a gold-backed currency issued not by a government but by a private exchange.

At its peak in 2006, e-gold had close to five million users and handled $2 billion of annual transactions. With the site being used for foreign exchange transactions, e-gold was emerging as a player to reckon with in international finance. However, its systems were prone to hacking and were used by fraudsters who sold fake goods and rapidly moved their gold earnings to lenient jurisdictions. The site was also a convenient medium for child pornography. In 2007, e-gold was charged with four violations of money laundering regulations and knowingly allowing a transaction for the purchase of child pornography.

Thiel believes that Satoshi Nakamoto, the elusive founder of the world's first cryptocurrency, the bitcoin, was on the beach in Anguilla in February 2000. Satoshi's true identity has not been conclusively established to this day, although rumours about possible suspects abound. Thiel conjectures that the fall of e-gold could have motivated Nakamoto to remain anonymous while developing the bitcoin.[18]

The timeline of events around the launch of the bitcoin is revealing. On 18 August 2008, eight years after the Anguilla meeting, the domain bitcoin.org was registered. In just under a month from the date of the registration, the Lehman crash would draw the curtains on the Global Financial Crisis. On 31 October that year, a paper authored by Satoshi Nakamoto, 'Bitcoin: A Peer-to-Peer Electronic Cash System' that explained the mechanics of the new currency was sent to a cryptography mailing list. The first block of transactions using bitcoin was uploaded to the public ledger on 3 January 2009. The notes accompanying the so called 'genesis block' included a headline from that day's *The Times*: 'Chancellor on the brink of second bail-out for banks.' That was the quote with which bitcoin challenged the official banking system, offering itself as a more reliable form of currency.[19]

The problem that Nakamoto set out to solve was to create a digital currency without the use of any central bank-like intermediary, without the use of a commodity such as gold being used as a monetary base, and with complete anonymity for the transactors. Techno-utopians cared deeply about preserving the anonymity of commercial transactions, even more so than the Austrians. To understand what he set out to achieve we need a short primer on the structure and functions of a monetary system and on the foundational principles of cryptocurrency.

The Monetary System and Cryptocurrency

A monetary system is in large part merely an accurate system of recordkeeping of commercial transactions. For instance, in the monetary system of the Yap in Micronesia, rai stones, each fairly large in size, were used as a form of money for thousands of years. Transactions were carried out without the physical movement of the stones themselves. Each stone was associated by stories of various transactions that had been carried out with its use. These stories established the identities of owners of that stone, the sequence of transactions and the portion they controlled. The trusted elders of the tribe were the custodians of the authenticity of the stories, a homegrown system of ledger-keeping that allowed the system to work.

In addition to accurately recording the balances of different entities resulting from the transactions that they undertook, thus acting as a unit of account, the rai stones were a universally accepted medium of exchange. Further, they served as a store of value, i.e., offered a convenient form in which entities could hold their wealth. These are the same functions that a monetary system in a modern economy must fulfil.

In order for money to be able to perform these functions it is imperative that there exists a set of trusted intermediaries, akin to the elders of Yap. First and foremost, the central bank and the central (federal) government together need to mandate universal acceptance of the currency by making it legal tender. They must also pursue policies that ensure stability in the value of the legal tender, for instance through low inflation. Second, the banking system plays an important role in multiplying the supply of money in the economy through credit creation. To take a simple example, deposits of ₹100 can be partly used to extend credit to borrowers as all depositors are unlikely to come at the same time to demand their deposits back. The borrowers in turn create fresh deposits which become a further source of credit creation. The banks thus serve as trusted intermediaries in honouring the balances of depositors and following prudential lending practices. Finally, beyond the traditional banking system, there are a host of entities and institutions in the financial services industry, that raise money from banks and other investors and channelize the funds for a variety of purposes including home loans, growth capital for emerging enterprises, and the revival of distressed corporations. These include non-banking financial corporations, corporate bond markets, and stock markets. It is the operation of all these trusted intermediaries, within and across countries, that allows the monetary system to work efficiently, allowing money to fulfil its expected functions.

The combination of cryptography, a field of study that aims to facilitate secure communication in the presence of an adversary, and 'distributed ledger technology' formed the foundation of Nakamoto's solution to the problem of creating a reliable monetary system without trusted intermediaries. The coding of messages sent during war time is an example of cryptography. To understand distributed ledger technology, imagine a group of people playing cards at a party. One way of keeping track of people's earnings is for one person to be designated as record keeper. But suppose no one is trustworthy enough for the role. Then one could devise a system in which each player keeps a record, and at the end of every round an entry is made in a central ledger after ensuring that it matches the noting made by every player. This is broadly the principle on which distributed ledger technology works.

In a cryptocurrency network, any transaction between two parties is protected by the passwords ('private keys') used by both of them. Next, there is a password generated for the transaction as a whole ('public key') that along with the signatures of the parties ensures that the parties did in fact carry out the transaction, i.e., the private keys were in fact used. A given number of such transactions constitute a 'block' that is uploaded to the distributed ledger. Coming back to the game of cards, it's like accounts are recorded after a fixed number of rounds (corresponding to transactions).

The process of uploading a block itself includes a number of checks and balances. The uploading is time stamped – hence, a person cannot use a bitcoin they have spent in the past to make another transaction. This addresses the 'double spend' problem in which one unit of currency is used twice, a possibility non-existent with paper money, but eminently possible with digital money. In this way a chain of blocks, i.e., a block chain, representing a series of time stamped transactions is created. But how does everyone trust the block chain is an authentic record? Can't someone tamper with the transaction details?

There are a large number of copies of this block chain. Any time someone tries to change a block, all the subsequent blocks on that copy of the block chain get 'broken', i.e., are marked as defective. Hence, in order to successfully change a block, one has to change all subsequent blocks as well. All this requires a significant amount of computing power as each change requires cracking a cryptographic code which in turn involves searching through an extremely large space of possibilities. But the challenges to a would-be hacker do not end here. In order for a change to be accepted, it has to be carried out in every copy of the block chain across thousands of 'nodes', in the network, i.e., computers. This makes the problem of hacking the block chain virtually intractable and ensures absolute faith in the record of transactions without the intervention of any trusted intermediary.

Innovations in Theory and Practice

The innovations of early cryptocurrencies such as Bitcoin and Ether can be divided into two categories – those that largely replicate features of existing monetary systems while doing away with the intermediary role of the central bank; and those that mark radical departures from existing systems. Innovations in the former category are important to techno-utopians but less important to those in the field of economics. This is because economists already have a bunch of tools that they believe can sufficiently curtail the power of central banks. For instance, as mentioned before, members of the Austrian School believe that the operation of free markets is capable of disintermediating central banks. For this reason, an economist would not regard the 'block chain' or distributed ledger technology, despite its pathbreaking algorithm for enabling trusted transactions without a trusted intermediary, as a radical innovation.* The real departure of the Bitcoin from previous monetary systems lies in something simpler – the manner in which the total number of bitcoins in circulation is determined.

The total number of coins of the cryptocurrency that are in circulation at any given time involves two parameters – the initial number of coins and the rule that governs the introduction of new coins into the system. At a time when the currency used to consist of gold coins, the introduction of new coins depended on the effort expended by competing miners on the mining of gold. In the bitcoin system, the introduction of new bitcoins depends on the computing power expended by competing programmers to crack a computer code. Here's how.

---

* However, in its power to bring about disintermediation, it is a game-changing innovation for other areas of commerce including for the creation of smart contracts.

After a block of transactions is created, several 'miners' have identical copies of the block. Miners compete with each other to upload the block to the distributed ledger, the block chain. The competition takes the form of cracking a code using computational power. The winner is the one who cracks the code first and thus demonstrates 'proof of work'. The winner is paid a commission for uploading the block and is also issued fresh bitcoins, in the manner of a traditional miner after a fresh discovery of gold. In this way, the number of bitcoins in circulation increases with each uploaded block of transactions.

But the number of bitcoins earned for uploading a block of transactions halves every two years. And, after a total of 21 million bitcoins are in circulation, the issuing of fresh bitcoins is programmed to stop. Thus, unlike in a system of fiat money, the total money in circulation cannot be increased indefinitely. Further, unlike in a system of competing private currencies à la the Austrian School, a software algorithm, and not the market mechanism, determines the total currency in circulation.

Limiting the number of units of currency is a good thing for those who believe that a monetary system where the money supply can go up indefinitely is prone to chronic inflation. However, as this limited currency becomes more widely used – as a means of payment, a medium in which contracts are drawn up, and a target for investment – its own value continuously increases. Thus, it seems inevitable that the prices of goods and services in terms of this currency would continuously decline. In other words, the currency, while not inflationary, runs the opposite risk – of being deflationary.

Therefore, a cryptocurrency such as the bitcoin appears to be inherently unsuitable as a means of payment or medium in which contracts are drawn up. As a medium of exchange, its main use would probably be restricted to transactions where anonymity is important. Such transactions often involve fraudulent or illegal activity.

These hypotheses seem to be borne out by the history of the bitcoin. The first marketplace that accepted bitcoins in return for goods and services was Silk Road, a platform that operated on the 'dark web'. Launched in 2011, it allowed users to communicate and conduct business while remaining anonymous and not revealing identifying information, such as location. Silk Road allowed anything to be traded, whether it was considered legal by the state or not. The trade was dominated by marijuana, hacked passwords, fake IDs, and drugs that normally could not be sold without a prescription. The US government seized Silk Road in 2013. Bitcoin was also used to make donations to WikiLeaks at a time when the US had banned donations to the site on account of the appearance of classified documents leaked by Edward Snowden.

Since 2014, it has been possible to purchase Windows games, Xbox games, music, movies, and other digital media from Microsoft using bitcoin. Companies such as Home Depot, US's largest home improvement chain, and Starbucks, the world's largest coffeehouse chain, also accept bitcoin payments in US-based stores. However, it would be fair to say that overall turnover remains small, and that it is dominated by goods and services where anonymity is important. Why then, given their apparent unsuitability for transactions, are cryptocurrencies bothering central bankers so much?

Concerns of Central Bankers

Today there are close to 9,000 private cryptocurrencies in circulation, somewhat analogous to the private currencies the Austrian School envisioned. On 14 November 2021, the combined market cap of all cryptocurrencies was as high as $2.8 trillion. This was nearly on par with the value of gold held as an investment. But on 27 January 2022, within just over three months, the total market cap of cryptocurrencies nearly halved to $1.7 trillion.[20]

It is possible that it is precisely the scale of speculative investment and the degree of volatility in the value of this asset class that central bankers are concerned about. This concern would reflect a measure of learning from the Great Financial Crisis of 2008, since before that the Fed believed that asset price volatility was none of its business.

Regulatory concern could also stem from the fact that far from decentralizing financial power, cryptocurrencies appear to have led to a concentration of power in the hands of a few private conglomerates and individuals.

We mentioned earlier that bitcoin mining involves expending computing power. Actually, the amount of computing power involved is substantial. The Bitcoin Energy Consumption Index suggested that the power required by a single bitcoin transaction in 2021 was equivalent to the total power consumption of an average US household over 50 days.[21] This power requirement has led to the concentration of ownership of the bitcoin as conglomerates of computing power compete with each other to win bitcoins.*

In this regard, the tweets of Jackson Palmer, the founder of one of the most successful cryptocurrencies, the Dogecoin, are instructive. Palmer tweeted: 'Despite claims of "decentralization", the cryptocurrency industry is controlled by a powerful cartel of wealthy figures who, with time, have evolved to incorporate many of the same institutions tied to the existing centralized financial system they supposedly set out to replace.'[22]

The value of cryptocurrencies has also been influenced by whimsical movements intended to trigger virality. For instance, in June 2020, influencers on TikTok, a video sharing site, launched an informal campaign to try to get the price of the Dogecoin to reach $1 per coin. They were able to drive up the value by 71% in a few days.[23] The pronouncements and actions of global influencers such as Elon Musk can make currencies shoot up or crash with a single tweet. The steep appreciation in the value of Dogecoin, of which a potentially unlimited quantity can be mined, shows that a limit on the number of coins is not necessary for appreciation of value, at least in the short term.

---

* The highly successful cryptocurrency Ether recently moved from a proof of work mechanism to a proof of stake mechanism. Under the proof of stake mechanism, the validator of the block is randomly chosen from a group of validators, each of whom has committed a certain amount of ether coins as collateral to ensure honourable behaviour. This mechanism reduces the energy requirements of the network and simultaneously increases the security as the network becomes more decentralized.

Finally, the average investor has been preyed upon by hackers and fraudsters. Mt. Gox, an early bitcoin exchange, had to declare itself bankrupt in 2014 when clients complained that they couldn't withdraw their bitcoins. Mark Karpelès, the CEO, found that a hacker had slowly and surely emptied out all of Mt. Gox's bitcoins without being noticed. The company lost 8,50,000 bitcoins – worth nearly $500 million.[24] In late 2014, Ryan Kennedy, an early investor in Dogecoin, started a Dogecoin exchange service called Moolah under the alias Alex Green. It was later found he was committing various types of frauds that led to the collapse of the exchanges.

It is true that central bankers could be looking askance at cryptocurrencies on account of their concerns for the fortunes of the average Joe. But, in my opinion, the concerns of central bankers are not limited to asset price volatility, concentration of power in a few hands, and the vulnerability of retail investors.

Naysayers about the potential of cryptocurrencies to act as a means of payment ignore the possibility that an entirely new universe of virtual goods and services could arise in parallel with the new currency. Cryptocurrencies could become a natural means of payment for such goods. Unlike traditional goods, the prices of these goods need not fall in terms of cryptocurrency.

Non-fungible tokens (NFTs) are a case in point. These are digital assets which include pieces of art, digital real estate, games and audio pieces whose ownership can be transferred from the owner to a buyer. In many cases, the copyright is not transferred, so the owner can create and sell duplicates of the original.

Artist Mike Winkelmann (known to the art world as Beeple)

sold 'Everydays: The First 5000 Days', a digital work of art comprising of 5,000 images created on a daily basis over 14 years for $69.3 million in 2021. The buyer paid 42,329 Ether for the artwork and displayed it in a digital museum within 'the metaverse'.*

Cryptocurrencies have been used to buy and sell online real estate located in game universes.

Some luxury brands such as Dolce & Gabbana, Jimmy Choo, Nike, Gucci, and Burberry have entered the world of NFTs by creating video game apparels and cosmetics that the avatars of gamers can don in the online world.[25] In November 2021, a report by Morgan Stanley claimed that this innovation has the potential to become a multi-billion-dollar market by 2030.[26]

An early successful blockchain online game was CryptoKitties, in which players adopted and traded virtual cats, with some kitties selling for over $100,000 each.

Thus, cryptocurrencies could become important as a means of payments and contracting in the digital universes coming into being. This, possibly, forms the basis of the bets speculators are making on cryptocurrencies as an asset class. This prospect could also be the real fear motivating the actions of central banks.

For, if cryptocurrencies become the currency of choice in the metaverse, and the metaverse continues to grow at its current rate, central banks will lose control over a significant portion of the currencies used for making transactions in the economy as a whole. This will limit their ability to manage the

---

* See Chapter 6 for a description of the metaverse.

money supply. Further, they will lose the seigniorage, i.e., the fees they earn for managing the mint. Meanwhile, the Treasury Departments of governments could lose a lot of tax revenue as transactions take place under the radar.

Finally, the Ukraine crisis has demonstrated that geopolitical transitions may result in certain countries losing access to markets and vital parts of the global financial infrastructure. The sanctions against Russia include cutting the country off from Society for Worldwide Interbank Financial Telecommunications (SWIFT), a messaging system that allows banks across borders to keep each other informed about transactions in real time, freezing Russian central bank dollar reserves, and decisions to stop trading with the country.

Russia's allies, such as China and India, would be willing to carry on trade with currencies other than the dollar. Private cryptocurrencies could also be used for such transactions. Further, with the threat of sanctions hanging over countries that previously obtained vital inputs from Russia, cryptocurrencies could emerge as a medium of exchange for proscribed transactions, in the black markets that are bound to arise following the sanctions.

Indeed, the war between central banks and cryptocurrency networks is part of a larger war being fought between the state and techno-utopians, a faceoff that is framed within the context of new geopolitical rivalries. There is reason for central bankers to be concerned.

4

TECTONIC SHIFTS IN GEOPOLITICS

The conception of the Middle East as an unlimited reservoir that exists to fulfil the ever-growing energy needs of consumerist Western societies was bound to come up against Islamism, a religio-political movement that believes that a puritanical conception of Islam 'should guide social and political as well as personal life'.[1] This confrontation between the ideology of enlightenment and a worldview that has come to represent its polar opposite has been referred to as a 'clash of civilizations'.[2] The clash was further ignited by the hubris of USA, the unipolar hegemon, that saw existential threats in Iraq where there were none, and assumed it had the bandwidth to effect a civilizational change in societies very different from its own.

In parallel, the US underestimated an old, resilient foe, Russia, and triggered a war in Ukraine – a war which suited an aging dictator determined to hold on to power. All these developments were, of course, music to the ears of the US arms industry, a key influencer of the political scene. Consumerism, democracy, the coalescing of geopolitical goals with the enrichment of the arms industry, and the desire to spread the ideology of rationality in Afghanistan and Ukraine reprise all the key registers of the age of rationality and highlight its deep fault lines.

Afghanistan: Grand Larceny in the Graveyard of Empires

On 11 September 2001, when the two planes crashed into the gleaming twin towers proudly soaring over Manhattan, they signified a tearing down of castle walls. Walls that protected privileged New Yorkers from the wretched of the earth – those living in far off hinterlands, objects of pity for anachronistic ways of life that seemed to be one-way tickets to nowhere, and useful only for the minerals lying deep within the bowels of their lands.

It was the moment when the American Dream cracked and splintered into a thousand pieces – each shard reflecting an image of bewilderment; each wail a dirge for the loss of innocence. It was an innocence that believed that American prosperity was a result of the American virtue of hard work and entrepreneurship, that the American way of life was a beacon of hope for the world, and that with God on its side, America's supremacy was here to stay.

And yet, perhaps it was not an innocence that was lost, rather a smugness that was shattered – a smugness that acknowledged that there was a world out there, forsaken and desolate, but that believed that it was inevitable that the weak lost out, that the incapable suffered, and the strong emerged victorious.

Actually, what was lost was not innocence, for then there would have been a humbling reappraisal of self-regard. Nor was it smugness that was surrendered, for then there would have been a pressing urge to correct wrongs. The moment marked the beginning of an age of insecurity that came on like a cloak, a creeping fear that killed chutzpah, a growing bitterness that took on idealism, and plunged a sword into the heart of America like nothing else could.

Within a few weeks, the US would begin a war against Afghanistan, the country whose government, led by the Taliban, had harboured Al-Qaeda, the terror group behind the attacks. Shortly thereafter, a non-Taliban interim government was installed to be followed in December 2004 by a democratically elected dispensation.[3] But, 20 years later, when American troops had to withdraw with the Taliban in control and the threat of another terror attack from Afghan territory very much in the realm of possibility, it was clear that the greatest country the world had ever seen had gone past the zenith of its power.

The story of the American defeat illustrates many pitfalls the US was unable to avoid as it navigated the post-Soviet world in which it held pre-eminent sway as the world's only superpower. The story of the combat operations in Afghanistan that earned Sergeant Clinton L. Romesha the Medal of Honour, the highest military decoration in the US, symbolizes the possibilities of US military strategy and its ultimate limits.

Winning the Battle of Kamdesh

It was 2009. The US had been present in Afghanistan for close to eight years. It had a new President, Obama, who was keen to win the war once and for all. The strategy was to build roads to the remotest corners of the country. The logic was that the road would enable the transportation of equipment, supplies, and soldiers that would help hold a position versus the Taliban.

However, there was also apprehension that on account of the mountainous terrain, the Taliban could easily set up ambushes or block the entire highway by controlling a small part of it.

Romesha, who hails from a family whose members have fought the Battle of Normandy in WWII as well as the Vietnam War, was stationed in Combat Outpost Keating, Kamdesh District, Nuristan Province, in Eastern Afghanistan, one of the remotest outposts of the US army. The outpost was situated in a valley at the foot of three hills. The difficulties of the terrain can be gauged by the fact that this location, difficult as it was, was the best among all possible alternatives.

What happened next had an air of inevitability about it.[4] At 6 a.m., on 3 October 2009, the camp came under attack from three sides. Armed with a recoilless rifle, rocket-propelled grenades, mortars, machine guns, and small arms, about 300 fighters mounted an attack. The International Security Assistance Force (ISAF) – comprising 85 soldiers from the United States Army, Afghan National Army, and Latvian Army was heavily outnumbered.

Very early on in the fighting, the ammunitions depot in the camp was destroyed. Within three hours of fighting, the compound had been breached and set on fire by the Taliban. With defeat and capture seeming imminent, Romesha decided they must reclaim the three entrances to the camp. Under heavy fire, he sent two parties to two gates and led one party to the third gate himself. The Taliban had not expected this counterattack. After 12 hours of fighting, they were beaten back with 150 casualties. The US lost eight soldiers. The battle had been won, and the Medal of Honour earned.

A few days later Camp Keating was wound up.

Losing the War

Holding Camp Keating was always going to be an uphill battle, given the difficulty of the topography. Obama's real plan was to capture the safe havens of the Taliban. In mid-2009, he sent in General Stanley McChrystal, head of Special Operations, to do the job. McChrystal asked for a surge of 15,000 US troops in order to secure a decisive victory; Obama reluctantly agreed. As a test case, the US alliance would attempt to take the town of Marjah in the Helmand Valley.

The target had been chosen for good reasons. In 2000, 10% of the global production of illicit opium originated from this area. It was the Taliban's treasure chest. While winning Marjah would have been a turning point in the war, the challenge was the strong local support Taliban enjoyed in the area.

Unlike in previous operations, the US command ensured that US soldiers formed a large proportion, almost a third, of the combined US–Afghan forces. The offensive that started in early 2010 was dubbed Operation Moshtarak ('together' in the Dari language). And yet, the US and Afghan fighters, despite initial success, could not hold Marjah.[5]

The Taliban kept making sneak attacks and laying more roadside bombs. McChrystal referred to it as a 'bleeding ulcer'. What was thought to be a war that could be turned around with a surge of troops started to look like it was fundamentally unwinnable. The US began to realize why Afghanistan had been a graveyard of empires as powerful as those commanded by the British and the Soviets.

In any case, the US had made its own task much harder with some utterly incomprehensible decisions as far back as 2003.

The Iraq War

The war against Iraq was part of the global war against terror that was initiated by President George W. Bush after the World Trade Center was attacked. It began in 2003 and continued till 2011. The ostensible causes were: Iraq's possession of weapons of mass destruction and President Saddam Hussein's links with the Al-Qaeda.[6]

The US Secretary of State, General Colin Powell, in a speech addressing the United Nations (UN), dramatically held up a vial which he claimed contained a biological weapon – Anthrax. He asserted that Saddam had the capability as well as the intention to unleash such weapons on the world. However, his theatrics stemmed in no small measure from a personal grouse held against Saddam by his Commander-in-Chief.

To be fair, President George W. Bush had inherited this grouse from his father who had been the President of the US from 1988–92. In January 1991, the senior Bush had ordered American planes to bomb Iraq in Operation Desert Storm, in response to Saddam's invasion of Jordan. The failure of that mission had weighed heavily on Bush Senior's re-election bid, which he ultimately lost.

In addition to the charge of possession of weapons of mass destruction, Bush Junior wanted the CIA to link Saddam Hussein to Al-Qaeda through Al Zarqawi, a Jordanian national who later became the founder of ISIS, a terror group described later in this chapter. The snag was that the CIA did not support the theory. Consequently, the war on Iraq was not firmly grounded in CIA intelligence as is usually the case in military operations.

Later, it became evident that questionable US intelligence

reports had been cherry picked to convince Americans that Iraq was a necessary target. UN Secretary General Kofi Annan said that the invasion of Iraq was illegal as per international law, because it violated the UN Charter.[7] Colin Powell would later refer to his 'anthrax speech' at the UN as a blot on his record.[8]

But a war was what Bush Junior wanted, and a war was what he got. In December 2003, Saddam Hussein was captured during Operation Red Dawn. He was executed three years later, after what was regarded as a sham trial.[9] At the peak of its engagement, in 2007, the US had stationed 1,70,000 soldiers in Iraq, even as a highly risky asymmetric war against the guerilla fighters of the Taliban raged in Afghanistan.

The Rise of ISIS

The first elected government following Saddam's ouster took power in 2006. It alienated the country's previously dominant Sunni minority and, consequently, worsened sectarian tensions between Shias and Sunnis. In the summer of 2014, the Islamic State of Iraq and the Levant (ISIL), which later came to be known as Islamic State of Iraq and Syria (ISIS), declared a worldwide Islamic caliphate after launching a military offensive in northern Iraq. Many members of ISIS were former soldiers from Saddam Hussein's army that had been disbanded by the new dispensation.[10]

In 2015, at the height of its power, ISIS controlled swathes of land in Libya, Egypt (Sinai Peninsula), Saudi Arabia, Yemen, Algeria, Afghanistan, Pakistan, Nigeria and the North Caucasus.[11] By then it had entirely eclipsed Al-Qaeda as a threat to the world order led by the US. Not just was it an incubator of terror attacks but a well ensconced quasi-state with its own government, military, and system of justice. The rapidly expanding power of the ISIS forced the US to increase its troop presence in Iraq once again in 2014.

But Iraq was not the only war diverting the attention of the US from Afghanistan.

Syria

A wave of armed rebellions, anti-government protests, and uprisings rippled across the Arab world in the early 2010s. Dubbed the 'Arab Spring', the protests against authoritarianism, corruption, and economic stagnation started from Tunisia, before they reached five other countries – Libya, Egypt, Yemen, Syria and Bahrain.[12] In Tunisia, the long-time president Zine El Abidine Ben Ali was deposed, and a democratic government came to power.

Following Ben Ali's fall, a group of teenagers in Syria, put up graffiti saying 'Your turn, Doctor'. This was a reference to their President Bashar al-Assad, who had been trained as an ophthalmologist. A brutal crackdown by the Syrian government followed. The US intervened with the ostensible aim of removing a dictator who had allegedly used chemical weapons against his population.

It should be pointed out that the US has a long history of supporting dictators – in the Middle East and beyond – to secure its strategic interests.[13] In 1953, the CIA toppled the democratic government of Iranian PM Mohammad Mossadegh to protect the fuel supply lines of the US. The last Shah of Iran, Mohammad Reza Pahlavi, who had close ties to the US, was installed instead.

Governments run by both Republican and Democratic parties have continuously supported authoritarian rule in Saudi Arabia for the same reason. However, starting with Hafez Al-Assad, a military officer who rose to become the President of Syria, they seem to have developed some problem with Syrian dictators. Their concerns seem to have spilled over to Assad Senior's son, Bashar al-Assad, as well.

Assad Senior was a votary of Arab unity in line with the philosophy of the Ba'ath Movement, an areligious movement espousing pan-Arabism and anti-imperialism, founded in 1947. He insisted that peace between Israel and the Arab world could only be predicated on a return of Palestinian refugees to Israel. But Henry Kissinger, the US Secretary of State, undermined Assad Senior's plans by creating a rupture in Arab unity through a separately negotiated peace deal between Egypt and Israel in 1975.[14] From this point on, Assad Senior would be a bitter foe of the US.

Assad Senior vowed to drive away American influence from the Middle East and is believed to have engineered a number of deadly terrorist attacks. Being wary of his power, the US largely chose to ignore him. Instead, they chose to demonize much weaker opponents such as Muammar Gaddaffi of Libya.

But after Assad Junior's crackdown on the Arab Spring Movement, the US decided to take on Syria. It fought the dictator alongside a bewildering array of forces, spanning a wide range of motivations.[15] The ISIS, US's enemy in Iraq, was opposed to Assad Junior as he ran a secular government. The Turkish-backed Free Syrian Army (FSA) was a loose collection of armed opposition groups founded in July 2011 by defecting Syrian military officers opposed to Assad. The

Kurdish-dominated Syrian Democratic Forces were fighting Assad Junior for greater autonomy in the region of Northern Syria where the ethnic group, the Kurds, were in a majority. The Kurds demand a separate homeland in a broad swathe of territory in West Asia, most prominently in Turkey, which is a member of the US-led NATO alliance in Syria, and has been vigorously opposing their demand. But they fought on the same side in Syria. The jihadi Hayat Tahrir al-Sham, similar to other Islamist groups, were opposed to Assad Junior's secular ideology, and fought alongside US forces. They were believed to have been propped up by Turkey to clip the wings of groups like ISIS.

Supporting the US were a host of countries including Saudi Arabia, Qatar, Britain, France, Israel, and the Netherlands. Ranged alongside the Syrian armed forces were Iran, Russia, and the Lebanese Hezbollah.

By 2014, with the Afghanistan problem still unresolved, the US-supported Iraq government losing ground to ISIS, and Syria in the midst of a conflagration involving virtually all the major powers of the world, the US had opened up a battlefront that stretched from the eastern border of Afghanistan all the way to the western border of Syria.

The Syrian war played an important role in cementing the axis of China, Russia, and Iran. Along with Russia, China vetoed UN resolutions condemning the Syrian government on several occasions. In 2020, Syria backed the national security law in Hong Kong at the UN, that China introduced in order to quell pro-democracy protests in Hong Kong.

This state of affairs made Pakistan, situated on the eastern border of Afghanistan, an indispensable partner of the US.

The Double-edged Sword of Pakistan

Afghanistan shares a porous border with Pakistan, and ethnic Pashtuns, the tribe to which the majority of the Taliban fighters belong, live on both sides of the Afghanistan–Pakistan border. The land mass of Pakistan is thus a crucial logistic corridor into and out of Afghanistan. Pakistan had been an ally of the US against the Soviet occupation of Afghanistan in the 1980s. Even before that, the US had a long history of supporting Pakistan to counterbalance its neighbour India's tilt toward the Soviet Union, and to prevent Pakistan from falling into China's sphere of influence. On its part, Pakistan has been only too willing to get US support in its continuous conflict with India.[16]

The Afghan war began after the refusal of the Taliban government to hand over Osama bin Laden and other leaders of Al-Qaeda to the US. In December 2001, US had come closest to bin Laden during the battle of Tora Bora (bin Laden's mountain stronghold), but he had eluded capture. It was speculated that he had slipped into Pakistan with the help of Afghan and Pakistani forces – that were supposedly US supporters.[17] In 2011, bin Laden was tracked down in Pakistan and killed in a bungalow in the military cantonment of Abbottabad where he had been comfortably ensconced for a few years.

This was not the first time that Pakistan would play on both sides. Nor was it the last.

The Taliban had by and large refused to speak to the Afghan government backed by the US, asserting that it was merely a puppet. This refusal marked a major roadblock to the goal of creating an Afghanistan where power would be shared between the liberal and hard-line elements.

Mullah Baradar was one of the few Taliban leaders who had shown a willingness to engage in talks. In February 2010, the administration of Afghan President Karzai reportedly held talks with Baradar. But things went downhill when Baradar was captured in Karachi, Pakistan, during a joint US–Pakistan raid. Karzai was outraged as this reeked of foul play by the Pakistani intelligence community, which was possibly opposed to Afghan peace talks that were being carried out independently of Pakistan.[18] Following this, the Taliban hardened its on-and-off stance that they would not speak to the Afghan government. Further, they made the exit of US troops a pre-condition for their coming to the negotiating table. These developments made them an attractive ally for Russia and China.

In fact, Pakistani territory remained in continuous use by the Taliban as a safe harbour, and a source of weapons, recruits, and other essential supplies from the beginning to the end of the conflict.[19]

From 2001 to 2021, Pakistan itself lost almost 70,000 lives in the war against terror.[20] However, despite suffering grievous losses, its intentions with regard to snuffing out terrorism are always suspect on account of its motivation to keep militancy ongoing in India, particularly in Jammu and Kashmir. The distinction the Pakistani establishment makes between good terrorists who stoke fires in India, and bad terrorists who engage in heinous activities in Pakistan in order to implement their hard-line vision of Islam, makes it difficult for them to proceed against either.[21]

Pakistan's motivations are also compromised by the vice like grip of the military on its policy making. According to World Bank data, in the period since 1995, about 16-28% of the annual budget of the Pakistan government has gone to the military.[22] Army generals run public sector companies operating across a wide range of businesses from cement to knitwear![23] Their retirement benefits include premium real estate plots. To legitimize their power, they work on two narratives. First, the spectre of a large external threat in the form of India. And second, the continuous presence of an inept civilian political leadership that is mired in corruption. Attempts by civilian leadership to normalize ties with India are generally followed by terrorist attacks in the neighbouring country.[24]

The US could have reduced its dependence on Pakistan by negotiating a deal with Iran, even though the two countries had been at loggerheads since the Islamic Revolution by Ayatollah Khomeini in 1980. In fact, in Iraq, the US and Iran share a common enemy. A deal with Iran would open some possibilities of controlling Afghanistan from its western borders.

It is true that US ties with Iran are constrained by the fact that it is considered an arch enemy by two important allies, Israel and Saudi Arabia. However, India has good relations with both Iran and Saudi Arabia due to its many civilian engagements including the development of roads, ports, dams, and hospitals. The good offices of India with Iran could have been used to ease American dependence on Pakistan.

However, the US did not use any of the available options to win over Iran in order to minimize its need for an unreliable Pakistan. Consequently, Pakistan continued as a safe haven for the Taliban as well as a key ally of the US.[25]

Negotiating an Exit

In May 2011, the US managed to kill Osama bin Laden and significantly weaken the Al-Qaeda. The main factor that had taken them to Afghanistan had been addressed.

The task of 'nation building' under which power would be vested in a liberal democratic government had been proceeding far too slowly, and the development of Afghan military was a challenge given the lack of ideological cohesion and the persistence of tribal loyalties of new recruits. The task was rendered more difficult by widespread corruption in the utilization of funds with individuals on both the Afghan and US sides gaining from the process. This made the creation of a committed cadre of Afghans difficult.[26]

Even though President Karzai had consistently made overtures to the Taliban since 2002, the US had been cagey, inserting conditions and clauses that made progress difficult. Till 2011, the US believed that the Taliban could be defeated militarily. However, after the failed operation in Marjah in 2011, Obama quietly started a process of peace negotiations and troop withdrawal.[27] A face-saving military presence that ensured a modicum of modernity in tiny enclaves while letting the large bulk of the landmass fester in a semi-autonomous state remained in place.

However, the secret talks ended inconclusively. In 2013, the Taliban opened a political office in Qatar, which was seen by President Hamid Karzai as an attempt to run a parallel government. When Pakistan hosted the first official peace talks between Taliban representatives and the Afghan government in 2015, US and China attended as observers. With violence on the rise, on 27 February 2018, the new President of Afghanistan, Ashraf Ghani, offered to recognize Taliban as a legal political party while also proposing unconditional peace talks. The release of the Taliban prisoners held in Afghan jails was also on offer. A conference of 20 countries in Tashkent, Uzbekistan, in March that year backed Ghani's peace offer.

However, the US had other plans. In July 2018, US officials secretly met Taliban's political commission in Qatar. In September, to promote intra-Afghan political peace process, Trump appointed Zalmay Khalilzad as special adviser on Afghanistan in the US State Department. The Taliban did not let the Afghan government join the talks. On 29 February 2020, the United States and the Taliban signed a peace agreement in Doha, Qatar.

The Unravelling of the Peace Agreement

The terms of the agreement seemed unexceptionable, both from the point of view of the US and the Taliban. They included complete prohibition of the use of Afghan soil for terrorist activities against the US, an agreement that the Taliban would begin negotiations with the Afghan government, and a commitment to completely withdraw US forces from Afghan soil in a phased manner *provided the peace negotiations between the government and the Taliban went well*. Troop numbers were to be reduced from 13,000 to 8,500 in 4.5 months, and then to zero in 9.5 months. As per the agreement, the US also intended to end economic sanctions on the Taliban by 27 August 2020. China, Russia, and Pakistan supported the deal, and it was unanimously endorsed by the UN Security Council.[28] However, the government of Afghanistan was not a part of this agreement.

One of the terms of the agreement was the release of 5,000 Taliban fighters held in Afghan prisons. In exchange, Taliban was required to return the 1,000 government soldiers it held.

The delay in the release of the prisoners, and the disagreement in the list of those to be released, led to talks between the Afghan Government and the Taliban being postponed till September 2019. In the interim, a sizeable portion of the US deployment had already been withdrawn. Hence the conditionality written into the treaty, that troop withdrawal depended on progress in peace talks between the Afghan government and the Taliban, ceased to be operative.

The absence of the Afghan government from the negotiation table was another major stumbling block preventing a successful transition of power. While the US would have been expected to negotiate on behalf of the Afghan government, it was clear that by 2021, the US was more focused on securing its borders from terrorist attacks originating in Afghanistan and ensuring safe passage for its remaining troops, than seeing its nation building activities through. Under the circumstances, the presence of the Afghan government at the negotiating table would have protected the interests of the Afghans who were committed to creating a democratic society in a manner that the US never did.

Meanwhile, the Taliban were growing in military strength. As early as September 2019, they controlled a large number of highways (mainly built by the US). The US–Afghan forces were focused on securing urban centres and provincial capitals, thus leaving rural areas to the militants. The month after the signing of the peace accord saw an escalation of hostilities by the Taliban even as the US–Afghan forces toned down their operations.

In April 2021, newly elected President Biden affirmed he would honour President Trump's commitment to evacuate the remaining 2,500 US forces by 11 September 2021, the 20th anniversary of the 9/11 attacks. This emboldened the Taliban further. Taking US–Afghan forces by surprise, they initiated their final surge from Northern Afghanistan, traditionally considered a stronghold of non-Taliban forces.*

One of the main elements of their strategy was arriving upon a negotiated settlement[29] with Afghan forces, mediated by tribal elders. The settlement involved soldiers receiving monetary rewards and a promise of safety or an induction into the ranks of the Taliban, provided they surrendered their equipment and abandoned their posts and bases.

Between April and August 2021, Taliban quickly expanded its control from 77 to 223 (out of 400) districts of Afghanistan. As the Taliban captured checkpoints, they began collecting large amounts of money from trucks and buses travelling on Afghan highways. Money, supplies, and support are also believed to have been sent by Pakistan, Russia and Iran. Apparently, their reinforcements included 10,000 to 20,000 Afghan volunteers that had been sent from Pakistan.[30] Meanwhile, Afghan villagers joined the militants by the thousands when it was clear they would win.

On 6 August, the lightly defended Zaranj in Nimruz Province became the first provincial capital to be toppled. With each victory, Taliban gained more fighters to attack bigger government provincial capitals. Their forces moved quickly on highways originally built to ferret them out from their hideouts, but now owned by them. Within nine days, 15 major provincial capitals had fallen. Though Kandahar and Lashkar Gah put up a tough fight, they collapsed on August 13. On August 15, Taliban marched into Kabul, the nation's capital, speeding down wide-

* For a good account of the final stages of the battle, see David Zucchino, 'Collapse and Conquest: The Taliban Strategy That Seized Afghanistan', *New York Times*, 18 August 2021.

open highways on motorcycles and captured government Humvees and police vehicles.[31]

A Post-mortem

As they say, hindsight is always 20/20. However, the following factors were crucial in ensuring that the Taliban returned to power in Afghanistan. (i) The settled conviction of the US till 2011 that they could defeat the Taliban militarily. (ii) The commitment of the Taliban to fight the long war with the steady support of Pakistan, China, and Russia. (iii) The non-representation of the Afghan government in the final peace process mediated by the US. (iv) The stratospheric levels of corruption that characterized US presence in Afghanistan[32]. (v) Unwise decisions of successive US governments that created an unmanageable front of conflict stretching from Pakistan to Syria, with a sole ally – Pakistan, that was fundamentally untrustworthy.

Even though the Taliban promises to turn over a new leaf in its new innings, initial indications are that many things will remain similar to their previous regime, including the lack of opportunities for women. Given the predilection of a series of American governments to take the high ground on such matters (despite their own lack of moral compass in matters such as corruption), it is likely that America will refuse to recognize the Taliban government, make every effort to cut off sources of funding, and maintain economic sanctions. Given this impasse, it is an open question whether US has indeed been able to secure its primary goal of protecting its borders from terrorist attacks incubated in Afghanistan.

Further, the US is powerful not just because of its military and economy but also because of its allies and soft power. During the hurried exit, the US paid no heed to what was in store for the locals who aided it in this war. The narrative of the US being a benevolent hegemon stands shattered, its allies are upset that their images have taken a hit, and in the wars to come, members of native populations might be more circumspect about going out of their way to help a country that has once demonstrated its proclivity to pack up and leave.

In hindsight, the Taliban did not just win back Afghanistan. They succeeded in significantly denting the prestige of the world's pre-eminent superpower.

Ukraine: Stuck Between Unipolar Hegemon, Revanchist Dictator and Corrupt Plutocrats

Since February 2022, Ukrainian President Volodymyr Zellensky has addressed legislatures of the most powerful countries of the world and the UN, as well as interacted with the most respected media houses, often from an unknown location inside Kyiv. His defiance in the face of an aging Russian dictator desperately trying to cling to power has struck a chord with many. On the other hand, the Russian President seems to also enjoy high approval ratings with several sections of the Russian population for his apparently heroic efforts to restore the lost glory of the Soviet Union. Finally, in the midst of generally dismal ratings, US President Biden managed to salvage a modicum of public approval for his financial and military support of Ukraine. And yet, despite all the leaders seemingly gaining from their stances, the war in Ukraine is a perfect example of entanglement.

Ukraine faces the prospect of immense loss of life and property on account of an invasion from a vastly stronger neighbour. The invader, Russia, faces enormous economic hardship on account of sanctions imposed by the Western alliance, besides a heavy toll in terms of military casualties. The US is faced with immense economic risks on account of the dismantling of the global economic system, as well as a loss of face emanating from its inability to deter Russia's invasion. Further, it must deal with the real possibility that the only country that will emerge stronger from this episode is China, its most formidable rival. But each member of the cast of characters has been complicit in this entanglement. The chain of complicity includes:

- a unipolar hegemon, USA, intent on encircling Russia and shrinking its sphere of influence, in the process overriding misgivings of its European partners, nervous about awakening the 'Russian bear', and its own military generals, concerned that newly acquired military allies would contribute far less to the alliance than they would receive from it.
- a dictator determined to retain power at any cost, and only too eager to capitalize on the narrative of Russian humiliation, offered to him on a platter by the West, yet stymied by the deterioration of his once fabled military force, a deterioration stemming from the cronyism his regime thrives upon.
- a country, Ukraine, historically divided between West and East, with a corrupt political elite hand in glove with their Russian paymasters.

The chain of causation stretches over decades, if not centuries. We pick up the story on 25 December 1991, the day that marked the end of the Cold War and the commencement of a unipolar world, with the Soviet Union announcing its dissolution.

NATO's Imprudent Eastern Expansion

The dissolution of the Soviet Union marked a major victory for Boris Yeltsin, a hard-drinking Russian who, in 1985, had been handpicked by the last President of the Soviet Union, Mikhail Gorbachev, to clean out corruption in the Moscow unit of the Communist Party. Yeltsin had emerged victorious against both his mentor, who advocated a more open and democratic federation, and hardliners, who wanted to restore totalitarian controls over the Union. But despite the victory, the troubles of the newly declared President of the Russian Federation seemed to have just begun. He was in desperate need of the support of the US to keep Gorbachev out of power, secure a place for Russia in the UN Security Council, and provide much needed resources to revive the Russian economy.

The US, on the other hand, as the sole survivor of the post-war global order, was faced with two options. It could either aim to assimilate Russia into the new liberal world order based on democracy and free markets. Or, it could embark on a strategy of isolation, taking advantage of its undoubted lead in economic and political power.

For a time, it appeared as if the US had chosen the former route. There were reports that James Baker, the US Secretary of State, had promised Mikhail Gorbachev that if he agreed to recall

Soviet troops from East Germany, the North Atlantic Treaty Organization (NATO), put into place in 1949 as the bulwark of the free world in Europe, would promise not to expand even one inch eastward beyond unified Germany. The camaraderie between the US President Bill Clinton and Yeltsin, evidenced over extended cruises, receptions, and summits, seemed to reflect a wider thawing out process that was underway. In the words of Yeltsin, the two heads of state had decided, 'We'll build the partnership on the basis of our friendship… and we'll do so for the sake of world peace.'[33]

In the midst of all the pressing of flesh, it was discovered that Boris Yeltsin's proclivity for the bottle made all meetings held after lunch time a waste of time. He was said to have once emerged on to the street from his luxurious suite in Washington, DC, clad only in underwear, to demand pizza. Immediately.[34]

Perhaps these could be categorized as minor irritations. However, Yeltsin's use of the military in 1993 to carry out a putsch against the members of the Russian parliament protesting against his economic policies did not go down well with his new friends. When the Russian Intelligence services covertly seized the Chechen capital of Grozny in an attempt to oust the government of Dzhokhar Dudayev, the US wondered whether the leopard had indeed change its spots.[35]

The 1999 war in Serbia and Montenegro marked a clear sign of the change in the attitude of the US. All Soviet Bloc countries had experienced the fissiparous tendencies of their patron in the 1980s and 1990s. In the 1980s, Yugoslavia, set up as a federation of six republics after WWII, broke up after a period of political and economic crisis. However, the republics continued to be roiled by ethnic strife and warfare. While the erstwhile communists had lost power in most republics, Slobodan Milosevic, a strongman of the vintage years of the Communist Party, acquired power in Serbia and Montenegro. He embarked on a program of centralizing power and reunifying Yugoslavia. He was opposed by the Kosovo Liberation Army, comprising the Albanians of Kosovo. In response, he launched a major offensive against the insurgents. The US-led NATO intervened in the war, citing a humanitarian crisis as justification for their aerial bombings. The US intervention created a groundswell of support for Milosevic, and he proceeded to initiate a brutal ethnic cleansing of the Kosovans.[36] Meanwhile, the US campaign did not get the approval of the UN Security Council and is believed to have caused approximately 500 civilian deaths.[37] Operations are said to have commenced even as the Russian foreign minister was flying into New York to meet his US counterpart for deliberations on the way forward.

However, the real irritations of Russia related to developments within an alliance that some thought had become irrelevant in the unipolar world: NATO.

The expansion of NATO and the position of Russia in the post-Soviet European security architecture had been a frequent topic of discussion between Russian and US interlocutors.[38] Right before Secretary of the State Warren Christopher's trip to meet Yeltsin in October 1993, the U.S. chargé d'affaires in Moscow, James Collins, had warned him, 'No matter how nuanced, if NATO adopts a policy which envisions expansion into Central and Eastern Europe without holding the door open to Russia, it would be universally interpreted in Moscow as directed against Russia and Russians alone – or "neo-containment".'[39] In a letter to Clinton sent on 15 September

1993, Yeltsin strongly advocated 'a pan-European security system instead of NATO'.[40]

Thus, there seemed to be two options that would be palatable to Russia: a dissolution of NATO and a new European security architecture inclusive of Russia; or, expansion of NATO starting with Russia. Instead, in 1999, amid strong Russian opposition, Poland, the Czech Republic, and Hungary were inducted into the NATO Alliance.

At approximately the same time, a former KGB officer, Vladimir Putin, became the acting Prime Minister of the Russian Federation.

Russian Revival after the Shambles of Soviet Dissolution

Putin was known to be a Yeltsin loyalist, but, in other respects, he was a largely unfamiliar figure for the public. He had come into prominence for his unrelenting approach in the Second Chechen War of 1999. After Yeltsin unexpectedly resigned in December 1999, Putin, largely due to Yeltsin's backing, won the presidential election and was sworn into office in May 2000.

The transition from a planned to a market economy in the 1990s had been chaotic to say the least. Russians were not used to making the choices that the free market frequently required them to make. A very small group of entrepreneurial, well-connected people learnt how to work the system in their favour, and built up sizeable fortunes. Entrepreneurial, well-connected people became the targets of a burgeoning criminal network that developed into the internationally feared 'Russian mafia'. Simultaneously, a vast apparatus of private security service providers came into being. Both the criminal network and the private security services were liberally peopled by former members of the Soviet military and intelligence establishment. Meanwhile, the withdrawal of the state from essential services such as housing and education without their replacement by the private sector caused widespread distress.

By the mid-1990s, the Russian government did not have the means to pay pensions or salaries, let alone alleviate the misery of the people. The beleaguered Yeltsin risked losing his 1996 re-election bid. In response, he devised a 'loan for shares' scheme under which the government was given loans by the companies of the oligarchs, and shares of public sector companies controlling critical natural resources became the means of repayment. Thus, critical resources got privatized on the cheap. The fact that the auction of the shares of public sector companies was conducted by banks controlled by some of the bidders created a conflict of interest that had become a routine part of the operating procedure in Russia.[41]

The oligarch-politician relationship was a marriage of convenience in which the oligarchs held the upper hand. The political elite needed the resources of the oligarchs, including the sizeable influence they could exercise on the masses through their control of the brand-new media networks created after liberalization. The oligarchs held sway, but they also had nagging fears about the return of communist regimes.

Putin brought about a decisive shift in the power equations. He allowed the continued operation of only those oligarchs who were willing to pledge absolute fealty to him.[42] In 2004, Mikhail Khodorkovsky, President of the Yukos, an oil and gas company, and then the richest man in Russia, became vocal about corruption in the government. He even indicated his interest in running for president. Within six months, he was arrested for fraud and tax evasion, and his company was driven into bankruptcy.[43] The company assets were auctioned at below market value with a state company, Rosneft, acquiring the largest share. Such operations led to a transformation of the energy industry into a highly concentrated structure controlled by Putin's handpicked cronies. Putin also targeted influential entrepreneurs in the media industry including Boris Berezovsky, a PhD in Mathematics and former engineer, and Vladimir Gusinsky, a graduate in theatre studies and former event manager.[44]

Since Russia was an exporter of natural gas, the global boom in energy prices in the 2000s galvanized the economy. Using the revenues accruing to the public exchequer, in 2005, the government was able to launch projects to revive Russia's healthcare, education, housing, and agricultural sectors.

Putin also checked the fissiparous tendencies of the nation. In 2000, the 89 units of the Russian Federation were replaced by seven administrative regions. Instead of being elected as was the practice, the Governors of these regions were appointed by Putin and approved by the respective regional legislatures. The stated aim was to purge the country of corrupt administrators. This move was an early sign of Putin's authoritarian tendencies.

But as far as NATO was concerned, Putin began as a believer. In 2000, three weeks before the election which made him president,[45] he said, 'Russia is part of European culture. And I cannot imagine my own country in isolation from Europe and what we often call the civilised world. So, it is hard for me to visualise NATO as an enemy.'[46] He asked the then NATO chief

George Robertson, 'When are you going to invite us to join NATO?'[47]

But slowly, Putin's attitude began to change.

Putin's Growing Discomfort with NATO

In 2004, the doors of NATO were opened to seven Central and Eastern European countries – Bulgaria, Estonia, Latvia, Lithuania, Romania, Slovakia, and Slovenia. Among these, Estonia, Latvia, and Lithuania were not merely Warsaw Pact countries that had been satellite states of the Soviet Union – they had, in fact, been an integral part of the erstwhile Soviet federation of states and had a large population of ethnic Russians. Besides, they shared borders with Russia. Thus, their inclusion meant that the Western alliance had reached Russia's doorstep.

In 2007, addressing the highly influential annual Security Policy Conference in Munich, Putin said, 'I think it is obvious that NATO expansion does not have any relation with the modernisation of the Alliance itself or with ensuring security in Europe. On the contrary, it represents a serious provocation that reduces the level of mutual trust. And we have the right to ask: against whom is this expansion intended?'[48]

He also dwelt at length on the prospect of a unipolar world calling it both infeasible on account of new rising power centres and unacceptable on moral grounds. Rather presciently, he said: '[A unipolar world] is pernicious not only for all those within this system, but also for the sovereign itself because it destroys itself from within.'[49] Finally, obliquely hinting at the war in

Kosovo and Iraq, he pointed out that 'unilateral and frequently illegitimate actions'[50] have caused new human tragedies and created new centres of tension.

In 2007, Putin suspended of the application of the (Adapted) Treaty on Conventional Armed Forces in Europe. The original treaty from 1990 attempted to achieve a balance of power between NATO and the Warsaw Pact countries with regard to the total number of conventional weapons and military presence of each bloc across their spheres of influence in Europe. In 1999, it was adapted to the post-Soviet scenario with limits placed at a country level. The Baltic States that had joined the NATO in 2004 were not signatories to the agreement. Thus, the treaty was not applicable to NATO's military presence in these states. This asymmetry was one of Putin's objections to the treaty.

By this time, Putin's increasing discomfort with the evolving security architecture in Europe was clear for all to see. And yet, on 3 April 2008 the heads of state and government at the North Atlantic Council issued the Bucharest Summit Declaration: 'NATO welcomes Ukraine's and Georgia's Euro-Atlantic aspirations for membership in NATO. We agreed today that these countries will become members of NATO.'[51]

The prospect of the loss of two vital allies was bad enough. But Putin's fears were not limited merely to strategic encroachment by the NATO.

The Personal Insecurities of Putin

At the time when Putin made his forceful Munich speech, it was thought that he was on his way out of power as the Russian constitution forbade the President from serving more than two consecutive four-year terms. But he had devised a way to bypass the rules.

In 2008, First Deputy Prime Minister Dmitry Medvedev was elected as Putin's successor. One day after the election, Medvedev announced that Putin would be his prime minister. In fact, the nomination of Putin as prime minister was one of the electoral promises that Medvedev had made during his campaign for President.

Even though the role of the President is more powerful than that of the prime minister, most Russians believed that power continued to be vested in Putin. And of course, Putin, had plans that stretched beyond his term as a prime minister. In 2011, Medvedev revealed that Putin and he had decided long ago that the latter would run for President in 2012.[52]

When Putin announced his 2012 candidacy, the urban centres of Russia erupted in protests over his attempts to extend his tenure. The protestors were inspired by the 'Colour Revolutions' (Orange in Ukraine, Rose in Georgia, Blue in Belarus) that attempted to strengthen democratic forces in erstwhile communist states, including Ukraine.* Nevertheless, in 2012, Putin returned as President and served two more terms. Medvedev, meanwhile, switched to being his prime minister. The tango of Putin and Medvedev was referred to as a 'tandemocracy'.[53]

From the standpoint of a politically insecure Putin, the provocations served up by NATO could not have come at a better time. Apart from inconvenient constitutional provisions

---

* Covered in detail later in the chapter.

that limited his tenure, there was an increasingly self-confident media and a rapidly maturing electorate that were complaining about electoral fraud. The economy was showing signs of weakness as Russian exports had shrunk in the wake of the 2008 Global Financial Crisis.[54] The gratitude that Putin had earned for rescuing Russia from the chaos of the 1990s could not last forever.

Russian aggression was also a natural outcome of their vastly improved domestic situation. By 2008, Putin had established control over oligarchs, the Russian economy was showing steady growth, and a measure of stability and social security had been restored. Therefore, the time was ripe for Russia to look outward to regain its international standing.

By convincing a large number of citizens that Russia had faced tremendous humiliation at the hands of foreign powers, and that only he could restore the once great country to its former heights, Putin was playing by an age-old play book. Several studies have established that dictators tend to use external threats, real or imaginary, and inter-state military operations as a tool to tighten their grip on power.[55]

And so it should not have come as a surprise that three months after the Bucharest Summit Declaration, in August 2008, Russia attacked Georgia. This was regarded as the first European war in the 21st century.

We now turn to Russia's interest in Ukraine. But first, we must understand the overall strategic context of Russia.

Russia's Geopolitical Compulsions

At 37,653 km, Russia's coastline is the fourth largest in the world, almost double that of the US. And yet, with the Arctic

Ocean frozen for several months of the year, much of this coastline is unusable as a conduit to access global maritime trade. One point of access is through the Black Sea via the Bosporus, which is controlled by Turkey, a member of NATO. Another outlet starts from Saint Petersburg, and passes through the Baltic Sea, where ships must sail through Danish waters – again, not a secure passageway. Thus, Russia, despite its long coastline remains landlocked, at least from a practical point of view. This held true even during the time of the Soviet Union. In this situation, Russia's western boundary is a critical element of its connectivity with the world.

Further, even demographically, Russia's population is concentrated along its western and southern borders that connect it to Europe and the Caucasus (the area between the Black Sea and Caspian Sea) respectively. This region is also the node of Russia's agriculture and economic activity.

While vital Russian interests are concentrated on its western borders, there are a few natural barriers to stop an enemy attack. Further, given its history as the economic anchor of the Soviet Union, the catchment area for Russia's economic activity is not limited by borders but extends beyond it into Europe. Thus, for reasons of security as well as economic well-being, Russia needs close ties with countries on its western border. Indeed, such ties could be said to constitute an existential necessity.

For NATO, on the other hand, establishing a presence along Russia's western border would virtually amount to a complete encirclement of Russia and be the best of all possible worlds. However, by no means would such an encirclement constitute an existential imperative that would match Russia's need to retain a buffer zone on its western border. In such a situation, with the balance of resolve tilted firmly in Russia's favour, we might ask if NATO's eastward expansion did not amount to overreach. Was it even militarily feasible, given that the new allies were themselves relatively weak and located far away from traditional Western power centres, but were in close proximity to Russia? Did it not increase rather than a decrease insecurity in Europe?

In sum, for Russia, the accession of Lithuania, Latvia, and Estonia to the NATO in 2004 constituted a triple whammy: there was the emotional blow of two former republics of the Soviet Union abandoning ship, heightened insecurity on its crucial western border, and the potential loosening of valuable economic ties. Having suffered such reverses, Russia was unwilling to see Ukraine and Georgia go down the same route.[56] And with Ukraine, its relationship extended beyond the cold logic of material gain.

Ukraine: A Contested Land

Bordering Russia on the west, Ukraine shares a tumultuous history with the world's largest country. Indeed, the Russia–Ukraine war can be regarded as the final act of a messy divorce.

Prior to the formation of the Soviet Union, Western and Eastern Ukraine (separated by the Dnieper River) had generally operated under different spheres of influence. While the Poles, Lithuanians, and Austrians vied for the western part, the eastern part was mostly under varying levels of Russian influence.*

* Under the Truce of Andrusovo, in 1667, Ukraine was partitioned along the Dnieper River, with the west reverting to Poland, while Russia took possession of the east, together with Kyiv. The Treaty of Eternal Peace

What is now called Ukraine is a portion of the greater Ukraine region which was divided between Poland and the Soviet Union after the Peace of Riga in 1922.*

During the Soviet regime, even though Russia was by far the most powerful republic in the Union, Ukraine exercised a level of social and political influence that was disproportionate to its economic power. The Black Sea coastline of Ukraine was a favourite holiday destination of the elites of the Communist Party.[57] After Stalin's death, Ukrainian politicians played a powerful role in the leadership of the Soviet Union. Leonid Brezhnev, who served as General Secretary of the Communist Party for 18 years, was of Ukrainian descent. So were Konstantin Chernenko, who had a short tenure, and Mikhail Gorbachev, the eighth and final leader of the Soviet Union, whose mother was Ukrainian. Nikita Khrushchev, who succeeded Stalin in 1953 and headed the Soviet Union for 11 years, was of Russian descent but was married to a Ukrainian woman. Ukraine held a special place in his heart.

In 1954, the Presidium of the Supreme Soviet of the Soviet Union, headed by Khrushchev, transferred the government of the Crimean Peninsula from the Russian Soviet Federative Socialist Republic to the Ukrainian Soviet Socialist Republic, even though Sevastopol, one of Russia's vital ports and a key resource of Soviet military power, fell in Crimea. Speaking of

---

between Poland and Russia in 1686 confirmed the division. Even though Kyiv falls under Western Ukraine, it has usually been part of the eastern sphere of influence.

* Apparently, between the Bolsheviks, white Russians (who supported the deposed Czar), Germany, and Poland, Kyiv was occupied 13 times in the two years prior to the peace.

her great-grandfather's approach to the transfer of Crimea to Ukraine, political scientist Nina Khrushcheva said: 'To some degree it was also a personal gesture toward his favorite republic. He was ethnically Russian, but he really felt great affinity with Ukraine.'[58]

But while the elites of the Kremlin may have adored Ukraine, the Ukrainian population had a mixed history with the powers that be. The Soviet Famine of 1932–33 claimed four million Ukrainian lives, out of a total of five million Soviet deaths, a consequence of punitive Soviet action against peasants resisting collectivization.[59]

In 1930, the Ukrainian Autocephalous Orthodox Church, a vital part of Ukrainian cultural life, was liquidated, as it was becoming a hub of nationalist aspirations. By late 1933, a policy of Russification had commenced. By 1936, as part of a wave of purges against supporters of Ukrainization, 99 of the 102 members of the Central Committee of Ukraine Communist Party had been shot.[60]

Hence, Ukrainians had a decidedly ambivalent view of the Soviet leadership, a view that persisted all the way up to and beyond the dissolution of the Soviet Union.

Russia's Wary but Compromised Ally

At the time of its dissolution, the Soviet Union was split into the Gorbachev faction that wanted a more open Union, the traditional communists who wanted to return to the command and control system of the pre-Gorbachev days, and the secessionists who wanted independence. Yeltsin, a Russian protégé of Gorbachev, led the secessionists, and won the day. Ukraine joined Russia and Belarus to form a part of the first wave of republics to stake their claims to independence.

Independent Ukraine consistently showed deep suspicion of Russian attempts at creating multilateral institutions in partnership with former Soviet republics and Warsaw Pact countries. Such attempts were viewed as an attempt to recreate a Soviet-style Union, violating Ukrainian sovereignty. Hence Ukrainian administrations sought a transactional relationship with Russia in order to manage their ongoing economic interlinkages, without compromising their independence or territorial integrity. Foremost among these dependencies has been Ukraine's reliance on energy imports from Russia.

Russia has always been the dominant supplier of gas to Ukraine.[61] In 1996, Ukraine imported 83% of its total consumption of natural gas. Even as late as 2018, this percentage was as high as 33%.[62] Possibilities of reducing dependence were circumscribed by Russian control of natural gas and oil reserves in possible alternatives sources such as Tajikistan, its ownership of the transmission infrastructure in transit countries, and its willingness to offer subsidised prices in return for fealty. Russia also cultivated the loyalty of a set of devoted Ukrainian oligarchs who gained from the fuel trade.

Of course, when crossed, the Russian sugar daddy could turn nasty, imposing high fuel prices on regimes such as that of Viktor Yushchenko, 2005–10 which attempted too close a dance with the EU or NATO. It is revealing that at one point Russia was said to have offered Ukraine a schedule of fuel prices as follows: low, if it joined the Russia–Belarus union; medium, if it joined the Russian-led Customs Union; and high, if it aligned with Western Europe.[63]

It is a critical element of the dynamics of the equation between the two countries that the fuel dependency, while constraining for Ukraine in the long term, was a source of personal enrichment for Ukrainian oligarchs. They built their empires through using their personal networks to secure contracts for importing fuel at cheap prices, selling fuel to energy-intensive industries at market prices, and buying the assets of companies reeling under fuel debt on the cheap while being themselves protected against a rise in the import price of fuel by government guarantees. They also profited from obtaining lucrative contracts for power distribution in prime urban areas. Finally, re-export of cheap oil and gas to other countries, although illegal, was also a standard practice at various points in time.[64] Thus, attempts to reduce fuel dependence, and liberalize the energy sector ran counter to the business interests of Ukrainian elites, although they were not averse to playing the nationalist card in order to protect their interests from Russian oligarchs attempting to control energy assets in Ukraine.

Politicians partook of the rents earned by oligarchs in the energy sector. They also adopted a pro-Russian stance, especially in the run-up to the elections, in order to secure support in the eastern and southern parts of the country that had a large population of ethnic Russians. Indeed, one of the contributing factors explaining President Petro Poroshenko losing the 2019 election may have been his projection of Ukrainian identity as mutually exclusive from Russian identity through his strong support for the Ukrainian language, and his attempt to stamp out all traces of communist influence in the culture.[65]

Politicians also relied on Russian support when they faced the increased moral opprobrium and reduced appetite for investment of the West in response to human rights abuses, such as the alleged murder of a journalist in 1999 by the regime of President Kuchma, or runaway corruption as seen in the regime of Yanukovych.[66]

But dependencies were present on the Russian side as well. As much as 80% of Russian exports of natural gas to Western Europe used transmission pipelines that ran through Ukraine.[67] Further, the vital Black Sea Fleet was docked at the Sevastopol port in Crimea which falls in Ukrainian territory. It appears that Ukraine was not able to take sufficient advantage of Russia's dependence on account of the compromised position of Ukrainian elites.

The West and Russia Compete over Ukraine

While Ukraine's attitude to Russia involved the adroit balancing of national dependencies and narrow personal ambitions, the dream of integration with the West was a deeply felt aspiration. The West represented 'civilization' and 'freedom', a counterpoint to the drudgery of the Soviet years. There were two main aspects to Western integration – economic and strategic. Economic integration through the membership of the EU had broad based support, not just in Western Ukraine, but also in the eastern and southern regions. On the other hand, support for strategic integration through NATO membership was lower, with opinions divided between the eastern and western parts and unpleasant memories associated with the

NATO bombing of Kosovo being a continuing turn-off.[68]

Russia's early attempts at creating multilateral institutions such as the Commonwealth of Independent States (CIS), the Common Economic Space, and the Eurasian Economic Community were characterized by non-binding, open structures. Such structures did not preclude Ukrainian participation in Western coalitions, that by contrast, required a fair amount of homogeneity of political institutions, economic policies, and regulatory structures across national boundaries. Thus, for many years, Ukraine could run with the hare and hunt with the hounds. However, as the EU began making active efforts at expanding eastwards, Russian-led blocs began to emulate the structures of Western multilateral institutions in order to force its allies to signal their definite commitment to the Russian-blocs.

In 2010, Russia, Belarus, and Kazakhstan became the founding members of a Customs Union, a term used to refer to a group of countries that share common trade and competition policies. The articles of association were incompatible with simultaneous participation of members in other multilateral institutions. This development brought matters to a head and catapulted a Ukrainian President into global attention.

His name was Viktor Yanukovych, and he was President from 2010 to 2014 after which he had to flee the country and take refuge in Russia.

The Much-maligned Yanukovych

In the last few years, Viktor Yanukovych has emerged in world media as the archetype of the corrupt communist boss concerned only with accumulating obscene amounts of wealth. There are good reasons for the opprobrium Yanukovych managed to earn. After he finally fled Ukraine, the public strolled unchallenged through Mezhyhirya Residence, Yanukovych's private estate set in the middle of a forest reserve on the borders of Kyiv. On the premises they discovered a private zoo, an underground shooting range, an 18-hole golf course, tennis courts, and a bowling alley. In addition, there were a number of chandeliers, each worth more than $1,00,000.[69]

But Yanukovych's undoing was as much a result of evolving structural inconsistencies that made the standard balancing act of Ukrainian administrations between the West and Russia incompatible, as a product of his personal excesses. Indeed, his life story is emblematic of an older way of being that Ukraine and its elites embodied for several years, a way that became anachronistic just as Yanukovych reached the peak of his power. Let's see how.

An impressive 6 feet 6 inches [2 metres] tall, Yanukovych was born in Eastern Ukraine in a poor family. He had a rough youth with a couple of jail terms thrown in, and rose through the ranks, from mechanic to executive, over a 20-year career in heavy industry. During this span, he also earned a degree in mechanical engineering.

He entered politics in 1996 and soon emerged as a favoured candidate of the business community in the face of rampant threats from organized crime. Between 1997 to 2002, he served as the Governor of Donetsk.

After the emergence of audio tapes proving the role of pro-Russian President Kuchma's role in the murder of a dissident journalist, Yanukovych was appointed his prime minister in 2002. The beleaguered Kuchma backed his candidacy for President, the highest post in the land, in the 2004 election. Yanukovych also had the support of Vladimir Putin.

In the middle of a bitter campaign, Yanukovych's chief opponent, the pro-Western Victor Yushchenko, fell ill after an apparent poisoning attempt. Yushchenko's popularity was greatly increased by images of him gallantly pressing on despite his disfigurement. But in spite of exit polls showing a clear lead for Yushchenko, Yanukovych was declared the victor.

There were allegations of massive corruption, voter intimidation, and electoral fraud sparking the 'Orange Revolution'. Thousands of protesters demonstrated daily in the capital city of Kyiv. Consequently, the results of the original election were annulled, and a revote was ordered by the Supreme Court.

The second iteration of the election was declared to be 'free and fair' by a large number of international observers. The final results showed a clear victory for Yushchenko, who had fought the election on the plank of integration with Europe, membership of the NATO, and the eradication of corruption.

Yushchenko's victory in the face of a repressive regime that controlled the media and had unlimited resources had been a masterpiece of strategy. Opposition parties had rallied behind a leader most likely to win. The marketing campaign had been slick and centred around the slogan 'Pora', meaning 'high time'. The logo of a ticking clock had been catchy. Stickers, spray paint, and websites had fuelled the voter outreach campaign in the days before social media. Street plays had struck a mocking defiant note, projecting irreverence, freshness, and a desire for change.

But the template was not new. The opposition had stuck to a formula that was allegedly developed by the US via previous trials in Serbia, Georgia (dubbed the Rose Revolution), and Belarus.* As per standard practice, the blueprint would be operationalized through the local US Ambassador, who in some cases would be transferred from one posting to another in order to spread the same magic dust.[70] The message of the Orange Revolution could not have been lost on an increasingly authoritarian figure in a neighbouring country, Vladimir Putin.

'If you can't beat em, join em,' is a 1940s adage about political contests. Yanukovych, whose youthful run-ins with the law, and gauche manners made him unacceptable to a sizeable swathe of Ukrainians, soon started undergoing a makeover under the guidance of Paul Manafort, a Republican political operative who would go on to chair the Trump presidential campaign from June to August 2016.† His remodelled look included a new wardrobe, a coiffed hairdo, and elocution lessons. His style of communication, approach to campaigning, and rallies started resembling those of the Republican Party in the US.

Meanwhile, the opposition parties that had swept to power on a united plank fell apart. In the melee, Yanukovych managed to become the prime minister from 2006 to 2007. Next, he won what international observers agreed was a free and fair election in 2010 to become the President of Ukraine.

---

* The efforts had succeeded in Serbia and Georgia but failed in Belarus where Alexander Lukashenko managed to win. He has held office for nearly three decades.

† Manafort was later charged in an investigation into Russian interference in the 2016 presidential election.

Increasingly Untenable Contradictions

The contradictions that had been adroitly managed by predecessors of Yanukovych became magnified and unmanageable during his tenure. These contradictions emanated from the strengthened aspiration for membership of the EU, based on the desire of a large and vocal section of the population to integrate with the civilized and prosperous West. This was accompanied by increasingly non-transparent processes of domestic resource allocation which seemed to have the enrichment of Yanukovych's family members as a prime motive, continued dependence on Russia for political support, energy supplies, and export markets, which served the existing oligarchic elites well, and a strengthened Russian desire to create and lead a monolithic East European bloc.

Among the first official acts of Yanukovych's tenure was to legally bar Ukraine from seeking NATO membership, a core demand of Russia. He also struck a deal to extend the Russian lease of Sevastopol till 2042 in return for steep discounts on supplies of natural gas from Russia to Ukraine. But simultaneously, he refused to join the Russian-led Customs Union and pressed forward with negotiations on the 'Association Agreement' that would align Ukraine's legal and regulatory systems more closely with the EU. To safeguard Ukrainian interests related to lower tariff barriers to access the Russian market, and to mollify Russia, Yanukovych advocated entering into a free trade agreement with its eastern neighbour.

In the summer of 2013, Yanukovych agreed to the political conditions of the EU (including demands for the release of Yulia Tymoshenko, a member of the government that came into power after the Orange Revolution) and seemed to be heading toward European integration. At this point, Russia launched a full-blown trade war, despite Yanukovych having attempted to mollify Russia by taking on observer status in the Russian-led CIS comprising Russia, Belarus, and Kazakhstan.

Instead of buckling down, Yanukovych initiated the 'Full Speed to Europe' program in September 2013. By October, with the draft of the association agreement finalized, it seemed the die had been conclusively cast in Europe's favour. Yet, Russia still had a lever that it could use as the Ukrainian economy was in tatters.

The International Monetary Fund (IMF) was ready to bail out Ukraine with a $15 billion loan, but it came with conditionalities that would involve reduced government spending and lead to short-term hardship. The EU too was prepared to help. But its offer of help based on its estimate of the cost of leaving the Russian fold that the Ukrainian economy would have to bear was much lower than Yanukovych's own estimates. Russia, on the other hand, adopted a carrot and stick approach. In two meetings held in October 2013, Yanukovych was warned that Ukraine would end up defaulting on its sovereign debt obligations in case it signed the Association Agreement. There were also some prospects of dire consequences arising for members of Yanukovych's family.[71] But, should Ukraine refuse to sign the Association Agreement, Russia promised immediate assistance to rescue the Ukrainian economy without any political conditions attached. In addition, Russian assistance would enable Yanukovych to raise the minimum wage, provide child benefits, and effect a public sector pay raise in the run up to his 2015 re-election bid. And of course, Russia also offered lower gas prices.

For an increasingly beleaguered Yanukovych, the choice was clear. On 21 November 2013, Ukraine formally announced postponing the signing of the Association Agreement on account of technical hitches. In December, two treaties with Russia were signed, and the first tranche of Russian assistance was released.

But Yanukovych had not reckoned with the fury of the people, who were reeling under his excesses and longing for European integration as a way to transition to a rules-based system.

A wave of popular protest erupted in the Euromaidan in Kyiv. Yanukovych responded with draconian anti-protest measures. But the protests only grew in strength, spreading out across Ukraine. When more than 70 people were killed in clashes with in February 2014, Yanukovych's support hit a new low, and the Parliament started impeachment proceedings against him. He responded by fleeing the capital and emerged a few weeks later in a safe haven in Russia.

At the height of the Euromaidan protests, Putin had held an all-night meeting with security service chiefs to discuss ways of assisting Yanukovych's exit from the country. On the day following the meeting, there were pro-Russian demonstrations in Sevastopol. Three days later, masked Russian troops with no insignia on the took over Crimea's Parliament and other strategic sites. By 16 March, a pro-Russian government had been installed, a referendum on Crimea's status had been held, and it was declared independent.

Meanwhile, in Yanukovych's absence, the full extent of his ill-gotten wealth soon started coming to light. When he was confronted with the evidence of his luxuriant lifestyle, including ostriches discovered in his petting zoo, Yanukovych is believed to have remarked: 'I supported the ostriches, what's wrong with that?'[72]

Thus, three forces gathering momentum over decades – the growing ambitions of the USA on the encirclement of Russia, the increasing personal insecurities of Putin, and the inevitable untenability of Ukraine's balancing act between the West and Russia – brought matters to a head the second decade of the new millennium. Things moved quickly thereafter.

Putin Amends the Constitution

Putin's second stint of two consecutive terms was scheduled to come to a close in 2020. In the same year, Putin held a referendum on a sweeping Constitutional amendment that would inter alia allow him to run again for two more six-year presidential terms, ensure patriotic education in schools, ban same-sex marriage, and make and place the Russian Constitution above international law. The referendum was a success.

By this stage, Putin was no longer a mere political leader. He had donned the mantle of a messiah with a mystical connection both to his country and its people.

He had made the transition by reaching back into history and tradition to revivify the Russian soul, to resurrect Russian pride battered after the dissolution of the Soviet Union, and tightened his grip on power. He referred to the dissolution of the Soviet Union as 'the greatest geopolitical catastrophe of the century',[73] and allied with the Russian Orthodox Church to serve up a heady cocktail of religious faith and patriotism. (This explains the inclusion of patriotic education and the ban on same-sex marriages in the Constitutional amendment).

A disproportionate share of his political opponents had suffered deaths and poisonings. However, Putin's position was secure because as far back as 2014, Putin knew that as long as he continued to reclaim Russia's lost greatness, he would continue to enjoy the unstinted adoration of vast masses of Russians.

And so, with Yanukovych's star plummeting, and Ukraine slipping away into the zone of Western influence, it was no surprise that Crimea was annexed and that on the day after the annexation, Russian soldiers in unmarked uniforms fanned across the Donbas region of Eastern Ukraine.[74] Within months, pro-Russian governments were installed in Donetsk and Luhansk and referendums were held that declared two provinces as independent states. These referendums were not accepted by the vast majority of countries. Russia said it would 'respect' the results.[75]

The Inevitability of the Russian Invasion

The trend of events after the Russian military operations of 2014 followed expected patterns, with a few noteworthy features. First, Petro Poroshenko, who succeeded Yanukovych, attempted to create a Ukrainian identity that was mutually exclusive from the Russian identity. Despite his apparent antipathy to Russification, after he lost the 2019 election, he was accused of corruption and illegal links with Viktor Medevedchuk, a pro-Russian tycoon. Second, his successor,

Volodymyr Zellensky, comedian-turned President, when faced with an intransigent Russia that was refusing to back off from Donbas and amassing troops on the border, threatened to step back from the Budapest Memorandum, under which Ukraine had given up nuclear arms. Third, when faced with a Russian dictator slowly and steadily progressing toward an inexorable attack with a military buildup extending for close to a year, and demanding that NATO pull back from Eastern Europe, the US made no concrete attempt at a compromise. And finally, the Ukrainians under Zellensky showed amazing stomach for a fight, repulsing Russian soldiers attempting to take Kyiv, and inflicting heavy casualties in operations across Kharkiv and Mariupol. Supported by an enormous supply of weapons from NATO countries, the Russians seem to have been pulled into a long-drawn operation with no clear winners.

It is pertinent that the once vaunted Russian military has declined precipitously and failed to undertake the modernization and reform needed to remain a formidable force. The vested interest of the military elite and their increasing political power are believed to be the main causes of the decline. Scholars have pointed out that this failure of the Russian army is not merely a product of the chaotic Yeltsin years, but largely true even of Putin's tenure. Putin consciously combined the deracination of the legislature and the judiciary, with an increased level of power accorded to the military.[76] His political compulsions blinded him to the fact that military top brass was misusing its privileges to maintain the status quo. By 2020, the state of Russian military preparedness was no secret.

Was Ukraine then the bait used to trap the Russian bear?

Post-Script: What Next for the Unipolar Hegemon?

From the rise of China, the defeat in Afghanistan, the re-assertion of Russia in the Ukraine war, and much else besides, it can be said that the unipolar hegemon is dead. Is it curtains down for the US? Or shall we say: 'Long live the unipolar hegemon?'

The events of the last 30 years represent the transition of the world from a bipolar formation split between the capitalist and communist camps to a unipolar structure led by the US. The bipolar formation itself came into being after WWII and was a successor to the unipolar world helmed by the UK that existed prior to WWI, with the with the inter-war period being a transitionary phase.

In the past three decades, as the United States attempted to expand into the vacuum created by the crumbling of the Soviet Union, it made a number of mistakes. It assumed its victory represented the triumph of its way of life and took it upon itself to perpetuate that way of life across the globe. The failure of this mission is most clearly visible in the events that unfolded in Afghanistan and Iraq. On the domestic front, it dismantled the checks and balances that ensure a society stays both economically dynamic in terms of rapid growth as well as humane in its concern for those left behind. The rise of a demagogue such as Trump makes the short-sightedness of its policies apparent. A storm of developments in technology and geopolitics served to amplify the contradictions inherent in its approach, but, undoubtedly, the US was guilty of hubris, overreach, naivety, and much more.

That the United States has fallen from its towering heights as the world's sole superpower is indubitably true. What lies next for the greatest superpower the world has ever seen?

While nobody can claim to have definite answers, let us start by comparing the decline of the world's previous unipolar hegemon, the United Kingdom (UK), and the circumstances surrounding that episode, with the current scenario.

WWI marked the beginning of the decline of UK and the rise of the US and Soviet Union as the two successors. This transition was cemented by WWII.

Although, at one time, it was said that the sun never set on the British Empire, global interlinkages were ripe for refashioning. International political and economic relations were based on asymmetric political power. The political subordination of the colonies was only too clear. Even economic interlinkages, to the extent that they existed, represented exploitative interconnections that consigned colonies to the role of producers of primary products. These nations were subject to the vagaries of declining prices relative to manufactured goods, as well as high levels of uncertainty on account of volatile meteorological conditions and global demand.

Hence, there was a strong desire to dismantle the political and economic structures attendant upon the hegemony of the UK. It was also a relatively simple move to new relationships as economic interrelationships were relatively rudimentary. The architecture of the post-WWII world comprising the NATO countries, the Warsaw Pact Nations, and the Non-Aligned Movement smoothly supplanted the old order and created new patterns of interrelationships.

However, the world that begins the transition from a unipolar world led by the US to multipolar world comprising a variety of great powers is deeply interconnected – economically, geopolitically, and with regard to the energy transition required to avert a climate crisis.

Unlike the colonies, the entities that are emerging as great powers in their own right have gained from the developments during the period of US hegemony, and they need to continue to retain old patterns of engagement even as they develop new avenues of future growth.

The US itself continues to be economically, militarily, and demographically strong. Although China is likely to become a larger economy by 2040, the US will continue to be richer in terms of per capita income, and its innovation engine remains robust. Militarily, its annual spending is larger than that of the next nine countries put together. Unlike Europe and China, it has a young population that is likely to power its growth into the next century.

The main vulnerability of the US at this time relates to its political system which is highly polarized, to the point that the chaotic transition of power of the kind witnessed in 2020 seems entirely possible in 2024. However, here too, the ability of the US judicial system to withstand the legal challenges posed by Donald Trump and the disappointing performance of candidates backed by Trump in the November 2022 midterm election appear to be signs that suggest that the US democracy may pull through.

Overall, it is too early to entirely write off the US. However, the prognosis is less sanguine for the continuation of the world system they have done so much to create.

5

MAN-MADE DISASTERS*

The gleaming city with its quietly humming climate control systems, futuristic metro rails, and cosmopolitan cultures far removed from the rustic countryside represents the crown jewel of the age of rationality. This chapter covers two entanglements emerging from right under the triumphal arc of urbanization. The first involves the twin challenges of air pollution and natural disasters that threaten to make cities unliveable. The second refers to the risk of viral outbreaks and the even more serious threats sometimes emanating from scientific attempts to control such eventualities. The city, thus, is the pinnacle as well as the deepest fault line of the prevailing worldview.

Gurugram: What Price the Millenium City?

The spectre of climate change looms over our civilization like a ticking time bomb. As island countries face the prospect of imminent submergence, agriculturists struggle with changing

* Given the overwhelmingly male-centric nature of the Age of Rationality, 'man-made' is a more accurate descriptor than the more politically correct 'human-made'.

and variable crop patterns, and urban agglomerations come face-to-face with the wrath of nature on a regular basis, the writing is on the wall.

It is easy to lose sight of our existential crisis in the midst of our busy lives, the dazzling developments of technology, and the challenge of freeing the world from pressing problems like poverty and want. And yet, some phenomena just cannot be ignored, even by the rich. An example is air pollution.

Every year, in the months of November and December, cities in Northern India acquire gas-chamber-like characteristics. The air quality index touches stratospheric levels, but residents don't really need air sensors to know that the air they are breathing is toxic. With windows tightly shut, they gaze gloomily at the grey haze spread everywhere. Those who are rich can buy air filters that work, but they soon learn that there are limits to the enjoyment of a life lived in a bubble. They discover that while death may be the great leveller, bad air effects a cutting down to size whose compulsions are equally compelling. Let's see how this problem plays out in Gurugram, aka Gurgaon – one of the fastest growing urban agglomerations in the world.

The Air Pollution Protest Rally

On a chilly morning in November 2019, I was in a group of about 3,000 people gathered on the grounds of Leisure Valley Park in Gurugram. Among the group, besides NGOs and activists, were a large number of children, many studying at exclusive private schools in the city, corporate bigwigs, and billionaire entrepreneurs. Manas Fuloria, the then CEO of Nagarro, a global digital product engineering company said on the occasion: 'Nagarro employs 5,000 people in Gurugram and the National Association of Software and Services Companies (NASSCOM) companies employ may be a hundred times this number here and form the main growth engine of the economy. And on behalf of NASSCOM, Haryana, I can state that we are suffering greatly on account of this air pollution. Our people are unwell, they are frustrated, they are leaving for other cities and countries. And our international clients are nervous. They are cancelling their trips to India.'[1]

The corporate leaders along with several other protesters were demanding their right to live and breathe clean air and urging the government to grow forests. 'Do not destroy a sacred forest,' said one poster. 'Trees forever,' said another. Many of the participants undertook a token hunger-strike at the venue. A group of clown artistes with two women in yellow t-shirts and yellow, pink, and green hair; and a young man in a black t-shirt with turquoise blue hair were also present. One of the girl clowns sang, '*Chidiya ki choch, choch mein sandesh, ped lagaao highway hataao, ped lagaao highway hataao*' (The bird's beak, hear what it says? Plant trees, banish highways. Plant trees, banish highways).'

What is noteworthy is that successful members of the corporate elite were a part of a street protest against the government, mouthing words that sound a bit like the utterances of a bleeding-heart NGO activist. Gurugram had often been held up as an example of government and entrepreneurs working well together to craft one of the most remarkable stories of urbanization of the last hundred years. How did things reach such a pass?

To understand this, we must delve into the history of the growth of Gurugram, a history whose key elements are similar to the histories of many urban agglomerations in emerging economies, except that events unfold in a highly compressed time frame.

Gurugram Rises as a Millennial City

Situated at the border of New Delhi, the national capital, Gurugram has been celebrated as the Millennium City, with its gleaming office spaces, plush gated communities, and diverse population comprising people from all over the world and all parts of India. And yet, till 2008, on account of its low population, Gurugram did not even have a municipal government, and was only just beginning to be recognized by the denizens of Delhi as something more than a dusty outcrop. But, in fact, while Delhi had been engaged in political confabulations, its usual pre-occupation, Gurugram had been racing ahead. It was precisely the lack of governance that became its greatest strength.

In Delhi, the Delhi Development Authority (DDA) set up in 1957, is the sole agency responsible for creating and managing the master plan for the city. Its functions include acquiring land and building residential and commercial spaces as well as public utilities like roads, parks, and bridges needed to support a burgeoning population.[2] But failures of implementation and planning led to a severe shortage of housing which was met by the mushrooming of a smorgasbord of structures including slums, and unauthorized colonies, some of which were later legalized.[3] In Gurugram, in the absence of a local government, the provincial (state) government sitting in the provincial capital, Chandigarh, teamed up with real estate developers, to cut through red tape and fashion a gleaming metropolis at breakneck speed.

The Haryana state government created a system of land acquisition from agriculture that was run by private entrepreneurs with full support from the Chief Minister's office. Given the barren and infertile nature of the land, local agricultural land owners were happy to accept the lucrative rates offered. Simultaneously, real estate developers were happy to find a liberal jurisdiction next to the national capital and close to an international airport to boot.

The industrial development of Gurugram began in the early 1980s, with a car factory being set up by Maruti, an Indian company originally floated by Sanjay Gandhi, the powerful scion of the Gandhi family, along with the Japanese car maker, Suzuki. The partnership between Hero Motors and Honda to manufacture motorcycles was another important development. Soon auto component companies, garment manufacturers, and a wide assortment of service industries set up shop in the burgeoning metropolis.[4]

A decisive turning point came when Jack Welch, the fabled CEO of General Electric (GE), bonded with KP Singh, the promoter of one of the big real estate players in Gurugram, DLF, over a common passion for golf.[5] One thing led to another, and soon GE opened a back office in one of the office spaces developed by DLF. In a few years, Gurugram became home to a vibrant industry of information technology-enabled services that mainly serviced overseas clients, making it a city that worked round the clock. The supply of world-class office infrastructure, and the rapidly developing linkages with overseas businesses, saw Gurugram emerge as a node for corporate offices of multinational corporations looking to expand in South Asian markets. By 2016, over half of the Fortune 500 companies had operations in Gurugram.[6]

Success and Complicity

The vacuum of urban governance was a boon for entrepreneurs, who had already been partly unshackled by the liberalization of the Indian economy in 1991. For them, Gurugram represented nothing less than a field of dreams. But despite the glitzy success, there was a hitch. The city had insufficient public goods required for sustainable urbanization – electricity provision, water supply, sewage lines, public transport, housing for workers, security...all were woefully inadequate.

Private enterprises attempted to provide each one of these public goods to the burgeoning population. Corporate parks and residential communities ran diesel generators for large parts of the day and built their own sewage treatment plants. Private water tankers crisscrossed the busy streets. Private bus services and auto rickshaws, loaded well beyond their capacity, stepped up to fill the gap in public transport. Original residents of Gurugram, who had made money through the sale of land, built tiny tenements to house the hordes of migrants pouring into the city. And security firms hired armies of people to protect individuals, residential communities, and corporate offices.

The private provision of public goods faced the challenges of inefficient scales of production, failure of coordination across different service providers, and the tendency to satisfy the needs of small groups of people while in the process imposing costs on the wider community. For instance, diesel generators were highly polluting, private provision of water resulted in the alarming depletion of groundwater, and sewage from septic tanks was routinely dumped on land that is a part of common property resources, contaminating the groundwater and spreading diseases.

One might believe that the onerous costs of taking over the provision of public goods would exert a chilling effect on the viability of private business. But nothing of the sort has happened, at least so far. For the most part, private enterprise more than made up for these costs by being remarkably productive, but also by playing fast and loose with the rules governing their operations. From my informal research conducted over 15 years of living in Gurugram, the following is only an indicative list of the wide varieties of transgressions that are fairly common:

- Building on unauthorized land.
- Getting the master plan modified to insert roads conveniently located next to proposed housing and commercial real estate projects in order to increase the value of real estate.
- Violating construction norms with regard to the permissible number of floors (this leads to further violations with respect to electricity, water, sewage, and gas connections).
- Utilizing a larger number of diesel generators than approved.
- Using unapproved bore wells, and going to greater depths than legally permissible.

- Dumping sewage on unauthorized lands without proper treatment.
- Not abiding by agreements stipulating the provision of housing for economically weaker sections in tandem with regular development for residential communities.
- Not following rules on construction activity including the treatment of waste water.

You will notice that most of the transgressions listed relate to the real estate sector. While businesses operating in the modern sectors such as IT and telecom, and those producing for foreign markets were far less violative of rules, most of them were operating from premises built on foundations inlaid with pelf.

All these transgressions were achieved through a cozy collusion among certain private entrepreneurs (many of whom were not originally from Gurugram), original inhabitants who had acquired wellbeing overnight through the sale of their agricultural lands, and some government officials who made sizeable personal fortunes through the simple act of turning a blind eye. And so it seemed that a solution had been found – private provision of public goods, 'under the table' enrichment of certain government officials, and a boom in private enterprise. Everyone was complicit, and no one seemed entangled.

But then the fumes started rolling in – wafting from farms burning crop stubble in the hinterlands, rising from car exhausts, spreading from factories running on dirty fuels, and emerging from incinerators disposing waste that should have been segregated and re-used.

The elite could no longer hide inside their gated communities.

Entanglement: The Angst of a Blue-blooded Entrepreneur

'It's depressing,' said Rohan Khanna, the founder of a travel company that is one of the great success stories of India's internet economy. Besides his success, Rohan is known for his efforts to promote entrepreneurship as well as for his company's generous support for a cleaner, greener Gurugram.

We are speaking in his office on Golf Course Road, Gurugram. It is 2020, and despite the rather noxious air outside, the air inside the office is remarkably fresh, thanks to the operation of a large number of air purifiers.

'It's depressing when my kids get sick on their trips back from their colleges overseas. Of course, the illness may be on account of a variety of causes, but doctors say that susceptibility to infection is higher, and recovery takes longer on account of the pollution. We are lucky to have air purifiers in every room at home, but one can't stay indoors all the time. My son is an athlete and needs to continue to train even while he is in India. He goes to the gym. We have a nice gym in our condo, but he would ideally like to train outdoors.'

'It's frustrating because unlike vaccination for dengue, this is a problem that can be solved quite easily. One needs to get vacuumizers and automatic sweeping machines to make sure that road dust doesn't rise into the air, move to electric public transport, create the ecosystem to allow private owners to move to electric cars, follow rules in construction activities... but the political will required seems to be lacking.'

I asked why he believes that there's no political will.

'I asked a friend of mine who is a former minister,' Rohan

responded. 'I said to him, "Politicians and Chief Ministers are all breathing the same air that we do. Why do they not seem concerned?" He told me, "It's because this is a rich man's problem. The poor have many other problems to think about. This is higher on the hierarchy of needs."'

I asked if he had personally gotten involved in promoting awareness about such issues. He mentioned his involvement with the many projects taken up by an NGO that was started by a group of former corporate executives and has been a force in the expansion of the public commons in the city. It has been involved in the revival of an ancient forest on land diverted to quarrying, known today as the Aravalli Biodiversity Park; created a linear forest and pedestrian walkway in a city focused on private cars; and has been working on restoring water bodies in another 80 acres of forest land.

Khanna also listed his role on the 'advisory board' of the Gurugram Metropolitan Development Authority (GMDA), a new municipal body created to facilitate better coordination between the chief minister's office and local municipal bodies, and Air Pollution Action Group, an organization set up by a private equity investor and philanthropist – Ashish Dhavan – to help governments create capacities to monitor the implementation of environmental laws.[7]

Since 2018, the NGO IamGurgaon has been involved in a campaign to prevent the construction of a road through the Aravalli Biodiversity Park. Rohan asserts his strong support for the cause. Meanwhile, NGOs such as the Aravalli Bachao Citizens Movement have been campaigning against a legislation that would allow over 60,000 acres of the Aravalli Range (on which Gurugram is built) to be developed for habitation and work. This is an issue with far wider ramifications than constructing a road through the park. I asked Rohan if he would be willing to throw his weight behind the larger cause.

'I am quite focused on my company,' Rohan replied. 'But I would love to see the emergence of a green party that makes this an agenda.'

Later, I also spoke to Latika Thukral, co-founder of IamGurgaon, and asked why her group is not more vocal about the larger issue of the colonization of the Aravalli Range. From her answer, I sensed Latika prefers not to project IamGurgaon as 'anti-development'. IamGurgaon chooses to work with the government to make tangible change happen on the ground, rather than take up large causes in a mode of 'resistance'.

When I asked Rohan if his travel business has been affected on account of pollution, he said that inbound traffic is definitely lower. A survey the company carried out among its employees showed significant health impact with sizeable monetary consequences. 'A number of employees would prefer to live in Bangalore (now Bengaluru) despite the traffic,' said Rohan. He went on to add that many Indians who returned to India on account of the tremendous business opportunities, may decide to move back. And definitely, many no longer want to make Gurugram their retirement option.

Internecine Differences: Old Money Stakes Out a Different Path

In our interview, referring to the proposed road through the Aravalli Park, Khanna had said, 'People who have property along the proposed road would want it to come up – in that case, let the government build the road below the ground. It will cost more but save the forest.'

To find out the views of such people I set out to meet Kishan ji, whose family owns large parcels of land in and around the forest restored by IamGurgoan.

After navigating potholed, overrun, and up and down streets, I suddenly enter a large spacious L-shaped compound with a five-storey building stretching along one arm of the 'L', like the side of a large ship, and a single storeyed office at the end of the other side with a large parking area in front. There are three cars parked outside – a Mercedes station wagon, a Toyota Fortuner, and a Toyota Innova. Also lying around are a couple of motorcycles, two hookahs, and a charpoy, which is a wooden cot strung with jute fibre. Through a small door one can see a yard where a few cows are lounging around, rhythmically working some balls of hay their mouths.

I am led through the little door leading into the cow yard. After crossing the mud pit, I find myself in a massive rectangular compound, which must be 2 acres in area, with a length about three times the breadth. Four large bungalows are stretched along one side, each with ample parking space inside. I see a Porche parked in one. In front of the row of houses, is a tarred road before which sits a long garden. On one end of the garden, is a gazebo, next to which is a circle of chairs. About five people are seated around, drinking tea, munching on snacks, and playing cards. Most are dressed in traditional Indian attire.

A couple of chairs and a table are arranged separately from the group. A gentleman in kurta pajama leaves the group and comes towards us. This is Kishan ji.

In the phone conversations to set up the meeting, I had been speaking to a gravel-voiced gentleman who seemed accustomed to rolling his tongue to give the usually soft 'n' the hard edge that makes even an entreaty or an encomium an expression of aggressive intent. But, in person, Kishan ji was compactly built, with a quiet air about him that exuded an understated confidence.

I mentioned I was a professor and, as part of some research I was conducting, had come to ask about the six-lane highway that was being planned through the park.

Kishan ji's response was immediate and emphatic. 'Look here now,' he said, 'A road should definitely be built.'

'At 5 p.m., it will take you three hours to travel the 20 kms from here to Vasant Kunj. The traffic is growing beyond all limits. Gurugram is growing day by day. Gurugram is the pride of Haryana, what does Haryana have other than Gurugram. I remember the days when Gurugram was in a bad shape. All this growth has happened only by cutting trees. Recently, lots of trees were cut down to build Sohna Road.'

'All the big companies will go away, if they have to remain stuck in these jams. This is a *kadva sach*, bitter truth. If a project of 200 crores is coming, why don't we spend 20 crores to plant trees, why are we not deploying dust cleaning machines, why aren't we maintaining the parks that are in the master plan? There are supposed to be 25 parks in Phase 3, Gurugram. Only the park inside the townhouse is developed. Other than that, there are no trees, no grass, no fences, no maintenance. The builder is not fulfilling his responsibilities.'

'But these are not merely trees are which are being cut. This is a forest which is being destroyed,' I interjected. 'A native forest painstakingly revived through citizen action.'

He said that sheesham* and keekar† came up on their own after the stone quarrying stopped. 'This growth is not the result of anybody's care,' he concluded.

'But sheesham and keekar are not native species,' I responded. 'IamGurgaon with the help of foresters such as Pradeep Kishan and Vijay Dashmana has attempted to regenerate a natural forest.'

'Those trees put up by Madam Latika, none of them is above 10 feet.' This damning indictment come from Inder, Kishan's heavy-set brother, who had joined our group. 'And this is after seven to eight years.'

I suddenly begin to appreciate the vast gulf in the outlook of IamGurgaon and the native dwellers of Gurugram. IamGurgaon believes in creating wilderness in the middle of the city, populated with native species of trees, bushes, shrubs, and insects, which would be an invaluable contribution to the civic life of the city. A 10-feet native species springing from a rock is much more integral to their plans than a 20-feet non-native species in a manicured garden. The native human dwellers of Gurugram on the other hand believe that trees must be a luxuriant green in colour, at least 20 feet high and must adorn well-planned parks, and gardens. Perhaps it should not be surprising that agriculturists who were at the vanguard of humanity's move from forests to agricultural settlements, regard the wilderness with a certain amount of impatience.

I wonder aloud if the difference between the stance of IamGurgaon and Kishan did not emerge from their very different class backgrounds – one from the newly rich settlers

---

* North Indian rosewood.

† A kind of acacia tree.

of Gurugram and the other belonging to older elites who came into a lot of money due to rapid urbanization.

Inder immediately read into my comments a subtle putdown and emphatically disabused me of any such notions: 'Ambani is my tenant,' he asserted, referring to India's most wealthy industrialist. 'I am Ambani's landlord,' he re-iterated, by way of abundant elucidation. 'The two tall buildings in Cyber Hub which house his telecom company, Reliance Jio, belong to me.'

I fall silent. Then Inder offered a compromise solution: 'The forest will not be spoilt, not if we build an elevated road.'

As I leave, I asked about their children. I am told they study in a school in Tijara, Rajasthan, a two-hour drive from Gurugram. The website of the school proudly boasts, 'Located on a picturesque 160 acres campus, the undulating green landscape has more than 2500 beautiful flowering trees, over 10,000 shrubs and fruit orchards.'[8] There is no mention of wilderness.

Thus, Rohan Khanna and Kishan differ almost on every point. Rohan feels business would suffer because of pollution, while Kishan believes it would suffer on account of lack of roads. Rohan values the ancient forest and wants it protected from modern development. Kishan does not even accept it is a forest, let alone something to be prioritized over essential infrastructure. Rohan offers an underground road as a compromise, Kishan an elevated road. The only point of agreement between them is that both have sent their children out of Gurugram for their studies.

In 2019, around the time of these conversations, I had gone to meet Mr V. Umashankar who was then the CEO of GMDA. Mr Umashankar is regarded as one of the brightest young members of the Indian Administrative Service, the extremely powerful bureaucratic machinery that undergirds the Indian state. We speak about developments in the civic governance of Gurugram and the innovative nature of GMDA, a body meant to provide better coordination between the state government and the local municipal government. The conversation veers towards the road passing through the biodiversity park. 'I think some people are being extremely selfish,' Uma says with an accusing tone. 'The road is essential for the development of Gurugram.'

In March 2022, the Aravalli Biodiversity Park was declared as India's first 'other effective area based conservation measures' site by the International Union for Conservation of Nature, one of the world's largest environment networks with 1400 members including governments, civil society organizations and experts.[9] This classification ensures that the park is identified as an area that is achieving long term and effective conservation of biodiversity, without giving it protected status. Realistically, as there has been no change in the legal status of the park, the development can only be seen as a temporary victory for the movement to stop a road being built through the park. In any case, with the entire Aravalli Range being in the cross hairs of developers, there are bigger challenges that lie ahead.

The Gurugram story is not an isolated phenomenon. The world's most polluted cities consist of 36 cities from India, 17 from China, and seven from Pakistan and Bangladesh. But air pollution is only one of the many environmental challenges facing urban dwellers – not just in India or emerging economies but across the world.

As urbanization accelerates across the world on account of economic development and the loss of rural livelihoods resulting from climate change, urban agglomerations are increasingly susceptible to natural disasters. Many of these agglomerations are situated in coastal areas where the risks of urban flooding due to a rise in water levels has been greatly magnified by global warming. Of course, populations in emerging economies are more susceptible than those in developed economies, on account of poor urban planning and disaster-prone infrastructure. But if the recent experience of forest fires in California, heat waves in Europe, and flooding in West Germany are anything to go by, urban areas in the developed world are very much in radar of unforeseen catastrophes.

The divisions between the native dwellers of Gurugram and immigrants are also being played out on the global stage in the form of differences between different segments of the global elite. The case of President Bolsonaro of Brazil authorizing the cutting down of Amazon forests, known as the 'lungs of the world', even as Europe chided the country for playing with a vital cog of global climate system, is an instance of this ongoing debate.

In other words, entanglement in urban areas and human complicity in that entanglement on account of man-made climate change is very much a global reality facing the elites of our age. To establish credibility in their advocacy for sustainable development, the elites who have gained the most from past patterns of growth, need to demonstrate willingness to forego material gain for the cause of sustainability. So far, despite the heroic exceptions, it seems to be a case of too little, too late.

The Lab in Wuhan: Brave New World or Technological Hubris?

It was perhaps inevitable that a society that prides itself on its mastery over nature would not remain content with the quest to identify and neutralize emerging viral strains. It needed to stay ahead of the curve of nature by targeting not only viruses that have already emerged but also viruses that that could possibly emerge in the future. This inexorable logic is embodied in the 'gain-of-function' research paradigm under which new viruses are manufactured in labs in order to evolve strategies to combat future threats. But the new research program is only the culmination of a quest that started 150 years ago, a quest as old as the Industrial Revolution.

One of the main objectives of the nascent science of urban planning in the late 1800s was the creation of a 'cordon sanitaire', a physical space separating the workers' town from the places where old and new money resided and from where the reins of power were controlled. The containment of viral outbreaks was one objective of the separation. But, in today's globalized world, where some of the objects we use on a day to day basis consist of components sourced from over hundred countries, where the number of international migrant workers has been estimated at 164 million[10], and where the number of annual tourist arrivals has increased 56-fold from 25 million in 1950 to 1.4 billion in 2018,[11] it is not enough to set up an effective cordon sanitaire within cities. It is imperative to proactively put in place measures for early identification and risk assessment of viral threats at a global level.

New viruses are likely to emerge in hotter climates, and in locations characterized by rapid urbanization and deforestation where the interaction between wildlife and human habitation is particularly intense. For instance, the Amazonian rainforest, given its rapid depletion for commercial use, might be a spot from where deadly viruses could emerge.[12] Hence, there is good reason for virology labs to emerge in the new hotspots of economic development.

Since the 1980s, these hotspots have been concentrated in non-traditional centres of growth such as Asia and Africa. The associated labs are often funded (at least partly) by entities in developed economies on account of the incentives of mitigating viral threats emanating from emerging economies. In a globalized world, a viral outbreak anywhere could quickly turn into a public health crisis everywhere.

Of course, the globalization of scientific research is not limited to virology but extends across the domain of natural as well as applied sciences. It is driven by several factors that include the emergence of global pools of scientific talent with significant cost differentials across geographies, increased government funding for scientific development in geographies other than the US and Europe, and the global nature of the challenges facing science (for instance, climate change). A global research presence also stems from the need of MNCs, which have acquired a dominant position in the world economy since the 1980s, to internationalize their R&D operations to tap global opportunities with greater speed and precision.

However, the globalization of research in virology, while a part of a larger trend of globalization and reflective of a dazzling development of technology, is associated with especially high risks as it involves the handling of lethal viruses across regions with disparate material resources and cultures with regard to safety.

In other words, while the high risk of the emergence of new viruses in far-flung geographies creates the need for a global network of laboratories, this global network in turn generates its own risks. Further, the specific scientific methodologies adopted to combat the future threat of viruses, while representing the pinnacle of scientific achievement, also magnify the risks. These methodologies and the structural duality between the dazzling scientific progress they represent on the one hand, and heightened vulnerability on the other form the subject matter of this section.

Another aspect of the structural duality is that the global development in virology research is accompanied by vast inequity in access to vaccines. This inequity could upset the most carefully designed strategies to combat the virus in advanced countries. While this duality is important, it will be addressed only in a peripheral manner.

Gain-of-function Research

The world at large first learnt of a new research paradigm in virology when news began to spread about the outbreak of the COVID-19 virus in Wuhan. This was a new strain of a 'coronavirus', so named because of its spiky surface that appears similar to a crown under a microscope. Simultaneously, an advanced research lab located in the same town came into the limelight.

As early as 2003, scientists at the Wuhan Institute of Virology (WIV), an affiliate of the Chinese Academy of Sciences, had successfully scoured bat caves and searched bat faecal matter to discover the coronavirus responsible for the deadly SARS outbreak that had infected 8,098 and killed 774 people. The head of the lab, Shi Zhengli, went by the moniker 'bat woman', on account of her single-minded dedication to finding reservoirs, including those located in remote caves and forests, that host dense populations of viruses originating in bats.[13]

There were two hypotheses about the COVID-19 outbreak. First, that it had reached human beings through a natural process of transmission from bats or an intermediary host. The wildlife markets of Wuhan, where civets, pangolins, crocodiles, and other wild animals were sold, were identified as a possible location where such transmission could have happened. Second, the virus could have been created in the Wuhan lab in a 'gain-of-function' experiment and leaked from there into the human populace.[14] All of a sudden, there was a possibility that scientific research had generated and unleashed a weapon of mass destruction!

The beginnings of this research paradigm were humble – it originated with unanswered questions about the deadly 'Spanish' influenza pandemic of 1918. In four waves spread out over two years, the flu infected over 30% of the world's population. Death estimates ranged between 17 to 50 million. The high death rate of healthy adults in the age group of 15 to 34 years of age puzzled the scientists.

For several decades, the question 'Why was the pandemic so deadly?' loomed over the scientific community. But without a physical specimen of the virus, their ability to answer the question was limited. Then in 1951, Johan Hultin, an enterprising PhD student at the University of Iowa began looking for traces of the virus frozen in time in a small oceanside village in Alaska – Brevig Mission, that had lost 72 of its 80 adults to the virus in 1918.[15] The bodies of the victims had been buried in a nondescript mass grave. After two days of digging through the permafrost, Hultin managed to obtain lung tissue from five bodies. To get the virus to grow, he injected it into chicken eggs. It didn't work.

Almost half a century later, in 1991, scientists at the Armed Forces Institute of Pathology in Washington, DC, managed to extract lung tissue from a 21-year-old male US soldier who had died in September 1918 in an army hospital. They used it to sequence a part of the genome – the complete genetic instructions that constitute the blueprint of an organism – of the 1918 virus.

Hultin read an account of this discovery that indicated that the work was still incomplete. So he wrote to Jeffery Taubenberger, the lead scientist on the study, and offered to help him get additional lung tissue from the Alaskan village he had visited decades ago. And thus, at age 72, Hultin went back to Brevig Mission at his own expense. After five days of excavation, he found the body of a woman whose lungs were perfectly preserved in the Alaskan permafrost. The hunt for a more complete understanding of the genome of the virus was on again!

Using the new sample of the virus, the scientist discovered that the virus had an origin in birds, but had developed a number of mammalian adaptations as a result of residing in mammalian hosts, human or swine. However, the authors could not identify any genetic features that would explain the exceptional virulence of the virus.

The saving grace was that by 2005, the entire genome of the virus has been sequenced. All the information required to reconstruct the deadly virus that caused the 1918 pandemic was in place. The same year, after considerable deliberation, the US government decided upon the Centre for Disease Control as the site for the reconstruction.

To ensure safety and security, only one person was granted permission and laboratory access for the process. That person was trained microbiologist Dr Terrence Tumpey.[16] Elaborate security measures were put into place, including the use of an iris scan to allow him access to the virus storage freezers. It had been agreed that if a situation arose in which Tumpey became infected with the virus, he would be quarantined and cut off from the outside world.

Tumpey injected genetic material from the eight sectors of virus' gene architecture into human kidney cells. The material was expected to instruct the cells to reconstruct the complete genome of the 1918 virus. After weeks of anxious waiting, Dr Tumpey observed the virus had indeed been reconstructed.

It was it was a historic moment, and, fittingly, Tumpey sent a message to his colleagues that echoed the message sent by Neil Armstrong after the moon mission: 'That's one small step for man, one giant leap for mankind.'[17]

Recreating a historical virus, was indeed only the first small step. Soon a 'gain-of-function' research program would be established under which scientists would attempt to genetically alter a disease-causing microorganism in ways that could enhance or alter its innate patterns of manifestation. For example, only humans and harbour seals are infected by influenza B. However, if a mutation can be introduced that allows the influenza B virus to infect rabbits in a controlled laboratory, it would be considered a gain-of-function experiment as it adds a function that the virus did not initially have. The experiment can then be used to study which parts of the virus are responsible for the range of hosts it can infect and this, in turn, can help create antiviral medicines which block this function.

For those troubled by the traditional seasonal flu, the year 2004 brought bad news. There were cases of Influenza A virus subtype (H5N1) avian flu spilling over to humans from birds. Virologists started wondering if H5N1 and the traditional seasonal flu virus could co-infect human and give rise to new strains of pathogens. Microbiologists started designing experiments to explore the question.

In September 2011, at a conference in Malta, Ron Fouchier presented data from experiments in which a human isolate of H5N1 avian-origin influenza had been modified to acquire some mutations that were expected to adapt it to human-to-human transmission.[18] Soon after, the laboratory of Prof. Yoshihiro Kawaoka reported similar developments.

The Dilemma

In 2004, a debate started about whether the new gain-of-function research programme was desirable, given the possibility of viral spillovers and the potential use of viruses as a biological weapon. In the beginning, these concerns were quite muted. However, in 2011, a major controversy broke out on the potential of the research to aid bio-terrorists or result in an accidental leak of potential pandemic pathogens (PPPs) that, by design, combine high virulence with high human-to-human transmissibility. Reports about mishaps and mishandling at high-containment federal laboratories in the US emerged, with some cases of human exposure to potentially lethal (but not highly transmissible) pathogens.[19] The debate split the research community into two camps.

The Cambridge Working Group (CWG) argued that the research posed unacceptable threats to safety and security and that its findings could be replicated by safer methods. Marc Lipsitch, convenor of CWG, wrote: 'The unique risk posed by gain of function or PPP creation is that such accidents will lead not only to individual infections but to ongoing transmission and, in the worst case, extensive global spread of the engineered pathogen... the existence of such risks should be counted, like great expense in time or money, as an important factor arguing against undertaking the experiment in the first place.'[20]

Scientists for Science that included stalwarts such as Karla Kirkegaard of Stanford University and Sean Whelan of Harvard University on the other hand, stated, 'If we expect to continue to improve our understanding of how microorganisms cause disease we cannot avoid working with potentially dangerous pathogens... Ensuring that these facilities operate safely and are staffed effectively so that risk is minimized is our most important line of defense, as opposed to limiting the types of experiments that are done.'[21]

From January 2012 to December 2017, the international scientific community went back and forth between voluntary pauses on this field of research activity, complete moratoriums, and approvals for projects that satisfied certain eligibility criteria. Ultimately, the research program went ahead. It was believed that after necessary precautions were taken, qualified researchers had 'a public health responsibility to resume this important work'.[22] The primary US agency responsible for public health research, National Institute of Health (NIH) asserted that gain-of-function research was 'important in helping us identify, understand, and develop strategies and effective countermeasures against rapidly evolving pathogens that pose a threat to public health'.[23] A series of international certifications Bio-safety Level (BSL) 1,2,3, and 4 were created to grade labs on their readiness to conduct research involving different levels of risk.

In parallel to these developments, a country regarded at that time as a backwater of cutting-edge research was making giant strides towards developing a level of scientific capability that would equal the best in the world.

The Wuhan Lab

The WIV came into being in 1956, and it was first called the Wuhan Microbiology Laboratory. In 2003, the institute received approval from the Chinese Academy of Sciences to construct a biosafety level 4 (BSL-4) laboratory. The lab, created in collaboration with Centre International de Recherche en Infectiologie (CIRI) in France, was completed in 2014, at a cost of ¥300 million (US$44 million).[24]

The National Biosafety Laboratory, as it came to be called, operated in close cooperation with Galveston National Laboratory in Texas and National Microbiology Laboratory in Canada. The collaboration included an exchange of research personnel. Two staff scientists at WIV, Xiangguo Qiu and her husband Keding Cheng, also worked at the Canadian lab and were remunerated by the Canadian government, until July 2019 when they were escorted out of the Canadian lab for undisclosed reasons. Researchers from the WIV such as Shi Zhengli have also collaborated in gain-of-function research on coronaviruses with American and British colleagues such as Peter Daszak, member of the Center for Infection and Immunity at the Columbia University Mailman School of Public Health, who we will encounter later in the chapter.

The BSL-4 facilities that were conceived in 2003 were put into operation in January 2018. This set the stage for the initiation of a specific research program led by Shi Zhengli that was later suspected of having resulted in the leak of the coronavirus. The program was being carried out in partnership with EcoHealth Alliance.[25]

A US-based NGO, EcoHealth Alliance aims to use scientific research to protect people, animals, and the environment from emerging infectious diseases. While it is known today for cutting-edge research in virology, it was founded by conservationist and author Gerald Durrell. Between 2014 and 2019, the EcoHealth Alliance channelled a sum of $598,611 provided to it by the NIH to the WIV. In the same period, EcoHealth Alliance received $815, 109 from the University of California-Davis which it transferred to WIH. The University in turn had received this money from the US Agency for

International Development (USAID), an independent agency of the US federal government that is primarily responsible for administering civilian foreign aid and development assistance. Thus, in a sense, the US government transferred over $1.4 million to a lab largely funded by the Chinese government through a partner that belonged to civil society.[26]

This institutional arrangement would be the cause of much controversy after the outbreak of the COVID-19 pandemic.

The Lab Leak Hypothesis

In January 2020, news emerged of a new virus outbreak in China. Belonging to the coronavirus family of viruses, it turned out to be the most serious public health threat since the Spanish flu.

To examine whether the virus had leaked from the lab, in February 2021, a group of top virologists who were a part of a WHO team undertook a visit to the Wuhan lab. They emphatically shot down the lab leak hypothesis.[27] However, the group in its report did not make full disclosure of the fact that one of its members, Peter Daszak, was heading EcoHealth Alliance that had funded gain-of-function research at WIF. Later, Daszak was recused from the work of a UN- backed commission on the origins of the pandemic.[28] The publication of an article in *The Lancet*, arguably the most prestigious medical journal of the world, rubbishing the possibility of a lab leak by a group of scientists including Daszak despite his obvious conflict of interest, and sans a disclaimer, suggested either slipshod processes or deeper levels of compromise that threaten the integrity of respected institutions in the world of academic research.[29] The apparent attempt to pre-empt a thorough investigation by Daszak et al. did not speak well of the scientific community.

In parallel, President Trump, with an equal paucity of hard evidence, actively espoused the theory that the virus had indeed leaked from the Wuhan lab.[30] There was only some circumstantial evidence available – including the fact that a member of the lab staff fell ill with coronavirus-like symptoms in October 2019. In April 2020, the Trump administration terminated the NIH grant that was meant to conduct research on how coronaviruses spread from bats to humans.

On 26 May 2021, US President Joe Biden ordered a 90-day US intelligence-community investigation into the origins of the coronavirus. The investigative committee, which included National Intelligence Council and four intelligence groups comprised anonymous third-party experts, could not come to a conclusion. While one group leaned towards lab accident as the cause, partly on the basis of the 'inherently risky nature of work on coronaviruses', two groups leaned toward natural spread being the cause. Each of these three groups had with low or moderate confidence in their finding. The majority of the investigators stated that more information was required to reach a firm conclusion. Cooperation from China that had resisted the investigation was held to be especially important in moving forward. There was only one unequivocal finding – the coronavirus was not developed as a biological weapon.[31]

In June 2022, in a report that marked a sharp reversal of its initial assessment of the pandemic's origins, an expert group of the WHO said that 'key pieces of data' required to gain an understanding of how the COVID-19 pandemic began were still missing.[32] The group issued the statement that they would, 'remain open to any and all scientific evidence that becomes available in the future to allow for comprehensive testing of all reasonable hypotheses'.[33] Co-chair of the 27-member international advisory group, Jean-Claude Manuguerra said scientists needed to be 'open-minded' enough to examine the lab leak hypothesis.[34] In response China's Foreign Ministry spokesperson Zhao Lijian said, 'The lab leak theory is totally a lie concocted by anti-China forces for political purposes, which has nothing to do with science.'[35]

Conclusion

In all likelihood, we will never know what really happened. In any case, even if the lab leak hypothesis is only one of the plausible causes, this possibility alone, combined with the tragic loss of life wreaked by the pandemic, suggests that we need to revisit our paradigms of scientific research.

The unfettered logic of technological progress aspires for a control over nature that seeks to remove human beings from the pale of unanticipated peril while keeping the prevailing logic of human behaviour unchanged. The controversy over Wuhan reflects the risks of this approach. Instead of seeking ever more sophisticated technological fixes to behavioural and systemic problems, it is perhaps useful to accept that technology is not the panacea we imagined it to be. The COVID-19 pandemic suggests that the problems of public health should not always be addressed by ever more dazzling technological virtuosity but also by rewiring our patterns of urbanization and economic expansion.

Further, the vast inequity in access to COVID-19 vaccines across the world, and the vastly differing priority levels for getting vaccinated, revealed another fault line, one that could trip up even the most prescient technological solutions. As per Global Dashboard for Vaccine Equity, a body established by UNDP, WHO, and Oxford University, by January 2022, only 4% of those in low-income countries had received at least one dose. In contrast, close to 70% of the population in high-income countries had been vaccinated.[36] With such a drastic difference, low-income zones can become hot spots for transmission and incubators for potentially dangerous variants of SARS-CoV-2.

However, actions to mitigate such risks are hampered by the fact that such regions have more pressing concerns than the coronavirus. Their leading causes of death are not COVID-19 but malnutrition, common childhood infections, and chronic diseases which the failing public health programs are unable to deal with.[37] For instance, from 2009 to 2019, Yemen has been suffering from the worst documented cholera epidemic in recorded history, with more than 2.5 million suspected cases and 3,000 deaths.[38]

The interconnectedness of global health combined with deep inequity of socioeconomic conditions threatens an entanglement that doesn't promise to go anywhere any time soon.

6

SURVEILLANCE CAPITALISM AND ITS DISCONTENTS

A central conceit of the age of rationality was that it would harness the power of nature for human progress. Nature was thus denied agency or priority in the new pecking order. In this chapter, we shall see how capitalism has similarly anonymized the vast mass of people becoming, in the process, a totalitarian force that mines the most intimate information about human beings in search of profits. This is merely a continuation of the colonial exploitation of faraway lands, except the realms being colonized are human bodies and minds everywhere. This development threatens even those who have played stellar roles in the creation of this system.

Further, the overweening power acquired by technology companies is facing resistance from governments everywhere, although these same governments have gained from their surveillance capabilities and played a key role in facilitating their rise. Thus, not even the tech behemoths, seemingly unsurpassed in today's world, are free from the threat of entanglement.

The Rather Messy Divorce of Jeff Bezos

On 1 May 2018, Jeff Bezos received a WhatsApp message with a video attachment on his mobile phone.[1] A name flashed across the dimly lit screen 'Muhammad bin Salman' aka MBS. Bezos had met MBS at a private dinner in Los Angeles in April 2018, but they were not in regular contact. The video file extolled the tremendous progress made by Saudi Arabia's economy under MBS.

One may imagine that it would be quite natural for MBS and Bezos, two members of the rarefied world of the global elite, to be in touch. The crown prince is seen by the world at large as the greatest hope for the modernization of Saudi Arabia. Bezos, of course, is an icon of the internet revolution. But there were more specific reasons that brought them together.

In 2013, Jeff Bezos had purchased the *Washington Post*, the iconic paper started by the legendary Katherine Graham, for $250 million. Starting in September 2017, the *Post* started running a column by Jamal Khashoggi, a Saudi Arabian dissident journalist, author, and editor of the liberal newspaper *Al Watan*.

Khashoggi's pieces in the *Washington Post* were critical of the Saudi government over a number of issues. He opposed its over-enthusiastic embrace of Donald Trump and exposed the exaggerated claims about reforms with regard to freedom of expression. He had teamed up on a range of projects with Omar Abdelaziz, who is among the most well-known public critics of the Saudi regime abroad and has received asylum in Canada. One of these projects was Geish al-Nahl (Army of the Bees) that aimed to create an alternative to the regime's propaganda machine – 'a network of pro-democracy activists who would post and amplify one another's messages about Saudi political issues'.[2]

On 2 October 2018, a squad of 15 assassins killed Khashoggi. He had been summoned to the Saudi consulate building in Turkey on the pretext of providing necessary documentation for his upcoming wedding. The squad ambushed him and suffocated him to death before dismembering his body.[3] Several investigations including by US and Turkey concluded that the assassination had been carried out by Saudi agents at the behest of the Saudi crown prince. The *Washington Post* began a relentless campaign against the Saudi establishment.

The campaign would soon face some unconventional challenges.

The National Enquirer Scoop

In early January 2019, Bezos and his wife MacKenzie Bezos announced they were seeking a divorce after 25 years of marriage. Later that month a story in a tabloid *National Enquirer* broke the news of Bezos' extramarital affair with former TV anchor Lauren Sanchez. Various text messages sent by him to her were revealed.

David Pecker, the owner of *National Enquirer*, was known to have business connections with the Saudi establishment. To coincide with the high-profile visit of MBS to the US in March 2018, *Enquirer* had put into circulation 2,00,000 copies of a 97-page glossy magazine on the crown prince's reformed Saudi Arabia.[4]

In February 2019, Bezos published a sensational blog post where he revealed that following the initial scoop, *Enquirer* had been extorting and blackmailing him over more of his intimate personal texts and photos that they claimed to possess. They were threatening to release the salacious content unless Bezos and his team committed to stopping all insinuations of electronic eavesdropping or political involvement of external parties (i.e., Saudi Arabia) in the tabloid's story about his affair. Bezos said he refused to be subjected to blackmail. He also mentioned that he had engaged an investigator to understand how his texts were obtained and what the motives of the *National Enquirer* were.[5]

The investigator was Gavin de Becker, an undisputed authority on security matters related to governments, large corporations, and public figures. In an article in *The Daily Beast* in March 2019[6] he asserted that while the *National Enquirer* was projecting Michael Sanchez, the brother of Lauren Sanchez, as the source of the leaked texts, his role could be compared to 'a low-level Watergate burglar', not to the architects of the Watergate scandal. De Becker was referring to the spying scandal that had brought down the government of President Nixon in 1974. He went on to claim that when the *Enquirer* approached Michael Sanchez, they had 'already been investigating whether Mr. Bezos and Ms. Sanchez were having an affair,' and had already 'seen text exchanges'[7] between the couple.

Sharing the details of the investigation, he stated, 'Our investigators and several experts concluded with high confidence that the Saudis had access to Bezos' phone, and gained private information. As of today, it is unclear to what degree, if any, AMI [American Media Inc., the holding company of National Enquirer] was aware of the details.'[8]

He further went on: 'Experts with whom we consulted confirmed *New York Times* reports on the Saudi capability to "collect vast amounts of previously inaccessible data from smartphones in the air without leaving a trace – including phone calls, texts, emails" – and confirmed that hacking was a key part of the Saudis' "extensive surveillance efforts that ultimately led to the killing of [Washington Post] journalist Jamal Khashoggi."'[9]

He also alluded to the elaborate Saudi social media program under which technology and paid surrogates were being used to create artificially trending hashtags. The surrogates included operatives working for companies such as Twitter.

The investigation into the hacking of Bezos' phone did not conclusively establish the specific spyware used. However, one particular surveillance company would soon find itself in the spotlight.

Niv, Shalev, and Omri (NSO)

In May 2019, three months after Bezos' allegations against the *National Enquirer*, WhatsApp Inc., and its parent company, Facebook Inc., filed a case in the United States District Court for the Northern District of California against the NSO Group Technologies Ltd., an Israeli limited liability company, and Q Cyber Technologies Ltd., an Israeli corporation and the majority shareholder in the NSO Group.[10] WhatsApp claimed that the NSO Group had developed spyware that was used to infect 1,400 mobile devices to enable remote access and control of information, including calls, messages, and locations of a targeted group of WhatsApp users. Of these users at least

100 were journalists, lawyers, human rights defenders, and political dissidents.

The alphabets in the company's name 'NSO', stand for Niv (Karmi), Shalev (Hulio) and Omri (Lavie) – names of the company's founders. It is primarily known for its proprietary spyware, Pegasus, that enables remote 'zero-click' surveillance of smartphones, i.e., key-presses, or mouse clicks are not needed for its operation.[11] Hence, it enables surveillance activities across borders and within countries without any act of volition by targeted entities.

The founders of NSO were previously a part of Unit 8200, the Israeli Intelligence Corps unit responsible for intelligence-gathering by interception of electronic signals. The Israeli government has classified Pegasus spyware as a weapon, and any export of the technology has to get official approval.[12] NSO claims that its technology is used by authorized governments as it helps them combat terror and crime.

It is noteworthy that both Israel and Saudi Arabia share a common enemy in Iran. The two countries have had close ties since the Arab Peace Initiative of 2002.[13] Therefore, the sale of the software by the Israeli government to Saudi Arabia would be consistent with broad strategic alignments in the West Asian region.

The Pegasus software has been associated with the capture of the Mexican drug lord, Joaquín Archivaldo Guzmán Loera, famously known as 'El Chapo' (meaning the short one, because of his physical stature).[14] However, with the approval of the Israeli government, the technology appears to also have been sold to governments that, in addition to justifiable deployments, have no compunctions in using it to quell dissent, target political opponents, and curtail democratic freedoms. Indeed, it is reasonable to assume that most governments would have used the software for both kinds of purposes, although to different degrees.

On 18 September 2018, Citizen Lab, an interdisciplinary laboratory at the University of Toronto, identified a total of 45 countries that might have been conducting surveillance operations using Pegasus. Prior to this, significant Pegasus operations had previously been linked to abusive use of spyware to target civil society in six countries – Bahrain, Kazakhstan, Mexico, Morocco, Saudi Arabia, and the United Arab Emirates.[15]

The NSO's defence against it being used in the Bezos phone hack was that its services do not work on US numbers. However, the inability to work on US numbers is a special concession wrested by the US from NSO, not an intractable technical issue. This particular clause in NSO's operational model could have been relaxed if the US government wanted. It is here that the possibilities become intriguing.

The *Washington Post* had been very critical of President Trump who in turn was scathing in his put-down of the *Post* and liberal media as a whole. He lumped all such media outlets under the label of 'fake news'. Simultaneously, he was soft on Saudi Arabia with regard to the Jamal Khashoggi murder as well as several other issues. Hence, MBS and Trump were natural allies against Bezos.

It is plausible that the infiltration of Bezos' phone could have been a one-off relaxation of the operational clauses governing NSO. In addition, to aid US government agencies in domestic spying, NSO had offered the Federal Bureau of Investigation a system called Phantom that could hack any US number. Thus, at the time of the break-in to Bezos's phone, the US probably possessed Pegasus-like capabilities that it could use on its own citizens.[16]

In sum, Bezos could well have become the victim of a closer dance between Israel, Saudi Arabia, and Trump. Mediating his infringement of privacy could have been a high technology company supported by the Israeli government and incubated by private capital sourced from Israel and Silicon Valley.

However, one has to say, this version of events is at best a plausible hypothesis.

Exegesis

In the absence of conclusive evidence, let's say that the US government was not involved. What is clear is that Bezos had serious fears that his phone might have been hacked, and that there is a probability this was indeed true. Even with this highly toned-down version of events, the episode has a number of significant features.

The start-up funding for NSO came from a group of investors headed by Eddy Shalev. Shalev is a partner in venture capital fund, Genesis Partners, that focuses on early-stage innovation-driven Israeli companies.[17] The surveillance company must have changed hands since its inception because in June 2017, Francisco Partners, an American private equity firm from San Francisco, put it up for sale for $1 billion. Francisco Partners is headed by Dipanjan Deb, a technologist and entrepreneur of Indian origin. Later, two of the founders of NSO, Shalev Hulio and Omri Lavie, partnered with a European private equity fund, Novalpina Capital, to acquire a majority stake in NSO in February 2019.[18]

The evolution of the NSO was enabled by a partnership between governments, most importantly the Israeli government, and the mainstream ecosystem of new venture development. It drew its resources from risk capital and personnel from the high-tech capitals of the world. In contrast, in India, the malware called NetWire reportedly used to target pro-Dalit activists gathered at Bhima Koregaon in 2018[19] was conceived, financed, and built in the underground economy.[20]

Bezos' own business and personal investments are not directly linked to surveillance technologies. A cursory look at the investments of the Jeff Bezos Foundation reveals an eclectic mix of egg producing companies, green energy innovators, and apps meant to simplify adulthood. However, the company he founded, and he himself, are pillars of the ecosystem of Silicon Valley in which NSO was incubated. Thus, NSO emerged from the very ecosystem Bezos did so much to create and nurture.

The pace of development of such technologies is bound to accelerate given their inclusion in mainstream innovation architectures. This would also result in a rapid enhancement of the capabilities of such software and a reduction of their price points. Thus, such technologies would become affordable for a larger set of countries, even as increased polarization around the world rapidly increases the demand for them.

It is true that surveillance is a weapon frequently used by leaders of the world's richest country and most influential democracy – the US. In 2013, Brazil complained that the US had hacked the phone of President Dilma Rousseff.[21] Edward Snowden's 2013 leaks of documents of the National Security Agency (NSA) indicated the depth and scale of US surveillance operations across the globe through agencies such as the NSA and the Central Intelligence Agency (CIA). But now such capabilities could be within reach of a variety of regimes from the liberal to the brutal.

It is noteworthy that the violation of the privacy of Bezos, if it did occur, was initiated by the leader of an authoritarian, repressive regime, and targeted at a member of the liberal elite of the world's largest democracy. The hacking of documents and emails from Hillary Clinton's 2016 presidential campaign as well as the Democratic National Committee by Russia, an action that created fresh challenges for an already beleaguered campaign,[22] was an even more consequential attack on liberal democracy. Thus, surveillance technologies created by the tech and financial elite of advanced economies are now weapons in the hands of authoritarian regimes against the democratic world.

The global war of cyber-infiltration is only the international version of the domestic threats to democracy from governments using heightened surveillance on their own citizens. The perceived adversaries are distributed across the spheres of politics, business, civil society, and the media. Recall, the Bezos episode began with the infiltration of the phone of Khashoggi, an enemy of the Saudi establishment. Many governments including that of India, the world's largest democracy, have been accused of using Pegasus against perceived critics.[*23]

A report on free speech with reference to the Bezos case, by the UN rapporteurs David Kaye and Agnes Callamard,

---

* The Supreme Court of India appointed a technical committee to examine if certain phones had been infected with Pegasus at the behest of the Indian government. It stated that the technical committee had found 'malware' in five of the 29 phones but was not able to say conclusively that the malware found was Pegasus. The Chief Justice also mentioned that the government refused to cooperate in the investigation.

stressed the need for a moratorium on the global sale and transfer of private surveillance technology. They urged that such technology needed to be subjected to the most stringent judicial controls.[24]

And yet, the threats to democracy from the possibilities of surveillance lie even deeper than the unfettered access of dictators to such technologies.

Corporate Surveillance: The Elephant in the Room

One objects to technologies such as Pegasus because they enable governments to access private information without consent. However, the threat of surveillance extends beyond the prospect of overweening states settling scores with enemies, overseas, and at home.

The elephant in the room is that a wide variety of corporations including internet companies, telecom operators, handset manufacturers, and producers of 'wearable' technology have (virtually) permission-free access to information about us. This is not just information that we generate while we are making choices on the internet or having a conversation on the phone. Our behaviour in the real world – beyond our usage of communication devices – in parks, restaurants, and in our bedrooms, is now being rendered into data. Physical parameters such as our blood pressure, heart beat, perspiration levels, who we are with at any point in time, and so on, are now part of the bitstream of cyberspace. Like telemetric devices used to track animals in the wild, the devices used to source such information are designed to be unobtrusive to avoid alarming us.[25]

The private information collected by corporations and the data analytics based on it is often shared with third parties. Indeed, the lucrative business models of product manufacturers and service providers rest upon the use of this data for purposes beyond improving direct services to the user. The business value of such data comes from its usefulness in predicting human behaviour, and, further, in shaping choices through an in-depth knowledge of our physical, social, and bodily contexts on a moment-to-moment basis. The aim is nothing less than to transform the entire world into a data source by creating a ubiquitous sensing and computing environment, and then to utilize the data to sell products with minimal time gap between desire and gratification.

In 2016, scholars from the Munk School of Global Affairs at the University of Toronto collaborated with Open Effect, a digital privacy and security nonprofit, to analyse the collection, processing, and usage activities associated with nine popular fitness trackers. They found that seven out of nine transmitted every logged fitness event to the company's servers – to allow sharing of fitness routines with one's friends but also enable 'data analytics' and distribution to third parties.[26]

Users usually have the option to opt-out of the data extraction process. Sometimes, under pressure from regulators, added protection is introduced, which allows companies to scrape personal data only when consumers explicitly 'opt-in' to such schemes. However, the details of the service contract lie hidden in reams of fine print. And, when one does opt-out, or refuses to opt-in, one risks losing access to much of the attractive service functionality. Ultimately, almost all of us choose to give in to the process of data capture and behaviour modification through a process of habituation.

Corporations stress that they only collect anonymized data, i.e., data from which the identity markers of the concerned parties have been removed and derive value by aggregating such data across a large number of people. However, re-identification science has shown that in the US it is possible to identify the name and location of a user with as little as three pieces of information – birthdate, zip code, and gender.[27]

Further, the process of developing intelligent machines involves training them by using vast amounts of data collected from humans. This data that includes voice recordings, still pictures, and moving images, has to be categorized, labelled, and contextualized by human beings. A vast worldwide ecosystem has sprung up to provide this service under the name of 'data annotation'. While we may opt-in to obtain certain advanced features under the illusion of data anonymization, we may not realize that images of ourselves, our homes, and offices can still be viewed by humans for the purpose of annotation. In 2020, there was widespread outrage when a series of images taken by a robotic cleaning device including that of a young woman on the toilet seat with a grainy picture of her face, and an eight- or nine-year-old boy with his face clearly visible appeared online.[28]

The marketers accept that they manipulate us but assert their objective is our empowerment.[29] To believe their claims in entirety, one would have to turn a blind eye to the formidable financial gains flowing to companies regarded as leaders of surveillance capitalism. For instance, in April 2021, Google-owner Alphabet Inc. had a cash pile of about $135 billion. Other internet behemoths were not doing too badly either. Apple Inc., Amazon.com Inc., Microsoft Corp., and Facebook Inc. had more than $300 billion combined.[30]

But the financial rewards may be regarded by some as being commensurate with the social benefits generated. One may choose to believe that surveillance by corporations is a benign activity designed to provide better products and promote human well-being, and that the loss of autonomy is a necessary sacrifice. However, a closer look will give us a sense of what is at stake.

In an experiment carried out by cognitive neuroscientists, participants lying in a scanner were asked to perform a decision-making task. They had to choose when to press one of two buttons, each of which was operated by a different hand. Simultaneously, a stream of letters was being shown on a screen at half second intervals, and participants had to remember the letter showing on the screen at the time they made their decision. Meanwhile, the scanner would monitor their brain patterns. The study revealed that brain signals in the frontal lobes predicted the time at which participants pressed the button a full seven seconds before the subject consciously made the choice.[31]

The seven seconds were presumably being used to process a decision that had already been made through the conscious mind. However, this does not imply that the conscious processing of decisions is irrelevant. Indeed, it represents a vital phase of our decision-making process in which we subject our prejudices and knee jerk responses to the test of reason and values, or, alternatively, validate our intuitive hunches.

To the extent that a metaverse comprising a network of sensors senses and responds to our sub-conscious processes faster than the time it takes for our conscious minds to arrive at a decision, it would by-pass our conscious minds and subvert our faculties of reflection. Thus, surveillance capitalism will impair our power of free choice in every aspect of our lives from the banal to the profound.

Democracy is not merely the freedom to choose a government. It also implies the existence of a private sphere for citizens that lies beyond the pale of the public gaze, whether of the government or corporations. It requires a space for autonomous, unconditioned activity. It is built on the recognition that social contracts must be consistent with conditions in which individuals can exercise their free will in the pursuit of 'life, liberty, and happiness'.[32] Thus, the foundational ideals of democracy are at threat.

Capitalism is not just the ability to access and afford a wider variety of material enjoyments. It is based on the sovereignty of the consumer, a faculty exercised to make unencumbered choices to consume or not consume any goods or services. Thus, the fundamental vision of capitalism is at threat.

A salubrious society is based on the existence of sanctuaries for individuals, families, friends that allow multifarious strains of sub-cultures to emerge and thrive. With sub-conscious processes exposed to surveillance capitalists, the sanctity of all sanctuaries is at risk.

In sum, the threat to human autonomy from a ubiquitous metaverse represents a profound challenge to the bedrock values of a free society, a system of which the *Washington Post*, the newspaper owned by Bezos, is a known guardian. While personalized services provided by private corporations have their own value, it is my belief that no value can be attached to human autonomy. And that nothing can compensate for the significant loss of free agency. Without realizing it, we appear to have been trapped in a Faustian bargain in which we give away what is most precious in exchange for, admittedly, an astonishing array of material possibilities.

In sum, both state and corporate surveillance have harmful effects on human society.

But there is more.

The very notion that these two kinds of surveillance constitute separate activities that are carried out in silos is flawed. To recognize the full nature of the threat, it is important to appreciate the partnership between the state and the corporation in the actualization of surveillance.

The Links Between Corporate and Government Surveillance

In 2000, one year before the 9/11 attacks, the Federal Trade Commission (FTC), the body responsible for competition regulation in the US, concluded that self-regulation by corporations would be insufficient to ensure adequate standards of privacy.[33] Had its proposals been translated into law, a number of violations of privacy that are currently commonplace would have become illegal.

However, after the 9/11 attacks, it became easy to make security the overriding consideration in the formulation of policy. In this environment, firms such as Google that were developing astonishing capabilities to scrape personal data to serve presciently accurate ads were no longer transgressors who needed restraining. Instead, they were recast as collaborators who needed to be co-opted in the state's overarching priority – safeguarding the homeland. Whether the measures taken were proportionate to the threat or even effective became moot. A state of 'exceptionalism' began to prevail in which the exigencies of security overrode the considerations of privacy, or autonomy.

The US government sidestepped tedious democratic processes by outsourcing development of surveillance technologies to firms such as Google. Keen to source new technologies emerging from the startup ecosystem in Silicon Valley, the CIA funded a venture firm called In-Q-Tel in Silicon Valley. Corporations were also co-opted to provide data for national security purposes, and there was a revolving door of expertise between the tech giants and the military. In this environment, Google and other such firms were free to go about their own businesses without regulatory oversight, provided they fulfilled the state's objective of 'Total Information Awareness'.[34]

The exceptionalism with regard to information in an environment of security paranoia mirrored itself within corporate structures. Google, once committed to the motto 'Do No Evil', enforced strict secrecy policies on its employees.[35] Founders of tech giants moved to establish complete control over their companies by establishing dual-class share structures. For instance, in 2004, at Google's public offering, founders Larry Page and Sergei Brin controlled the super-class 'B' voting stock, shares that each carried ten votes, as compared to the 'A' class of shares, which each carried only one vote. Note, investors with lower voting weights were assigned the more privileged letter – 'A' – a classic case of misleading branding. The founders claimed such moves would inoculate them from outside pressures.[36] Conveniently, these steps also cemented their complete control over the company. Along with the range of secretive practices followed by the company, the pedestal on which the founders placed themselves invited comparisons to cults.[37]

Complicity for the Noblest of Reasons

Regarding his purchase of the *Washington Post*, Bezos had said: 'When I'm 90, it's going to be one of the things I'm most proud of, that I took on the *Washington Post* and helped them through a very rough transition.'[38] In September 2018, *Time* magazine was acquired by Salesforce.com Inc. founder Marc Benioff and his wife Lynne. Benioff paid $190 million in cash to Meredith Corp.[39] to join Jeff Bezos among the group of tech billionaires buying highly esteemed print publications. The temptation to control valuable and venerable media properties seems to be catching. However, tech moguls must also know that their hobby of acquiring stakes in liberal media publications could put them in the cross hairs of global powers in a world of renewed great power rivalry with shifting sands of alliances.

Their vulnerability is heightened with the development of surveillance technologies in the high-tech ecosystems that they themselves did so much to create. Further, surveillance forms an integral element of their own business models and poses a threat to the liberal principles that so many of them espouse. Thus, they find themselves caught in an in an entanglement of their own making.

In her divorce, Mackenzie Bezos, the ex-wife of Jeff Bezos, received $38 billion. In retrospect, Bezos may have regretted the price he ended up paying for his purchase of the *Post*.

But, of course, the real tears must be shed for the common citizen. A blogpost by Bezos is cautionary in highlighting the extent of the threat. He wrote: 'If in my position I can't stand up to this kind of extortion, how many people can?'[40]

The Global War on Big Tech and Mr Musk's Intriguing Curveball

It is indeed true that breathtaking possibilities have been put within reach of human beings through the combination of accelerated computing, anytime connectivity, and a vast value network of interconnected devices and services. The question is – could such possibilities have been put within our reach without the tentacles of surveillance capitalism extending into every aspect of our lives? If we want the baby, must we accept the bathwater as well? Is the continued march of surveillance capitalism indeed inexorable? This question acquires significance because even though transformational progress has already been made towards a world of ubiquitous computing, we are still only at the start of the journey.

Indeed, the prospects in front of us are truly staggering. Today, with fifth-generation (5G) technology, we are entering a world where the volume of communication between intelligent machines will exceed human-to-human communication. Our intelligent automobile will communicate with our intelligent garage door to ensure it opens just when we arrive, warehouses will send messages to suppliers to restock items just in time, and sensors will enable remote monitoring of equipment and systems. However, this reality, disruptive as it is, appears to be only the start of a longer voyage as the digital world gears up for an even more unfamiliar terrain – the metaverse.

The metaverse presents the prospect of a single universal 'mixed reality world', a world comprising millions of people, each with a 'digital avatar', i.e., a digital representation of themselves which they can control just like they control actions in the real world, billions of sensor-equipped intelligent machines and objects of our everyday world – automobiles, clothes, shoes, currency, even trees, and a verisimilitude of virtual objects such as cryptocurrency, and non-fungible tokens. Interactions in this world include both online and offline elements. For example, a wedding in a physical court of law could be beamed on to a virtual wedding venue where digital avatars of guests mingle with the newlyweds and are issued NFTs as wedding gifts.

This world is coming into being using technologies such as augmented reality, artificial intelligence, 5G mobile technology, and blockchain. It aims to create the platform – the environment in which we will live our lives. The natural world will only be one of the many elements in this environment; perhaps not the most important one. So while 'datafication', the rendering of all our actions into data which can be used for marketable insight, aims to extend the reach of sensors into the 'real world', the vision of the metaverse is nothing less than creating a new reality by combining physical and virtual worlds in a seamless whole.

The term metaverse was first seen in a science fiction novel *Snow Crash*, published in 1992.[41] It was a portmanteau that combined 'meta' and 'universe'. It's most highly developed operationalization can be seen in massively multiplayer video games such as Roblox. The game had over 202 million monthly active users as of June 2023 – it was estimated that half of all American children aged under 16 were playing it.[42] Within the gaming universe, players use a virtual currency called Robux for in-game purchases of things such as rentals of premium servers that would enable faster connectivity for closed group play.

The nascent stages of the development of the metaverse hint at the vast universes that technology entrepreneurs are in the process of creating and colonizing. So, we are only at the start of a journey of infinite possibilities. But it is precisely the scale of what is being envisioned, and its location outside the traditional modes of regulation, that presents the most serious threat to its actualization.

In *The New Digital Age: Transforming Nations, Businesses, and Our Lives*, Eric Schmidt and Jared Cohen state, 'The online world is not truly bound by terrestrial laws…it's the world's largest ungoverned space'.[43] The digital space is indeed the new Wild West, the ungoverned, ever-expanding frontier of human exploration. But Schmidt and Cohen failed to touch upon an important nuance. If the online world is not bound by terrestrial laws, it is not merely because governments cannot keep up with new technologies. It is also because they have chosen to turn a blind eye, and in fact, become active partners in the creation of an online realm free from regulation.

We have seen earlier how the government collaborated with companies and allowed the stated objective of security to override considerations of privacy. But regulatory forbearance with regard to competition is an even more important factor.

An essential enabler of world that is coming into being is the vertical and horizontal integration of companies that facilitate the creation of a multidimensional profile of users across a wide variety of services including search, e-commerce portals, social media, and location-based services. It is this integration across behavioural domains that enables seemingly magical choice prediction and choice modification and creates insurmountable barriers for the entry of competitors. The regulation of internet search is an instance where regulators chose to allow the creation of vertically integrated behemoths instead of taking the stance that had led to the breakup of AT&T in 1982.

The Federal Trade Commission's Regulation of Search

A significant percentage of the traffic on the internet begins with a search referral. The Google search engine is the dominant player in the space. Data released by Statista in April 2021 shows that Google enjoys 82.95% market share in the United States, 83.9% in Germany, 92.58% in Brazil and 75.71% in Japan.[44] In addition to Google Search, Alphabet, Google's holding company, also has a number of other services that seek to show up in search returns. For instance, Google has a restaurant comparison service. This may create a conflict of interest of the search engine with respect to Yelp, Google's competitor in restaurant ratings. This conflict may reflect in a search bias.

The FTC carried out a two-year investigation into claims that Google 'manipulated its search algorithms to harm vertical websites and unfairly promote its own competing vertical properties'. However, the investigation ended without a formal complaint against Google. It was unanimously agreed that Google's 'practice of favoring its own content in the presentation of search results' was not in violation of US antitrust laws.[45]

Thus, the emergence of behemoths that create and monopolize the space of surveillance capitalism is not an inexorable fact of nature, but the result of several regulatory stances such as the one above. Different approaches may have allowed us to experience a digital revolution that we could celebrate.

In any case, the past is not necessarily the way things are going to play out in the future. In the US, a series of events has united politicians across the aisle with the common agenda of cutting Big Tech down to size.

Facebook Used to Meddle with Elections

In 2018, Christpher Wylie exposed Cambridge Analytica, a political consultancy firm and his former employer. Wylie revealed that the company illegally used the private information of Facebook users for targeted political communication by candidates, including Donald Trump, for the 2016 US presidential election. Apparently, the data of as many as 87 million Facebook profiles was mined to create the advertising campaign.[46]

Of course, advertising agencies have been implementing various forms of psychological targeting for years. However, the scale of the reported operation and the high stakes involved in its application eclipsed anything done before.

In April 2018, the US Senate Judiciary Committee summoned Facebook to testify about the data breach and the issue of data privacy in general. In his testimony, Mark Zuckerberg accepted that it was his personal mistake that he had not done enough to prevent malicious uses of Facebook. 'That goes for fake news, foreign interference in elections and hate speech,' he said.[47]

The UK's Information Commissioner's Office found Facebook guilty in the data breach case in July 2018. It charged Facebook with a fine of £500,000 ($663,000) – the maximum permissible amount. The office said that Facebook 'contravened the law by failing to safeguard people's information'.[48] A year later, in the US, the FTC approved a fine of $5 billion and sweeping new privacy regulations.[49] Once again, this was one of the largest penalties ever levied by the US government for any violation. Facebook agreed to pay $100 million to US Securities and Exchange Commission for 'misleading investors about the risks it faced from misuse of user data'.[50]

In the US, while both the Republican Party and the Democratic Party took umbrage at the breach of privacy, it was the latter that was the more exercised, given that most of the advantages of the breach of privacy seemed to have accrued to the Republicans. However, soon it was the turn of the Republicans to feel like they were the more aggrieved party.

Trump's Right to Free Speech

Upon declaration of Joe Biden as the victor in 2020 US Presidential election, Trump filed dozens of lawsuits challenging the results of the elections in the states of Georgia, Arizona, and Pennsylvania. Almost all the lawsuits were thrown out of court. The Attorney General, William Barr, declared that he found no evidence of tampering on a scale that would overturn the result of the election. A number of states carried out recounts and ratified the results. In mid-December, after the electoral college confirmed Biden's victory, the Senate majority leader Mitch McConnell formally congratulated Joe Biden on his victory.

Yet, Trump continued to peddle his claims. Egged on by him, a 2000-strong group of protestors stormed the Capitol building on 6 January 2021.*

Trump watched the scenes of violence from the White House.[51] It wasn't until an hour after the Capitol was put on lockdown that he intervened. He tweeted that the protesters should 'remain peaceful'.[52] However, despite advisers urging him to do more to calm down sentiments, he continued to claim the election had been stolen.

'I know you're hurt. We had an election that was stolen from us. It was a landslide election,' he said. 'But you have to go home now... We have to have law and order.'[53] In another message that called the mob 'great patriots' who were reacting to an election victory 'viciously stripped away'.[54]

The same day Twitter intervened as per its public interest framework and Twitter Rules and made it clear that further incitement of violence could potentially result in suspension from Twitter. Two days later, Trump tweeted, 'The 75,000,000 great American Patriots...will not be disrespected or treated unfairly in any way, shape or form!!!' [55] He further mentioned: 'To all of those who have asked, I will not be going to the Inauguration on January 20th.'[56]

At this point, citing their glorification of violence policy, Twitter permanently suspended Trump's account which had 88.9 million followers. They stated: 'These two Tweets must be read in the context of broader events in the country and the ways in which the President's statements can be mobilized by

---

* For more details, see Chapter 1.

different audiences, including to incite violence, as well as in the context of the pattern of behavior from this account in recent weeks.'[57]

On 7 January, 2021, Facebook followed suit, suspending Trump's Facebook and Instagram accounts 'for at least the next two weeks'[58] on account of the risks his usage of these social media platforms posed to the peaceful transition of power. Later Facebook extended the ban for an indefinite period[59] and referred the matter to its oversight board which included former Danish prime minister, Helle Thorning-Schmidt. The oversight board faulted Facebook for its decision of an indefinite ban, and fixed the period of suspension for two years from the date of the insurrection.[60]

Trump challenged all his suspensions in court citing the US Constitution's first amendment rules promoting free speech. As of August 2023, the matter is sub judice. Meanwhile, Republicans have developed a major grouse against the ability of tech giants to curb what they consider 'free speech'.[61]

The Bipartisan Consensus

In June 2021, lawmakers at the US House of Representatives, where Democrats had a comfortable majority, introduced four bills aimed at reining in the power of the tech giants. The measures sought to rein in conflict of interest by banning platforms from owning subsidiaries that operate on their platform and making it illegal for a platform to give preference to its own products, with strict fines in case of non-compliance.[62] A platform was also required to refrain from any acquisition unless it could show the acquired company did not compete with any product or service the platform was already providing. Facebook's acquisition of Instagram and WhatsApp would most likely have not gone through had such proscriptions been in place when those transactions took place.

Even in the Senate that is evenly split between Republicans and Democrats, the worries about influence cut across the aisles. Republican Senator Mike Lee, a ranking member of the Senate Judiciary Subcommittee on Competition Policy, Antitrust, and Consumer Rights, had this to say when a Facebook executive asserted that criticism about his company's harmful effects missed the mark: 'How does it miss the mark, any more than revelations years ago about tobacco companies concealing the dangers of tobacco?... And what tobacco companies knew about what they were doing to their own users?'[63] The Senator was referring to Facebook leaks that had revealed internal research findings showing the harmful effects of the photo sharing app, Instagram (owned by Facebook), on girls' mental health with regard to issues such as body image and self-esteem.

Things certainly seem to have come a long way from the time when tech was accorded the status of a religion, and its torchbearers were seen as no less than evangelists heralding the future with their awe-inspiring revelations.

The transition to an administration run by Democrats following the 2020 Presidential election is another warning bell for large internet companies. Traditionally, the Democrats are far more concerned than Republicans about the possible anti-competitive impact of large firms. In June 2021, the Biden administration appointed Lina Khan as the head of the Federal Trade Commission, the US competition regulator. Khan is known for her strong views against Big Tech companies. She has advocated bringing back possibility of structural separation of platforms from firms operating on those platforms.[64]

Facebook and Amazon contested Khan's participation in FTC's antitrust investigations into their companies. They cited her past criticism of them as an indicator that she could 'not be a neutral and impartial evaluator'.[65]

But, of course, the appointment continued, another sign that the cozy handshake between government and Big Tech in the US appears to have well and truly run its course. It is ironic that recent events in China mirror the developments in the US.

China Builds and Then Dismantles Big Tech

In China, the names Google Inc., Facebook Inc., Twitter Inc., and Amazon.com, Inc. don't evoke quite the same sense of awe as they do in the world at large. Instead, the country with the largest number of internet subscribers in the world (1,012 million as of January 2023 with India a distant second at 692 million and US third at 311 million[66]) worships at the altar of Baidu, WeChat, Sina Weibo, Alibaba, Tencent, Didi and Tik Tok.

The growth of these entities was driven by a thriving economy, a raft of financial support from the government, and most of all, the Great Firewall of China behind which Chinese companies were allowed to thrive without any fear of foreign competition. Thus, the state has played an important role in the rise of Big Tech in China, as it has in the US.

Further, China has shown an even greater proclivity for migrating to online modes of operation than the US. For instance, in 2016, China's total mobile payments from third-party providers (with Tencent's Tenpay and Alibaba's Alipay being the dominant players) totalled an estimated $ 5.5 trillion – over 50 times the equivalent value in the US[67]. As a result, today, China's top tech firms have a market capitalization of trillions of dollars and are among the largest global companies. The rise of the tech industry has meant founders such as Jack Ma of Alibaba, Pony Ma of Tencent Holdings Ltd, Colin Huang of Pinduoduo Inc, Cheng Wei of Didi, and Richard Liu of JD.com Inc. have acquired billionaire status.

As in other parts of the world, many of these companies have moved beyond the initial avatars with which they entered the market to create vibrant digital ecosystems catering to a portfolio of customer needs. Alibaba, initially an e-commerce company has diversified into cloud computing, payments, and advertising.[68] Tencent, originally an online gaming company, now also includes a social network (WeChat), a venture capital firm, and a web portal.[69] Didi, originally a ride-hailing company, has diversified into the sale and lease of automobiles.[70] WeChat, Tencent's social media platform, has over 900 million users, and various applications of Alibaba have a combined total of 500 million-plus users.

In conformance with global trends, the growth of Chinese tech giants has been fuelled by their data collection and processing capabilities. Today, they sit on vast quantities of data and are poised to capture even greater amounts and more sensitive kinds of data. The growing clout of internet firms through their access to citizen data is being seen as a threat to the Chinese political system itself.

The huge cash reserves that the tech giants possess have granted them the power to acquire or take strategic stakes in emerging businesses outside of China. This brings them under the regulatory ambit of foreign governments, a source of concern to Chinese authorities. There is a fear that foreign governments will gain access to the data of Chinese citizens.

Finally, Chinese firms have also raised capital from overseas, including from the US stock market. In doing so they have stepped around regulations of the Chinese government barring foreign shareholding in sectors such as the internet, education and media.

Increasingly, this has had serious consequences.

On 30 June 2021, Chinese ride-hailing giant Didi Global Inc. raised $4.4 billion in an initial public offering on the New York Stock Exchange (NYSE). This moved Beijing to launch a full-scale cybersecurity investigation into not only Didi but several other Chinese tech firms that had recently listed in New York. By 4 July, Didi had been banned from all app stores, including super apps such as WeChat. It could not access any new customers. Subsequently, new rules were announced for firms listing overseas under which all 262 Chinese firms listed in the US with a market capitalization of $2.1 trillion could be delisted.[71] However, while new listings have slowed down, no action had been taken till mid-2023.

China adopted a new data security law in September 2021 that lays out what kind of data needs to be protected and prevented from being accessed outside of the nation's borders. The law also put an end to free harvesting of data by defining how companies that are gathering huge chunks of data can harvest it, and how they can slice, dice, analyse or sell that data for profit. This law could put a brake on the growth of the Chinese tech giants and the tech sector, an important driver of growth in an economy suffering from a buildup of debt and facing the imperative of sourcing new avenues of demand.

However, the poster boy of China's crackdown on Big Tech has to be Jack Ma, Chairperson of Alibaba. In October 2021, with Alibaba valued at well over $1 trillion, Ma was planning to reach the peak of his career with a public offering of his company, the Ant Group, the largest financial technology company globally. On 24 October, he bluntly criticized the Chinese financial establishment. Days later, the authorities summoned Ma to Beijing for 'regulatory interviews' and cancelled the Ant IPO.[72] That was the last reliable piece of information on Jack Ma.

Since then, he has appeared in a video shot at a remote rural school where he says he has been studying and thinking, and has become more determined to devote himself to education and public welfare. There have been reports that he is working on his golf game, and that he is spending his time painting.[73] Meanwhile the conglomerate he set up is being dismantled and is losing hundreds of billions of market value.

Big Tech is facing regulatory heat in Europe as well.

Europe Tightens Privacy Regulation

The General Data Protection Regulation (GDPR), 2016, put into place measures for data protection and privacy in the EU and the European Economic Area (EEA). While the regulation made exceptions for the processing of personal data for national security or law enforcement, it introduced a number of privacy-oriented measures.

These include the following: If informed consent is used as the lawful basis for data processing, consent must be sought explicitly for all data collected and for each purpose for which data is used. An online form which has consent options structured as an opt-in (agreement to data being used) selected by default is a violation of the GDPR, as the consent is not unambiguously affirmed by the user. In addition, multiple types of processing may not be 'bundled' together into a single affirmation prompt, as this is not specific to each use of data and the individual permissions are not freely given. Data subjects must be allowed to withdraw this consent at any time and the process of doing so must not be harder than it was to opt in. A data controller may not refuse service to users who decline consent to processing that is not strictly necessary in order to use the service.[74]

Thus, the growing insecurities of the state seem to pose significant challenge to the unbridled, runaway growth of surveillance capitalism. It is likely that the US will go the way of Europe in increasing curbs on internet companies. However, China is likely to take a different approach. It is likely to transfer power from the captains of industry to the Chinese state without reducing the level of surveillance. It is possible this approach may enable faster technological progress in China than in the US, although technology companies in both jurisdictions are likely to progress at a slower pace as compared to what they would have in an unfettered world.

The uncertainties internet companies are facing do not stop at the increasing insecurities of states.

The growing schisms in the global world order in the wake of the rise of China and the Ukrainian conflict (see Chapter 4) present a mixed prospect for tech giants. On the one hand, the use of surveillance as a tool to further geopolitical interests will increase. Hence, tech giants will become useful to governments as in the days following the 9/11 attacks. Yet, the unfettered progression of technology company across global boundaries, with the full exploitation of synergies of work, play, and commerce, is likely to face severe hurdles. The downside risk appears to outweigh the upside.

And then there are the systemic risks.

In an episode in his series 'Everything is Stupid', Malaysian comedian Ronny Chieng says this about the metaverse: 'Yes, the metaverse is coming...not that anyone asked for it.'[75] And he's right. The metaverse is not a response to consumer demand, but an initiative of technology companies. In an economy where income inequality is growing, there is likely to be a paucity of consumer demand as there is a limit on the consumption that the upper echelons of society can undertake. Business investment through avenues such as the metaverse serves to keep the engine of demand humming despite huge amounts of inequality. Indeed, it is a necessity for internet giants sitting on huge piles of cash.

As of May 2021, Apple had close to $200 billion, Alphabet $136 billion, Microsoft $132 billion, Amazon $82 billion, and Alibaba $79 billion.[76] Such huge reserves require some avenue of investment. There is only so much that the distribution of dividends or buy back of shares can do. The metaverse serves as that fertile avenue of investment.

Recall from Chapter 1, how financial engineering was used to catalyse housing demand to revive the economy after the technologically fuelled dot-com boom went south. The metaverse can be seen as a similar phenomenon, though this time it is a technological boom that is meant to revive the economy after the housing boom went bust.

Like all speculative investments, it promises to subject the global economy to high levels of volatility and create extreme levels of distress for the average citizen. It remains to be seen how long this pattern of development characterized by high inequality, technological progress, financial speculation, and volatility will repeat itself.

But as of now, one thing is clear. The unimpeded run of Big Tech is facing significant headwinds on account of its own success. Its awe-inspiring achievements stand in contrast with the increasing social complexity and political instability it has spawned.

But the threats stem not merely from governments insecure about the ground slipping beneath their feet, geopolitical ruptures, or systemic fault lines. They also flow from within the club of the tech elite, a bunch of mavericks, if there ever was one. And no one fits the definition of a maverick better than Elon Musk. Indeed, in retrospect, the surprise is not that Musk chose to take on some of his fellow tech billionaires. The wonder is that it took so long for him to get around to it. But even as he geared up for a frontal assault on Twitter, there were some surprises in store for him as well.

Musk's Curve Ball

Even though he is a card-carrying member of the exceptionally gifted, headstrong, and driven group of tech billionaires, Elon Musk, South Africa-born entrepreneur, who periodically tops the list of the richest people in the world, stands out by virtue of his dreaminess and ability to fashion outrageous fancies that others would perhaps not even dare to articulate in the full glare of the public gaze. His plans to build a human settlement on Mars, create a network of tunnels under Los Angeles (to beat traffic), and develop 'friendly AI' so that 'unfriendly AI' (a nagging fear of his) does not destroy the human race, are the stuff of Silicon Valley legend.[77] And, of course, his biggest engine of success is the electric car company, Tesla, that has made the prospect of transition to cleaner fuels a reality. But as always, he has always had more cards up his sleeve than people give him credit for.

In April 2022, Elon Musk announced his decision to bid to acquire Twitter and make it a privately held company, taking it off the stock market. He mentioned three radical changes he would bring to the platform: first, the promotion of 'free speech'; second, making the ranking algorithm, which ranks tweets in order of popularity, open source (thus, users would be able to understand what factors determine the ranking); third, purging Twitter of messages generated by spambots, i.e., robots engaged in generating mass messages in order to effect trending patterns and influence public opinion.[78]

His intentions earned him the ire of both Democrats and Republicans. The former believed that his promotion of free speech would be a thinly veiled attempt to allow hate speech, misinformation, pornography, and pseudo-science unrestricted access. A natural implication of such a stance would be the return of Donald Trump to the platform. Some also complained[79] that Musk's concern about free speech only extended to reducing moderation on Twitter and did not include combating government censorship around the world including in countries such as China where Musk's flagship company, electric car maker Tesla, has sizeable economic interests.

A number of Silicon Valley movers and shakers expressed their concerns as well. Bill Gates was worried about Twitter becoming a haven of anti-vaxxers, who have been refuse to take the COVID-19 vaccine.[80] Mark Zuckerberg, founder of Meta, expressed confusion and uncertainty. Jeff Bezos wondered if Tesla's business interest in China would give the Chinese government leverage over Twitter via Musk.[81]

Meanwhile, Musk kept everyone guessing about his true intentions. After making the Twitter stock price increase by 22.2% one day after his announcement of a takeover bid, he walked back on his declaration citing insufficient action taken by Twitter to curb the operation of spambots. However, the legal agreement he had signed with regard to the takeover did not allow him renege on the deal without significant penalties. Hence, on 27 October 2022, facing the prospect of a difficult legal battle, and a court deadline of 28 October 2022 for the acquisition, he consummated the deal.

The episode shows that in today's world, tech companies can never be too sure where their next threats are coming from.

7

THE ERODING HUMAN CONNECT

When the logic of rationality becomes pervasive, it makes even the most intimate human relationships transactional. Markets naturally emerge to service these new modes of connection. Simultaneously, a vast ecosystem of relationship technologies offers new possibilities of individual gratification. The combination of markets and technology robs relationships of their nurturing and nourishing functions. The result is a pandemic of loneliness in the midst of a profusion of sexual exploration, a phenomenon that threatens the foundations of social stability.

The Post-sex World

Like many other couples, Abhay and his wife Vera were separated during the pandemic. He was in Seoul, while she was in Estonia. And the visa rules did not allow them to travel to each other's location.

It was tough. They had only just gotten engaged after a one-year transcontinental courtship and romance. Now, they could not physically meet.

Their relationship was saved by digital technology. Not just FaceTime, WhatsApp, and Zoom, but technologies specifically designed to assuage the loneliness of long-distance relationships. Pillow Talk,[1] a wristband they wore when they slept, recognized their heartbeats and sent it to the partner in real time, so both of them could go to sleep to the rhythm of the other's heartbeat. The Kissenger, a kiss messenger, allowed them to kiss each other remotely using a device that sensed the pressure of the partner's kiss and transmitted it in real time to the other.[2] And yes, the remote-controlled vibrators allowed them to simulate sex with each other, which turned out to be quite enjoyable after the technical glitches were sorted out.

But this chapter is not about the joys of sex-tech. It is about the decline of the humanizing power of sex in a society built on the foundations of individualism. Actually, it's not just sex that is to blame. But hang on, you'll see!

To be clear, I am neither a sociologist of sex, nor a sexologist. So, as a writer sallying forth where I should perhaps fear to tread, let me make some of my beliefs clear. First, I am not favourably inclined to the stance of religious denominations (including my own) that assert that the fundamental purpose of sex is procreation. For this reason, while I appreciate the promotion of the rhythm method as a well-meaning way to allow the faithful to have a lot of sex without interfering with the essential reproductive function of sex, i.e., a way of bending the rules, I disagree with its fundamental premise. On the other hand, I am also a little hesitant about going rah-rah about the credo sex for sex's sake, or sex as a hedonistic pursuit of pleasure.

I am a romantic at heart who believes sex is both a means of procreation of the species as well as one of the greatest expressions of intimacy between two people, married or unmarried, whether aiming to make babies or not. I am also a liberal who believes that matters in the bedroom should be decided primarily by the free choice of people present in that room.

So, I am a reasonably broad-minded guy, although my expansive ideological positions may be tested when my children get older.

I do have one rigid position on this is matter though – and it's not the missionary position, as would have become clear by now. And it is this: sex is about human interaction. Somewhere underneath the chaotic energies, the utilization of the other as a means to satisfy one's own lust, and the desperate search for emotional release, must lie the possibility, however remote, of an authentic human encounter. And while sex-tech saved Abhay and Vera's relationship, at least for now, on the whole, I believe it forms a part of a dazzling ecosystem of medical and technological possibilities that strikes at the root of human relationships.

Hence, I refer to our society as a post-sex society, one where sex has become more plentiful, accessible, varied, and technologically sophisticated but has decoupled from, and indeed become antagonistic to, the possibilities of sustained human relationships. If we define sex as a human activity which retains a relationship, however tenuous, to sustained intimacy and companionship, then we can assert that we are now in a post-sex society.

In his immensely popular recent song 'Got You' Daniel Cesar, the Canadian R&B artiste, sings:

'And when we're making love...It's only the two of us
Everything I need's between those thighs.'[3]

And then he goes on to lament:

'...it winds down into
The memories, It's all just memories.'

Close to 50 years ago, at the beginning of the flower power revolution of the 1960s, the Beatles had sung in a song entitled 'And I love her':

'A love like ours, Could never die, As long as I, Have you near me.'[4]

The contrast could not be starker – one song celebrates lovemaking, the other celebrates love. One, inevitably, ends with only memories to live by, while the other holds the promise of eternity. It is important to notice that neither song celebrates the joys of parenthood in the manner of the hit from the British pop charts where Joan Regan sang,

...Just a year from the day they were married
Came a gift from the girl to the boy
Looking proud as a queen as she carried
Such a wonderful bundle of joy...
Papa he loves mama...Mama she loves papa'[5]

Joan Regan's 'Papa He Loves Mama' came out in 1960. The Beatles released 'And I Love Her' in 1964. Daniel Cesar celebrated his conquest with 'Got You' in 2017. The three songs are emblematic of three different world views. In 1960, the world celebrated the family, no matter how repressive that family often was to members living within it, especially the women. With blinding speed, in 1964, the greatest phenomenon the music world had ever seen, The Beatles, sang of an idealized romantic love. And today, the successors of the stars of yesteryear celebrate with unbridled joy, the pleasures to be mined in specific parts of the human anatomy.

How did the shift happen? And how are we to reconcile the structural dualities of the transformation – the revolutionary achievement it represents in the form of the dramatic empowerment of women and the weakening of the hetero-normative consensus – with the equally disturbing social fallout in the form of unsatisfactory relationships, infertility, and loneliness.

This is a story which is about much more than sex-tech. To understand the present situation, we have to go back fifty years.

Sex Decoupled from Reproduction

The story of the decoupling of sex from human relationships starts with the decoupling of sex from reproduction. Two important developments that have characterized this process deserve mention.

The Pill

The American biologist Dr Gregory Pincus is usually given credit for developing the contraceptive pill in the 1950s.

However, it has a much older history dating back to the search for an inexpensive source of steroid hormones such as oestrogen and progesterone as an alternative to the supply from powerful European pharmaceutical companies. Before being used for contraception, these 'female' hormones were used for various medical purposes such as treating menstrual disorders and symptoms of menopause such as hot flashes, the use of which continues till today. The vision of using hormones for contraception dates back to the 1920s, and its development took place through the efforts of several scientists and social activists including Margaret Sanger, an advocate for women's reproductive rights and a collaborator of Pincus.

A professor from Penn State University, Russell Marker, found a relatively inexpensive source of progesterone in inedible Mexican yams and finally broke the monopoly of the European cartel. His company Syntex, founded in 1944, succeeded in reducing the price of progesterone almost 200-fold in eight years.[6] This helped to expedite Pincus' efforts to develop 'The Pill' that was finally approved for release by US's Food and Drug Administration (FDA) in 1960.[7]

In less than two years 1.2 million American women had started using the pill. The NHS introduced it in the UK in 1961 for married women only, and this lasted until 1967. By 2007, it was being taken by 3.5 million women in Britain between the ages of 16 and 49.[8]

The pill allowed women to take charge of their fertility without sacrificing sexual relationships. Soon after its legalization, college attendance and graduation rates for women increased sharply.[9] Although there were many victories that had already been secured by the suffragette movement including the right to vote, nevertheless, the pill transformed women's role in modern economy as it delayed the age of matrimony, allowing women to invest in education and prioritize their careers.[10]

Sex no longer remained just a means of reproduction. With the pill, intercourse could be an expression of love, or a means of physical pleasure, or a way of satisfying one of the wide variety of needs fulfilled by sex including the assertion of power. Though previous contraceptives also facilitated this transition, their relatively high failure rates failed to emphasize the distinction between sex and reproduction as clearly.

The legalization of abortion via the 1973 Roe v. Wade judgment in which the US Supreme Court declared that a set of Texas statutes criminalizing abortion in most instances violated the constitutional right of privacy came as yet another affirmation of a woman's ownership of her body. Curiously, abortion, especially on health grounds or in the case of rape, has always been easier in many societies where the position of women is regarded as worse than in the US, including Middle Eastern countries.[11]

In-vitro Fertilization

If the pill and the legalization of abortion offered ways to ensure that sex did not inevitably lead to reproduction, in-vitro fertilization (IVF) offered the possibility of reproduction without sex. In-vitro fertilization is a process in which an egg is drawn from the female, while sperm is taken from the male, and the fertilization of the egg takes place 'in vitro', i.e., in glass, outside the woman's body. The fertilized egg is allowed to grow for some time in an artificial medium before being transferred to the uterus, either of the mother or a surrogate, to establish a successful pregnancy.

Interestingly, Dr Pincus, a key player in the development of the pill, was also involved in research in IVF. As early as 1934, along with Ernst Vincenz Enzmann, a scientist at the Haskins Laboratories located in New Haven, Connecticut, he was trying to carry out IVF in rabbits. However, it was only on 25 July 1978 that the first human baby to be conceived by IVF, Louise Brown, was born thanks to the efforts of Patrick Steptoe, Robert Edwards, and Jean Purdy. Patrick Steptoe was an obstetrician and gynaecologist, while Robert Edwards was a biologist and physiologist. Jean Purdy assisted them as a nurse.

A few months later, Subhash Mukhopadhyay, a physician from India working on his own, used basic instruments and a household refrigerator to successfully create the world's second IVF baby.*

Sperm has been frozen for generations.[12] However, the ability to freeze and preserve a woman's eggs is a relatively recent development. In 1986, the first successful in-vitro procedure using frozen eggs was reported.[13] This advance meant couples could delay the birth of their children till long after the decline of fertility.

There has been a widespread uptake of IVF, especially IVF along with surrogacy, in recent years due to a pandemic of infertility in couples. Indeed, IVF is used mainly by couples who cannot reproduce by natural means.

---

* While Edwards received a Nobel Prize in physiology or medicine for his achievement (his collaborators could not be awarded as the Nobel Prize is not given posthumously), Mukhopadhyay faced disbelief and criticism for his efforts and finally died by suicide in 1981.

But the decoupling of sex from reproduction had consequences that went far beyond the obvious gains.

The Pure Relationship

According to British sociologist Anthony Giddens, the differentiation of sex from the exigencies of reproduction and the rise of artificial conception made sex 'fully autonomous' from reproduction.[14] Giddens argues that this development signalled a deep transition in personal life. It gave birth to what he calls the 'pure relationship', in which a 'relation is entered into for its own sake, for what can be derived by each person [and] is continued only insofar as it is thought by both parties to deliver enough satisfaction for each individual to stay within it.'[15] Such a relationship was based on the 'contractual assumption' that two individuals with equal rights were uniting for emotional and individualistic purposes. Commitment to the relationship never usurps individual privacy and free will.[16,*]

It is evident that in a 'pure relationship' both parties would need to be malleable about their expectations and flexible about their behaviours. The men constitute the party in the relationship that, after thousands of years, needs to accept an unfamiliar assertion of agency by the women. Women face the challenge of finding their balance in a world where possibilities

---

* Of course, the decoupling of reproduction from sex does not necessarily make a relationship 'pure'. In cases where there is financial dependence of one partner on another, power relations will usually be skewed, and the scenario of 'equal rights' is a chimera. But, of course, to the extent that the decoupling facilitated greater financial independence of women, it would usher in an age of pure relationships.

have dramatically expanded. It is quite plausible that the process would be hard on men who have to give up privileges that they had taken for granted, and that their inability to do so would result in a certain amount of rockiness in the landscape of relationships. Unfortunately, the process of finding a new normal does not seem to be going well, at least in the US.

The 'date' is the central social event around which the beginnings of the pure relationship are played out. It has an infinite number of variations but at its heart it involves a couple socializing with each other to derive mutual satisfactions of various kinds – physical, emotional, and even financial. Let's see how this institution is faring in the US. My reason for focusing on the US, in the discussion on both dating and marriage, is that the relevant data is readily available.

Dating and its Discontents

About three out of ten American adults are single. This group includes a disproportionate share of the 18–29-year-olds and the over 65 group. There are huge differences by gender: 51% of men younger than 30 are single. In contrast, women are more likely to be single later in life – 49% of women who are 65 or above are unpartnered, while only 19% of 30–49-year-olds are likely to be single.[17]

According to a 2019 Pew survey,[18] about half the single adults in US say they are looking for a committed relationship or casual dates. Of these, 67% say their dating life is going not too well or not well at all. This perception is true of a majority of daters across gender, age, race and ethnicity, education, sexual orientation and marital history. Moreover, 75% say it's been difficult to find people to date in the past year. Difficulty of finding someone looking for the same type of relationship (53%), finding it hard to approach people (46%) and the challenge of finding someone who meets their expectations (43%) were cited as the top reasons.

Given the difficulties faced by people who are looking to find dates, it is not surprising that half of the single population say they aren't currently looking for a relationship or dates. When asked to list the important reasons they were not interested, 47% said they had other priorities, and 44% said they just liked being single. There was also a significant number of people whose responses explicitly suggested that past disappointment or feelings of inadequacy were the deterrents – 18% said they hadn't had luck in the past, 17% said they felt like no one would be interested, 17% said they felt they were too old, while 11% said they had health problems that made it difficult.

Men and women had similar responses, with one notable exception. Non-dating men were twice as likely as non-dating women to cite the feeling that no one would be interested in dating them as the major reason.

It's clear that the dating scene is not doing too well in generating relationships. Let's see how the institution of committed relationships is faring.

Marriage: Delayed Beginnings, Uncertain Ends

In the 1980s, it was said that roughly half of all American marriages would end in divorce.[19] If this statistic is likely to get less alarming in the next few years, it is because young Americans are becoming highly selective about marriage – cohabiting for a few years and going their separate ways if things do not go well.

American divorce rates are up in the 55–60-year age group but down among the younger generation.[20] The rise of divorces in the older age group is on account of the baby boomers, those born from 1950–65 during the heady days of the sexual revolution. They were responsible for spikes in the divorce rates among young people in the 1980s when they started marrying and are now responsible for similar trends in older populations.[21]

Data shows that people who remarry after being divorced, as the baby boomers tend to be doing, are more likely to get divorced again.[22] Perhaps the baby boomers retain a rose-tinted view of marriage. And don't learn from their mistakes! The same is not true of young Americans who are delaying the age at which they first marry or are foregoing the option altogether.[23]

Getting married and having children are important but not essential for leading a fulfilling life – say more than half the Americans. On the other hand, 57% consider having a job or career they enjoy is essential for a man, and 46% say it is essential for a woman.[24]

Whatever be the reasons for the scepticism toward marriage, a Pew survey shows that married couples express a greater amount of trust in the partners and higher levels of satisfaction with their relationships than those in committed relationships without marriage – 58% say things are going very well in their marriage compared to 41% of the unmarried cohabiters.[25]

In any case, one could argue that a process involving the overturning of gender roles and relationships that had been institutionalized for thousands of years would inevitably involve a measure of churning. And that once this churning is complete, a new, more egalitarian, and humanitarian norm will emerge.

Seen in this light, the current discomforts are merely necessary evils that must be borne in order to give birth to a new dawn.

But can we expect the process to give birth to the new relationship norm that we seek? Is the process of transition fraught with a level of instability that threatens social sustainability?

To answer these questions we have to recognize that the 'pure relationship' is being impacted by a number of powerful forces.

The Logic of the Pure Relationship in an Internet-enabled World

If a long-term commitment or marriage represents the voluntary giving up of certain freedoms in order to benefit from the joys of mutually beneficial exchange within the institution of the relationship, the cold logic of transactions requires each party to examine whether they could enjoy similar exchanges without the accompanying restrictions – either by remaining single, or by switching to another relationship.

Here, the notion of 'transaction costs' provides some clarity. In the parlance of economics, transaction costs are costs not directly related to the service being exchanged, but attendant on the provision of those services. The costs of monitoring a software maintenance contract or pursuing legal remedies related to it are examples of transaction costs. The actual cost of providing the service, i.e., maintenance, is central to the transaction and distinct from the transaction costs.

An important structural change has taken place since the dawn of the age of the pure relationship – there has been a dramatic reduction in the transaction costs related to the mutual satisfactions traditionally provided within the context of a committed relationship. A somewhat trivial example relates to 'cuddling', a form of loving touch between couples that is known to release feel-good hormones.

Earlier one would have to enter into at least a casual relationship with someone in order to access the joys of cuddling. This would involve the cost of dating, the loss of freedom due to commitment, and so on. Such attendant costs would represent the transaction costs of cuddling, comprising both monetary and non-monetary elements. Since the transaction costs were high (taking both monetary and psychological elements into account), it did not make sense for human beings to constantly strike new relationships within which they could enjoy cuddles but to forge a relatively long-term associations within which these joys could be obtained. Now, with a number of cuddling services on offer, all that one has to do is to find one such service located nearby, check the user ratings, and pay the necessary fees. In other words, due to the vastly reduced transaction costs related to cuddling, a relationship is no longer necessary to obtain this particular satisfaction.

Cuddles represent just the tip of the iceberg in terms of tradable offerings available outside relationships. The list includes highly varied and plentiful experiences of sex, paid conversations, consort services, and so on. Given that the number, variety, and quality of such services has acquired critical mass, a number of people are happy to remain single.

Not just have the transactions costs of obtaining services usually found within relationships reduced for single people, but the costs associated with breaking relationships including the emotional costs of a commitment gone awry, the social stigma associated with a failed relationship, and the dreariness of a single life have also come down. Today, alimony expenses could represent the major disincentive to divorce but, in most cases, the pre-nuptial agreement, yet another innovation of the market economy, eliminates that too.

The reduction in transaction costs of services typically obtained within relationships and the reduced stigma associated with breaking relationships implies that the world of pure relationships, given its present trajectory of evolution, is bound to be transient and unstable – to a far greater extent than it would have been before the advent of the internet, the time when the phrase was coined by Giddens.

The structural transience and instability of the modern relationship play out in different ways in different instances. But two avenues of conflict stand out and need further exploration – the challenges posed by the world of work, and the expectations related to physical intercourse.

To start with, a trip down the new highways and by-lanes of modern sexual practice is in order.

Sex Then and Now: What a Long, Strange Trip Turn Over Been

The modern world of sex is characterized by four interrelated trends: the sexualization of the secular, the virtualisation of the sexual, the individualisation of the virtual, and the emancipation of the individual.

The Sexualization of the Secular

Modern societies are characterized by an increasing proportion of spaces unmarked by religious influence, i.e., by an increasing secularization of society. Increasingly, such spaces have become sexualized, primarily through the ubiquitous commoditization of the female body. Everything from soap to stationery has to be made sexy in order to sell it.

In this connection, the words of feminist Luce Irigaray are thought provoking. In *An Ethics of Sexual Difference*,[26] Irigaray asks: 'Has a worldwide erosion of big gains won in women's struggles occurred because of the failure to lay foundations different from those on which the world of men is constructed?' In other words, by attempting to out-do men in traditional bastons of privilege rather than establishing new forms of power, are women fighting the wrong battles, and, thereby, losing the war?

In the context of the pure relationship, the sexualization of the secular has transformed sex into an art form, a 'performative act' that has acquired immense weight in the success of a relationship. The widespread transformation of sexologists into sex coaches testifies to this fact.[27]

This focus on sex could in any case have been problematic given that no relationship can consistently satisfy the unrealistic expectations stoked by mass media. However, the challenge becomes even more pressing in view of the vast number of alternatives emerging on the horizon.

The Virtualization of the Sexual

At the start of the chapter, the ability to simulate sexual activity without actual physical presence was alluded to. But human mating can be described as a long and elaborate dance leading up to the final act of consummation. Today, every step of that process has been virtualized.

Online dating services in the US were projected to grow to a $3 billion a year business in 2018. Around 15% of US adults use websites or mobile dating apps in their pursuit of romance. According to the Pew Research Centre, online dating usage tripled among those between the ages of 18 and 24 between 2013 and 2015. The older generation wasn't lagging behind either – for 55- to 64-year-olds usage doubled from 6% to 12%.[28] As per Nielsen data, 10% American adults spend over an hour every day on a dating app. Over 1,500 dating apps or websites are already trying to draw single men and women and match them.[29]

When the virtual interaction site Second Life came up in 2003, it offered users a chance to interact with others through their online avatars.[30] It was believed that this site included spaces where avatars could engage in sexual activity with one another.[31] However, users could merely watch their avatars chat and engage in audio exchanges without experiencing any of the real sensual pleasures that would be in play in the real world. Almost 20 years later, things are changing rapidly. Even before COVID-19 pandemic, significant progress was being made, but after it, the process of allowing physically separated human being to simulate shared sensual experiences through bits and bytes hurtling across cyberspace was turbocharged.

The space of possibilities makes sustained coupling a challenge. But the virtual options are not just restricted to coupling with other people.

The Individualization of the Virtual

Although people rave about social media networks, pornography may be the internet's biggest and most enduring 'killer app'. While it is difficult to define and correctly estimate the size of the industry on account of blurred boundaries between adult content and porn, in 2018, a conservative estimate placed the size of the industry at $15 billion. That made online porn bigger than Netflix ($11.7 billion), Hollywood ($11.1 billion), and Viacom ($13.3 billion).[32]

User surveillance technology and data analytics invented by the Big Tech companies are being masterfully used by porn companies to closely monitor the consumption of free porn to assess the kinds of content users will be ready to pay for.[33] Countries across the world seemed to be equal opportunity offenders in terms of serving up traffic to porn sites, with developing countries exhibiting the greatest traffic by volume and advanced countries providing the traffic with the highest willingness to pay.[34]

There is also a new kind of porn site, the user-generated video-sharing platform that can be understood as YouTube for sexual content.[35] Users create content based on their own sexual activity and upload it for widespread viewing. On such platforms, a large proportion of the uploaded content consists of participants engaged in solo sex. Evidently, there is a sizeable market for the viewing of such activity.

The Emancipation of the Individual

The outcome of the above trends is the unshackling of the individual from the relationship. Recall, the logic of transaction costs makes the 'pure relationship' unstable. But there is more. The logic of transaction costs redefines the nature of the relationship itself and drives a renegotiation about the set of services that are expected to be provided within a relationship. Services that are not satisfactorily provided within a committed relationship would begin to move outside its ambit even as it appears to continue.

Sociologists such as Esther Perel have written about how the attitudes associated with parenting – security, stability, surety – militate against attitudes that promote desirable sexual experiences – risk, danger, adventure.[36] Thus, sustaining a satisfying sex life is a challenge for most married couples, especially those with children. Therefore, the norms around relationships are beginning to include concepts such as open relationships (in which both partners have the freedom to find sexual partners outside the relationship), polyamory (in which each partner can simultaneously enter into several relationships), swinging (in which two couples swap partners), and optional monogamy (in which partners retain the option of venturing outside the relationship without necessarily exercising the option; apparently the added risk entailed helps retain excitement in the monogamous relationship).

Thus, sex has come a long way. At one time it was seen as a functional pursuit for the propagation of the species or a handmaiden of undying love. Today, it forms a part of the substratum percolating through all of daily human experiences, a virtual pursuit of shared pleasure, an individual quest for physical gratification. And it has refashioned the relationship between couples in fundamental ways.

Can relations survive the erotic boredom that is inevitable

for a human being fed on a constant diet of sexual messaging and having access to a dizzying variety of alternatives?

And can they sustain themselves despite the constant presence of the workplace and its demands, an 'other' that insinuates itself into every moment?

Work: The Elephant in the Bedroom

The hypercompetitive workplace has imposed itself into the space between two human beings, a space meant to be relatively inviolate. Whether one belongs to elite groups in society that are doing well or the masses who are having to struggle, professional stress is a constant companion. And while relationships can play an important role in mitigating stress, the latter puts enormous pressure on relationships.

The nature of stress for those doing well and those who are struggling to get by is different. Relationships for those who are struggling often represent convenient arrangements to split the costs of essential items such as housing. Recall, cohabitation was said to be less satisfying than marriage. A possible reason is that financial compulsion is more often a driving force for cohabitation than it is for marriage. In a 2019 Pew survey in the US, 13% of married adults stated staying with their partner made sense financially and 10% said it was convenient. In contrast, as many as 38% of those cohabiting without marriage cited finances, and 37% cited convenience as major reasons.[37] A relationship formed to escape financial stress cannot be said to be well grounded.

For those who are doing well, the professional and financial expectations that each partner has of the other and of themselves and the immense pressures at work in a winner-takes-all world act as significant obstacles to the forging of human relationships free of material concerns.

In a situation where the paradigm of a mutually beneficial 'transaction' lies at the heart of a relationship, the logic of commerce dominates not just before a relationship is struck (as it did in feudal times when 'alliances' were made purely on the basis of materialistic factors) but also after it is forged. Since human beings, despite all their claims of modernity, need their relationships to provide refuge and serve as a sanctuary from an increasingly competitive and inequitable world, they are unable to find satisfaction in the new modes of intimacy they are presented with.

Given such stiff competition, it is no surprise that human relations are not doing so well, either in terms of romantic satisfaction or long-term commitment. The result is, to use the words of former US Surgeon General, Dr Vivek Murthy, an 'epidemic of loneliness and isolation'.[38]

Loneliness Within and Without Commitment

The coronavirus pandemic brought with it a sharp increase in the levels of loneliness in the US. But loneliness was a serious issue even before the pandemic. Almost 60 million Americans said they often or always felt lonely as per a study conducted by the Kaiser Family Foundation.[39] It was worse for older adults. A report by National Academies of Sciences found that more than a third of those over 45 and 43% of those over 60 were lonely.[40]

Dr Vivek Murthy writes of his visits to communities across the USA during his tenure as US Surgeon General: 'Loneliness ran like a dark thread through many of the more obvious issues that people brought to my attention, like addiction, violence, anxiety, and depression.'[41]

Dr Murthy believes that the individualistic culture of modern society has a lot to do with the problem. He states:

> 'In an individualistic culture, your successes and your failures are entirely yours. That can place an extraordinary burden on individuals who may experience failure, not simply due to their individual efforts but because of complex circumstances. There are some people who might respond well to that, but a lot of people end up doing worse because they just beat themselves up further. That leads to further erosion of self-esteem and confidence, and creates that downward spiral of loneliness.'[42]

Thus, loneliness is often caused by an innate lack of self-esteem that renders it difficult for people to reach out to others to establish human connections that are essential for our emotional well-being. The isolation further exacerbates the problem making it even more difficult to make human contact.

Recall, a large number of single people who had opted out of the dating market did so because of lack of self-esteem. This was especially true of men.

Loneliness is experienced not merely by single adults but also by teenagers, and those in committed relationships including marriage. A 2020 study by Making Caring Common revealed that 61% of those aged 18 to 25 experienced high levels of loneliness.[43] Data released by the Center for Disease Control and Prevention in June 2021 showed that 63% of young individuals were experiencing substantial symptoms of anxiety and depression.[44]

In 1966, a student sniper climbed up a clock tower at the University of Texas and fired down on passers-by from the observation deck. By the time police could take him down, 17 other people were dead or dying. In the 50 years preceding this incident, only a total of 25 mass shootings – those in which four or more people were killed – had occurred. In the 55 years since, there have been 189 shootings, more than three a year, with 1,332 people killed.[45]

The frequent school shootings in the US, the pandemic of mental health issues, and even terrorist involvement – loneliness plays an important role in all of these, manifesting sometimes as hurt over perceived slights, at other times as rage over remote world events.

Events in the US represent more fully formed versions of developments taking place across the world. More traditional societies, for instance those in South Asia, will probably continue to maintain the illusion of the traditional family for some time. The difference with advanced economies will be in the levels of hypocrisy involved not in the actual content of human experience.

Does the Faustian bargain in which we seem to trade progress and women's empowerment for crippling loneliness have no possible alternatives?

Hope, ironically, stems from the fault lines emerging in the system of which relationships are but a part. More of this in Chapter 8. But first let's join a late night conversation to further validate our findings.

After Hours with an Intimacy Coach

Are the phenomena referred to earlier in the chapter limited to advanced Western societies? Are societies regarded as more grounded in tradition immune to these new relationship pressures? With not much data to source, I turned to the oldest method for gathering information – the knowledgeable informant. For this purpose, I sought out Aili Seghetti, an intimacy coach and sex coach based in India.

Aili is 48-years-old, half Finnish, half Italian. She is a slim blonde with blue eyes and a ready smile. She is wearing what appear to be coffee-coloured, steel-rimmed cat-eye frames. At one stage in our conversation, a furry white cat gracefully glides across the screen onto her lap.

Aili's English is curiously Indian. She rolls her r's and often uses a Hindi word for emphasis. I learn that she has lived five years in Finland, 13 years in Italy, 13 years in the UK, and the rest in India. She obtained a bachelor's and master's degree in Hindi from the SOAS University, London. She was interested in Indian philosophy and had wanted to enrol in the comparative religion program, but a professor sold her on the Hindi degree because it included a third year that was to be spent abroad. Her master's dissertation was on the representation of Black people in Hindi films. Soon after her master's she got into a relationship with an Indian man. They got married in a year.

After her master's degree, she worked at Whistling Woods, a film school promoted by famous Indian film director, Subhash Ghai. Then, she got into market research and worked for firms such as Happy Thinking People and Flamingo. Her clients included dating app firms such as Bumble and Tinder. While doing research on the customers of these apps she got to understand the changing world of relationships in India. She found she was not interested in research, but enjoyed speaking to people about their relationships and sex-related issues. Meanwhile, her marriage broke up when she found her husband was cheating on her.

She wanted to start helping people who used dating apps. But, at the stage of life she was in, she did not want to spend time earning a degree in sex therapy, a fairly long drawn-out process. In any case, she was less interested in a pathological approach and instead wanted to help clients solve their problems using a mixture of psychotherapy and tools and techniques drawn from the realm of sex coaching.

There are no institutes in India where one can learn to become a sex coach. Most coaching institutes are located in the US, with a few in Australia and Europe. Although the courses are expensive, up to €5,000 for a six-month course, the certification does not count for much.

Nevertheless, Aili decided to take a Sex Coaching Certification course with a US-based institute called Somatica and calls herself a Somatica sex coach, one who uses touch-based coaching in body parts that are not genitalia.

She divides the entire area of coaching services related to sex into four groups – sexological body workers, those who use hands to touch genitalia for the purpose of arousing sexual energy; sex surrogates, who engage in full-blown acts of sex; sex/intimacy coaches, who talk to clients to address their sexual issues; and Somatica sex coaches.

Aili has been an intimacy coach for the last eight years. She got into Somatica sex coaching only in the last three years. Soliciting for sex work is illegal in India, although the work itself is legal. Thus, sex work often comes into a grey zone where some sort of police protection has to be purchased.

As her life trajectory shows, Aili has played many roles in Indian society, including a market research analyst, the wife of an Indian man, and a Somatica sex coach. Her testimony is not meant to be seen an evidence-based revelation about the truths of Indian society, but rather as a set of hints from someone with first-hand experience of the instabilities of Indian relationships. The experience she draws upon is coloured no doubt by her Western gaze, her own involvement in a failed marriage to an Indian man, and the inevitable limitedness of one person's perspective. Nevertheless, I found her insights enhanced my own intuitions about changes underway in Indian society. Hence, I decided to include her perspectives as a conversation starter on the changing mores in a traditional society.

Aili says about 70% of her clients are men, 20% are couples, and 10% are women. The men are generally 25–35 years old. They suffer from a variety of problems including erectile dysfunction, premature ejaculation, unsatisfactory sex lives within their relationships, and porn addiction.

The women are older; they suffer from vaginismus, the inability to have penetrative sex, they can be single women looking to get dating coaching, married ones wanting to open up their marriages, or women who have not experienced orgasms.

The couples are generally in the early 30s or 40s. They are often in sexless marriages, although Aili says the problem usually lies somewhere else in the overall relationship. They are looking to transition to open monogamy or polyamory.

After four years as an intimacy coach, Aili added Somatica sex coaching to her service portfolio because she felt talking about solutions to sexual dysfunctions was less effective than showing people through touch. She had grown up in a very conservative sect of Lutheran Christians called Conservative Laestadianism. They are not even allowed to watch television. 'If my father had been alive, I would never have been able to do this work,' laughs Aili. 'He would have killed me.' Aili's friends worried about her move to Somatica sex coaching because they felt inviting people home for such encounters would expose her to physical danger. However, Aili has found that clients needing such services are usually painfully shy, and far from being a threat in any way.

She has worked with approximately 700 clients over the last eight years. This is her take on the state of relationships in India:

1. She estimates that many men are cheating on their partners, and believes that this has always been common in India*. According to her, the figure as of now could be higher than 50%. Half of the men who cheat go to sex workers; the other half enter into relationships outside marriage. Men often use massage parlours to source sex. Trips to Thailand or Nepal are also much in demand. Martial arts clubs double up as ways of sourcing sex overseas in the course of travel for tournaments.
2. Men from small towns are also looking for options outside marriage. However, they have to come to a big city to avail the options.
3. With financial independence, women are not accepting this state of affairs any more. They are also not willing to continue in the old patterns of relationships in which they are expected merely to serve their mother-in-law, manage

* I interpret her comments as insights into urban India, the milieu in which she works.

the kitchen and fulfil child rearing responsibilities. They are choosing divorce, staying single for longer periods of time, and seeking to open up the relationship.[46]

4. Cheating among women is on the increase. However, it continues to be much lower than cheating among men.
5. The contours of long-term relationships are changing. There is a high level of interest in exploring what is loosely referred to as 'non-monogamy'. These include the freedom to engage in single encounters, casual hook-ups, light dating, non-sexual romantic relationships, non-romantic sexual relationships, romantic and sexual relationships, triads, polycules, i.e., three or more people who are connected romantically and/or sexually, etc.*
6. Contraception is still mainly restricted to the morning after pill taken by the woman. Men feel the condom interferes with sensation. They don't use a condom even with a sex worker. Women, too, often regard the condom as a foreign object. Therefore, the risk of infection high. Despite that, getting tested for Sexually Transmitted Infections (STIs) is really difficult.
7. There are many active swingers clubs in which couples bond sexually with other couples.
8. The path of seeking greater sexual freedom used to be lonely but is less so at present because of being able to find communities on the internet.
9. She feels it is too early to tell if greater sexual freedom will lead to more sexual satisfaction or more sustainable relationships.

* Taken from a document 'Guidelines for a Poly Agreement' shared by Aili.

10. She doesn't feel virtual sex through online sex toys will work without the sense of smell.

Aili's testimony suggests that some of the trends observed in western countries are also operating in India. The traditional Indian marriage was tilted in favour of the man. The growing financial independence and decision-making power of women is changing the equation. More women are opting to remain single, exiting the marriage, or demanding that it be opened up for them too.

India is a country with very low rates of divorce overall, even below 1%. However, in metropolitan cities the rate of divorce is more than 30%.[47] Family court officials say that the number of divorce applications has doubled (even tripled in some cases) in cities such as Mumbai, Delhi, Bengaluru, Kolkata and Lucknow in the period from 2010 to 2015.[48]

Aili feels that in India, the institution of family will endure as it is deeply embedded in our cultural fabric. Also, it will remain relevant as there is little societal support or infrastructure for old people. However, underneath the façade of the family, the equations will be very different. Aili herself is in a poly-amorous relationship; she has multiple male partners. I asked her about the security of children in such relationships. Aili feels children may not suffer in families practicing polyamory as such families have a much higher appreciation for feelings, and boundaries.

The world Aili inhabits – of open monogamy, polyamory – may still be a marginal phenomenon. But, surely, it is suggestive of broader fissures appearing in the Indian marriage and indicates that the thumbprints of the age of rationality are appearing all over the world, not just in advanced Western countries with relatively limited demands made by tradition.

The theory of innovation proposed by the late Clayton M. Christensen, celebrated American academic and business consultant, states that disruptive change often comes from small new companies as innovative ideas get lost on the fringes of mainstream organizations.[49] As we begin the process in the next chapter of synthesizing the learnings from the case studies covered so far, it is perhaps fitting that the last word has come from the margins of our society. I end with a quote from the famous Urdu poet, Nida Fazli who wrote in his poem 'Communal Harmony' (my translation):

'That woman of the night
has known many manners of men
perhaps that is why
she understands the world
a little bit better...'[50]

SECTION 2

8

THE SEVEN UNRAVELMENTS

The world today exhibits seven kinds of unravelment which suggest that the ideas, conceptions, goals, institutions, and technologies that have powered human development for over two hundred years have outlived their utility. And that a new imagination must come into being to lead the world into the next epoch of growth. The dynamics of these unravelments have been covered in detail in the previous section. In this chapter, we summarize and synthesize the main themes.

Economic Unravelment

The last thirty years have led to the creation of a more equitable world as China and the emerging economies such as India, Brazil, and Mexico have made rapid strides in increasing both the size of their economies and their per capita incomes. However, levels of inequality within countries have risen.

Further, the deregulation of the financial sector and the digital economy has created winner-takes-all markets where a few successful firms command vast war chests while most flounder and disappear.

Inequality of income and wealth between households creates a paucity of purchasing power of the masses. Since the consumption levels of the wealthy cannot increase in proportion to their wealth, there is a likelihood that a shortfall of demand for consumption may occur.

With regard to business investment, the leading technology companies that are sitting on huge stockpiles of cash are often unable to identify investment opportunities to utilize their investible resources. Meanwhile, as geopolitical realignments lead to increased protectionism, exports are drying up. In response, countries such as China are trying to rebalance their economies towards infrastructure investment. However, viable opportunities are proving to be hard to find. Thus, there appears to be a shortfall of demand for investment in technology, infrastructure, and industry in general.

A key solution devised by the modern economy to address these shortfalls of demand is a rise in debt levels and an expansion of equity investment in technology startups.

The Nixon shock of 1971 that decoupled the dollar from gold gave the US central bank the ability to print dollars in order to tide over economic crises. This led to periodic surges of liquidity in the world. Further, as emerging economies such as China and the oil exporting countries developed export surpluses in the 1990s and invested those surpluses in US treasury securities, savings flowed from emerging economies and resource-rich countries to the US. Simultaneously, there was a wave of financial deregulation that allowed the growth of financial derivatives, especially in the USA. These derivatives which were indiscriminately used by financial institutions like banks, in turn, facilitated borrowing by people who had limited financial prospects. All three phenomena – the surges of liquidity, the global transfer of savings to the USA, and the growth of financial derivatives – enabled the growth of debt. In some cases, there was a surge in household debt. In others, there was a rise in corporate or government debt.

American households immiserated by the outsourcing of manufacturing jobs borrowed to buy homes, Chinese goods, college education, and automobiles. Perversely, their unsustainable debt was necessary to keep the Chinese growth engine humming. Across emerging economies, loans were extended for the build-up of infrastructure.

As export markets shrank after the 2008 Global Financial Crisis, China substituted export demand with demand for domestic infrastructure and infrastructure in countries associated with the Belt and Road Initiative. A surge of corporate and sovereign debt ensued.[1]

Technology companies gained from the availability of funds without the expectation of profits or even revenues in the short to medium term. An ecosystem of private capital comprising angel investors, venture capital funds, and private equity funds sprang up to mobilize the wealth of a generation of entrepreneurs and executives who had gained from the global developments of the 1980s and 1990s. The war chests of the Big Tech companies also added to the availability of funds for tech start-ups. A large proportion of the resources flowing to technology start-ups took the form of convertible debt, i.e., debt that could be converted into equity at the discretion of the investor. Periodic speculative bubbles on stock markets provided a safety valve that assured investors that at least a few of their investments would come good, making them rich beyond their wildest dreams.

A rise in household debt is sustainable if it is backed by the income potential of the borrower. Given the decline in the fortunes of the working class across the globe, this is often not the case. A rise in corporate debt is sustainable if the ensuing investment can be expected to yield healthy returns. However, given the high level of speculative investment in technology or infrastructure, this is often not the case. A rise in government debt is sustainable if it is linked to well-designed welfare programs or infrastructure schemes. Given the rise in populist politics across the globe as a reaction to high levels of inequality, this is often not the case.

As the true picture of household finances is revealed, as the flimsy fundamentals of technology start-ups are exposed, and as the spectre of ghost towns mocks the hubris of lenders and investors in infrastructure, the debt crisis spreads its tentacles across the world.

The COVID-19 pandemic led to yet another surge in both government as well as private debt. Supported by low interest rates, governments in advanced economies as well as certain emerging economies like China borrowed to contain the devastation caused by the virus. Facilitative conditions for the uptake of private debt were also put in place. As a result, private debt also ballooned. Meanwhile, on account of their low credit ratings, low-income economies were unable to increase public debt to provide relief measures even during the pandemic. However, they also experienced elevated debt-GDP ratios on account of a reduction in their nominal GDPs.[2]

When debt is unsustainable in a country or a block of countries, rescue by unaffected countries is possible. This was what happened after the 2008 financial crisis when countries such as Germany bailed out the flailing economies of Portugal, Ireland, Greece and Spain through the European central bank. However, when a critical mass of countries comprising both advanced and emerging centres of economic power suffers from an unsustainable build-up of debt, there is no reprieve.

Data from the institute of international finance shows that total global debt by the end of 2021 was over 350% of global GDP.[3] This was an increase from 220% in 1999. If the average growth rate of the past 15 years continues, rough estimates suggest that the global debt would be more than four times global output in 2030.[4] Assuming a conservative interest rate of 5%, this would mean that at least 20% of annual global income would be spent in debt servicing. These levels of debt were necessary for the shoring up of demand to facilitate continued GDP growth, but, surely, they have now become unsustainable.

So, there is every possibility of a cutback in spending on account of the blowing up of the debt bubble. Then, there will be no place to hide from the fact that a world characterized by growing inequalities and by winner-takes-all markets is a demand constrained world.

But the demand constraint is not the only issue. With global supply chains broken on account of COVID-19, the faceoff between the US and China, and the Ukraine war, we are also in the middle of a potential crisis of supply.

With challenges on both the demand and supply sides, the world is staring at the real risk of stagflation, i.e., a decline in output accompanied by high price levels. The situation we face today is intrinsically linked to the market-led pattern of development of the last 40 years.

Political Unravelment

The world's largest democracy and brightest beacon of freedom, the US, is sharply polarized. It should not be surprising that social polarization characterizes many other respected democracies in the world, including Brazil and India. And if we include the countries where democracy has been practiced with varying levels of success over the last fifty years, the list of sharply divided societies only expands to include Russia, Philippines, Turkey and Pakistan.

In these sharply polarized societies, the playbook is roughly similar. Power is captured through the ballot box by one or other of the factions existing in society. The faction in power then proceeds to govern the country in a manner that is highly appreciated by its voter base but deeply disliked by the other faction. Often, members of the other faction are especially targeted with legal and criminal proceedings. Since corruption is endemic in the operation of most electoral democracies, accusations of pelf form a convenient stick with which the government targets the opposition. Freedoms considered to be an integral part of modern democracies such as the freedom of speech or the right to liberty are given short shrift.

Given the prevalence of such practices, it would not be an exaggeration to say that the template of democracy is broken. And except for a few honourable exceptions such as Canada, all that remains is the model of an electoral autocracy or an illiberal democracy.

Economic divides between those who have gained from the processes of globalization and those who feel left out are certainly an important cause of polarization in society. However, polarization is equally a function of cultural factors.

The winners in the globalized world see themselves as part of a global collective with universal values and concerns. They are deeply concerned about climate change, sensitive about race, gender and sexual identities, and somewhat sceptical of the institutions of organized religion and the family as vehicles to promote a non-patriarchal society. On the other hand, economic laggards often cling to older ways of being and relating with people. They are discomfited with global values and get impatient with sensitivities around race and gender, especially when sensitivity for their own economic predicament appears to be lacking among the winners.

A society characterized by such divides is prone to unbalanced preoccupations, unsubstantiated accusations, deep moral outrage, breakdown of trust, and shrill echo chambers that amplify polarities. The internet only facilitates such schisms.

There can be no better sign that democracy is at siege – from within and without – than the emergence of the view that the Chinese model of 'democracy' is not such a bad thing after all, at least for the Chinese.[5] Indeed, classical democracy is in a competition with other systems, and it must answer along the dimensions of political stability, economic performance, geopolitical power, and social cohesion.

The jury is still out on which system will prevail.

Social Unravelment

In November 2022, India was shocked by the murder of Shraddha, a 25-year-old woman, by her boyfriend, Aftab. Shraddha's parents had refused to acknowledge the relationship, and the couple had recently moved from Mumbai to Delhi. Aftab had a reasonably successful career as a food blogger. Shraddha had worked as a journalist. Allegedly, Aftab killed Shraddha in a fit of rage after her repeated pleas that they should get married. This was not the first such scandal emerging from middle-class India in current times. Earlier, such lurid tales were the preserve of the upper crust, and were breathlessly followed by the middle classes, or were the sorry features of life among the underclasses, usually ignored. Sadly, across the world, such trends are now becoming common within the middle classes.

The literature on economic inequality generally focuses on the widening gulf between the top and bottom 10% of the population. The fortunes of the other segments are often ignored. This is unfortunate.

The middle classes, the heterogeneous group of people who fall between the social elites and the toiling masses, used to be the glue that held societies together. These were people who believed they were neither needy like the poor, nor corrupted by an overabundance of material riches like the elite. They prided themselves on a worldview that was based on broader humanitarian concerns.

Their self-respect and their belief that they were 'better' than the upper crust or the toiling masses was a great source of social and political stability. They mitigated the class struggle, promoted social harmony, and generally served as a force to protect humanitarian mores. Their value system became the mainstream value system of society. With their emphasis on upward mobility, they were also a positive force for economic development.[6]

Indeed, the middle-class outlook was based on material achievement as well as a sense of being above material concerns.

The dichotomy was expressed in inter-generational harmony as the younger generation would strive to get ahead without losing respect for the older generation that had achieved only middling gains during its own career. A shift in values across generations would happen in a gradual, harmonious way.

However, today those in the middle of the income spectrum find it hard to pay for housing, education, and healthcare. Costs have gone up much faster than their incomes. For instance, while the incomes of US working class households have been stagnant since the 1980s, medical costs have gone up by more than two and a half times, and college educational expenses have increased almost six times.[7] Employment opportunities are shrinking and volatile in a world of rapid automation. Thus, the middle classes no longer sit on a perch far above material concerns, in the world but not of it. They no longer are able to fulfil their vital role in nourishing their communities.

A study shows that in Europe, even before the Great Financial Recession, the size of the middle class, defined as those with incomes between 60% and 200% of the median income in their countries, was declining in 13 out of 26 countries.[8] Major economies such as Germany and the UK were part of the group of countries experiencing an erosion of the middle class. After the financial crisis, the erosion of the middle class only accelerated – 19 countries experienced a decline in the size of their core middle class.[9] Similarly, in the US, the income share of the middle class went down from 62% to 43% between 1970 and 2014.[10] Thus, the middle class has been decreasing in population share as well as earning a disproportionately small share of the income pie.

A society with a vanishing middle class becomes an unstable

formation prone to polarization and disharmony. From being reliable guardians of the middle ground, the middle classes become abettors of sharp political and social divisions. Waves of immigration – a result of climate change and geopolitical conflict – only add to the pressures on the middle-class way of life. The rise of far-right formations in Europe and the US shows the impacts of a constrained middle class.

However, while the middle class is shrinking in the US and Europe, it is expanding in emerging economies, at least in terms of income. In India, the size of the middle class is expected to increase three-fold in percentage terms from 13% of the population in 2010 to just under 40% of the population in 2025.[11] The rapid growth of spending on non-essentials is slated to make India the most exciting consumer market in the world.[12]

Unfortunately, societies with a large and growing middle class are not immune to the instabilities that characterize societies, with shrinking middle classes. In such societies it is possible that there can be a large number of middle-class incomes without the accompanying values that promote stability. An important cause of this new trend is the stratospheric rise in the aspirations of young members of the middle class without anywhere close to a matching rise in stable professional opportunities.

Speaking of the drivers of illegal migration of poor people from Bangladesh to European countries, the novelist and sociologist Amitav Ghosh argues that the digital revolution has reduced the distance between different classes of society in terms of awareness about the good things of life. A paddy cultivator in Bangladesh is more aware of the lifestyles and indulgences of the rich than ever before. He or she is even familiar with the cityscapes of European cities where their brethren have emigrated. On the other hand, the digital economy has simultaneously widened the gulf between classes in terms of the actual opportunities needed to bridge the ever-increasing material divides.[13]

This dichotomy is as true of the burgeoning middle classes as it is of the poor. In fact, the predicament of the middle class may be even worse than that of the poor, because while the poor may look upon opulence as an unreachable fairy tale, the middle-class youth may view it as tantalizingly attainable. The resulting dissonance sweeps away the last vestiges of middle-class values. A manifestation of this phenomenon is the increasing reports of abuse of parents by adult children. A survey by the NGO, HelpAge Asia stated that in India 35% and 21% elders faced abuse from their sons and daughters-in-law respectively, a startling statistic for a culture that prides itself on family values.[14]

The rapid urbanization that is being experienced by emerging economies is bringing droves of young people from rural areas into urban agglomerations where they have very little institutional support. Thus, urban areas are becoming home to masses of drifting young people with very few social moorings or stable support structures. In the face of such rapidly changing urban people-scapes, the middle class fails to form a bulwark against the washing away of essential moral architectures.

In both kinds of societies – those with shrinking as well as expanding middle classes – there is a breakdown of traditional support structures such as the family and the state without compensation in the form of newly formed communities.

The family was the citadel of the middle classes, its trophy quietly held aloft amidst the opulence of the rich and the squalor of the poor. The decline of the family signals the breach of its bastion, the disappearance of a way of life that held society together.

Both Aftab and Shraddha had broken free of family structures and struck out in a new city. Cut off from her family, Shraddha reported warning signals about Aftab's dysfunctional behaviour to a therapist.[15] His advice that the couple start practicing yogic breathing and come back to see him doesn't seem to have helped.[16]

With all the dazzling growth of technology and opportunities, something vital seems to have been lost.

Ecological Unravelment

Floods ravage Pakistan. A third of the population affected.[17]

Kenya's Lake Turkana is flooding even as East Africa hit by drought.[18]

The 2022 floods in Kerala bring painful memories of the 2018 floods.[19]

European populations exposed to unprecedented heatwaves in 2022, all-time national temperature records in multiple European countries broken.[20]

Fast moving wildfires in California force thousands to evacuate homes.[21]

The news items above represent a mere fraction of the havoc caused by extreme weather events. In the period from

1970 to 2019 more than 11,000 reported disasters attributed to climate change-related hazards occurred globally, with over two million deaths and financial losses of $3.64 trillion. The number of disasters increased by a factor of five over the 50-year period.[22]

But what is to come could be far worse than anything we've seen.

Let's start at the beginning. According to our best available science, the world's atmospheric concentrations of carbon dioxide, methane, and nitrous oxide have increased significantly since 1750. The increase in carbon dioxide concentration has happened mainly because of the use of fossil fuels and the changes in land use. The increase in methane and nitrous oxide levels are primarily due to agriculture. The increasing concentration of these gases in the atmosphere prevents the heat of the sun from escaping back into space, thus increasing the Earth's temperatures.

The rising temperatures have a variety of harmful effects: heat waves, extreme weather events such as floods, droughts, and wildfires. They also affect the agricultural calendar, leading to widespread rural distress, and forced migration.

Further, atmospheric pollution has become a major health hazard all over the world.

Under the Paris Agreement signed by 196 parties in 2016, countries were legally bound to limit carbon emissions in order to ensure temperature rise remained limited to 2 degree Celsius above pre-industrial levels, and pursue efforts to achieve an even more ambitious goal of restricting the rise in temperature to 1.5 degree Celsius.[23]

However, in spite of the legally binding commitments made at the conference, an October 2022 report of the United

Nations Environment Programme (UNEP) asserts that there is 'no credible pathway to 1.5 C in place'.[24] Inger Andersen, Executive Director of UNEP stated, 'We had our chance to make incremental changes, but that time is over. Only a root-and-branch transformation of our economies and societies can save us from accelerating climate disaster.'[25] To examine the possibilities of such a transformation, an examination of the economics and geopolitics of renewable energy is in order.

The cost of renewable energy has dropped dramatically over the last few years, solar power by 90% and wind power by 71% since 2010.[26] The natural resources on which these sources of power are based, sunshine and wind, are free, hence it is possible for improvements in technology and increases in the scale of production to result in sharp decreases in costs. Fossil fuel technologies are unable to generate similar reductions in cost on account of the fact that natural resources account for a much higher percentage, close to 40%, of their total expenses. As a result, in 2019, 72% of *new* global energy capacity came from renewable sources. However, as UNEP states, the transition is not happening fast enough.

While the cost of renewable sources of energy may compare favourably to fossil fuels, when comparing the alternatives of building new renewable energy plants versus utilizing fossil fuel plants that are already in existence, the balance is tilted in favour of traditional energy sources. The business imperative of recouping sunk investments in traditional energy and the long-term power purchase agreements that are not linked to transitions to clean energy reduce incentives for moving to clean energy. Continuing power subsidies to politically sensitive groups also increase energy consumption and greenhouse gas emissions.

Thus, despite the reduction in the cost of renewables, energy transition is an expensive process that requires compensating investors for sunk investments in traditional forms. However, as of now, it does not appear as if our world has resources to finance it.

As explained in an earlier section, the globe is looking at the prospect of a simultaneous deceleration of growth and inflation, i.e., stagflation. A deceleration in growth makes it difficult to raise tax revenues. The spectre of inflation makes it difficult to countenance an easy money regime that would generate finances for renewables. There are vast stores of wealth available among the elite of society. However, the political will to impose a levy on wealth does not appear to be forthcoming. Simultaneously, political polarization makes it difficult to dismantle subsidies for important political constituencies such as farmers.

The prospects for a clean energy transition are also muddied by new geopolitical divides. Increasing tensions between the US and China raise a question mark regarding the sustainability of solar power given that over 80% of the solar panels are sourced from China[27]; along with 60% of the rare earth metals (used in solar photo voltaic cells) and 90% of their processing capacity.[28]

And then there is the fallout of the Ukraine war. In 2020, 25% of Europe's energy consumption came from Russia – the biggest external source, second only to EU's own resources that accounted for 42%.[29] Russia is also the world's largest exporter of natural gas, the second-largest supplier of crude oil after Saudi Arabia, and the third-largest coal exporter behind Indonesia and Australia.[30] Moving away from dependence on Russia for critical energy requirements requires the identification of new sources of supply, the buildout of new infrastructure related to transportation – including pipelines, and ports, further development of renewable energy technologies, and investments in energy transitions.

Energy transition is made easier in situations where energy security, i.e., the stable sourcing of energy to fulfil domestic needs in the near and medium term, is relatively assured, the economy is stable, and the polity is operating in a business-as-usual mode.

Currently, none of these conditions hold.

Despite REPowerEU, the European Commission's plan to end dependency on fossil fuels by 2027 and accelerate the green transition, several EU members have increased the use of coal-fired power plants as quick alternatives to Russian oil and gas. They have also declared gas powered plants and nuclear plants as eligible for green investments.[31]

Before the recent geopolitical developments, the US seemed to have become an energy surplus nation on account of the shale energy revolution. Experts believed that this attainment would mark the end of its dependence on the Middle East and be a game changer for international geopolitics.[32] However, the new cold war with Russia and China has vastly increased its responsibilities with respect to the energy needs of its allies. While it may try to accelerate its energy transition to fulfil its responsibilities, it is quite possible that strategic pressures would force its hand toward greater reliance on traditional fuels.

Meanwhile Russia's own transition to clean energy stands in peril due to the tremendous economic pressures it faces. Even with regard to the fossil fuel industry, it was heavily dependent on technology and capital from the US and EU. The dependence was going to be even greater with green energies. Now, the schism with the West deprives it of important inputs and makes it ever more dependent on Chinese technology and investments. But, given its high dependence on China with respect of geopolitical and economic support, Russia will want to calibrate its dependence on its neighbour for its green transition so as to keep its overall dependence at a manageable level.

Along with climate mitigation initiatives that reduce the human carbon footprint, climate adaptation measures to guard against increasingly common natural disasters are urgently needed. As per some estimates, an investment of $1.8 trillion in measures like early warning systems, climate-resilient infrastructure, and resilient water resources could result in avoided costs and social and environmental benefits that would amount to savings of $7.1 trillion.[33]

However, as of 2023, only 21% of climate finance provided by wealthier countries to assist developing nations, i.e., about $16.8 billion a year, goes towards adaptation and resilience.[34] The reason is probably that returns on investment in developing new clean technologies, i.e., climate mitigation, are higher than in climate adaptation initiatives. The fact that the effects of climate catastrophes are disproportionately borne by developing countries could also be a contributing factor to the neglect of climate adaptation.

Overall, given that the transition to clean energy must take place within a certain time horizon, the prospects look dim.

Perhaps, Mr Musk was right after all. Those who can, should hitch a ride to Mars.

Managerial Unravelment

A man walked to his field one day to find the crop had been consumed by the cattle of the neighbouring plot which belonged to his brother. He went back to his father, who was respected not just the family but by the community at large.

'Father,' he said, 'Brother's cattle have destroyed my crop. The hard work of a whole year has been eaten away.'

The father said, 'I feel for you my son, but I will have to consult the elders of the village who are very sensitive about the health of the livestock and might get annoyed if we take precipitate action.'

So, the father and son went to the head of the Village Elders' Council. The head heard them out patiently.

'My brothers, I feel for your problem, but we will have to talk to the authorities in the capital who have issued the directive that cattle are not to be restrained,' he said.

So, the son, the father and the village elder went to the national capital. In the capital they found a lot of support, but in the end, the political representative said, 'Our political party believes in protecting the sanctity of the family so we cannot interfere in family relations. These are to be kept entirely outside of the political and judicial mechanism. Maybe you can approach the Council of Nations which lays great store by the sanctity of private property.'

So, the son, the father, the village elder and the political representative went to the head of the Council of Nations. The door of his office was open. All four entered with beating hearts only to find the office empty.

They waited for a long while for someone to show up. Finally, a tired looking old man entered the room. 'Can I help you?' he asked. They explained their problem to him.

He thought over their issue for a while. Then he said, 'You will have to settle it with your brother, I am afraid. Local problems must be solved locally.'

The son looked at his father. 'It's all up to you,' he said. The father shook his head sadly, 'You know the situation as well as I do, son. After your brother decided to marry a girl from a different religion, no one in our family is speaking with him.'

The fable demonstrates an important truth of our world. The managerial unit, whether a family, a firm, an NGO, a government, or a multilateral institution, is no longer equipped to solve the problems that lie within its jurisdiction.

The following are some instances of managerial unravelment: Central bankers can't control debt problems within their country without controlling cross border flows, over which they have little control. The IMF, which is supposed to control cross-border flows, can't do so without reining in the US Fed over which it has little control. The US Fed cannot check cross-border flows without regulating financial markets which it has often found difficult to do because of the lobby of the financial services industry.

Of course, managerial unravelment is not limited to economics. The UN, the overarching organization tasked with the maintenance of international peace and security, is similarly entangled. Its institutional structure consists of a Security Council and a General Assembly. The Security Council has five permanent members – US, Russia, China, France and UK – and ten elected representatives. Decisions of the Council are binding on all members of the UN, but they require nine assenting votes. Further, except in votes on procedural questions, a decision cannot be made if a permanent member abstains or vetoes a resolution. The veto power cripples the possibilities of decision making in a geopolitically divided world. Most recently, this was reflected in the inability of the Security Council to pass a resolution on the Ukraine war.[35]

Governments the world over are hampered by the reality of dealing with global corporations that in many cases match them in financial strength and political heft. A firm's decision-making power is severely challenged by the high levels of geopolitical, macroeconomic, financial, and public health volatility. Firms are also challenged by new paradigms of performance evaluation in which their success depends not on attaining the traditional targets of profit but on the more nebulous target of long-term value creation. In most cases, this requires them to convince a small group of private equity investors on the basis of non-traditional metrics like the number of users that the firm is on the right track.

The uncertainties besetting firms are also faced by families that are also grappling with changing structures and far lower levels of cohesion.

It's not an easy time to be a manager.

Technological Unravelment

They say if you go to a surgeon, they will advise surgery, even for a common cold. Every civilization searches for solutions in restricted spaces that reflect its values and beliefs.

Human societies have never witnessed the level of technological advancement that we observe in our age. And, therefore, we invariably seek technological solutions to problems, even those created by technology in the first place. Thus, if addiction to mobile devices creates a pandemic of stress among the youth, a host of new digital apps promise to cure addiction by better monitoring of online habits. If fossil fuel-based technologies threaten the existence of human civilization, then renewable energy technologies step in to allow the smooth progress of the human race. And finally, if the prospects of renewable energy being able to counter global warming seem weak, a moonshot to Mars aims to create human settlements far away from an unsustainable planet Earth.

But, today, technological solutions seem to solve narrowly defined problems, only to magnify larger systemic risks. For instance, the 'gain of function' research paradigm that aims to anticipate future viral threats by manufacturing viruses creates unacceptable risks of viral outbreaks.

Noah Yuval Harari speaks about the risks of a world where mechanization of everything leads to a ceding of power by humans to algorithms.[36] With their deep knowledge of our predilections, technology-enabled firms are not merely violating our privacy. They are subtly modifying our behaviours to conform to their business objectives to a degree that amounts to a violation of our autonomy. Search algorithms and algorithms that push content on social media sites are creating echo chambers that threaten social stability. Complex decision-making algorithms meant to increase the efficiency and speed of decisions are creating unacceptable risks of catastrophic events. For instance, financial algorithms that order the purchase and sale of billions of dollars of financial assets in seconds are believed to have played an important role in the 2008 financial crisis.[37]

Harari asserts that while human feeling and intelligence displaced the omnipotent God as the final arbiter of right and wrong in the age of humanism, a similar transition is taking place in our time, except that now the human mind is ceding power to algorithms powered by cloud computing technologies run by Big Tech companies.[38] Some technologists warn of a future 'technological singularity' in which the intelligence of machines would exceed the intelligence of human beings, and human beings will be controlled by automatons more intelligent than them.[39]

To a certain extent it is to be expected that solutions to problems would come with their own attendant issues which would need to be addressed at some point. However, when the problems generated by solutions become more serious than the original problem itself, then there is a reason to believe that one is looking for solutions in the wrong place. Or, if a particular problem is required to be addressed by solutions with increasing levels of complexity, then one has cause to ask if one is moving in the right direction.

It is time to ask ourselves if the solution to our problems is to be found in the realm of technology, or if we need to look beyond technological solutions to ask fundamental questions with regard to the ways of being and relating that we have accepted as axiomatic.

But the techno-utopians, a tribe that believes in ever more dazzling displays of technical virtuosity, still search for the magic technology to cure the ills of our age. They are in denial, and so are most of us.

Geopolitical Unravelment

Till the fall of the Soviet Union, the need to secure energy supplies and other natural resources was a prime determinant of international geopolitics. The US policy toward West Asia, China's interests in Africa, and Europe's relations with the erstwhile Soviet Union were driven by this motive. But today, after more than 30 years of globalization, the situation has reversed: new developments in international geopolitics now constrain the strategies of a country with regard to energy security and access to natural resources. This is both a risk and the saving grace of the current geopolitical scenario.

Thirty years of globalization have led to a deeply interconnected world: China, the US's greatest rival, is the largest holder of US dollar reserves worth $3.2 trillion.[40] Russia, now being touted as a 'rogue state', is fourth largest holder of US dollar reserves.[41] A crash in the US dollar will hurt both the US and its rivals.

Close to a quarter of EU energy supplies come from Russia.[42] It also supplies the metals – nickel, copper, cobalt – used in the production of semiconductors that power digital economies everywhere. China has a monopoly in the processing of rare earth metals that are essential for the digital economy and the transition to renewable energy.[43] And the Middle East, that is critical to the supply of fossil fuels, is neatly divided between the US and EU on one side and China and Russia on the other –

Saudi Arabia, UAE, Bahrain are aligned with the Western bloc, while Iran, Iraq, and Syria with China and Russia.

Thus, today's geopolitical unravelment involves the unspooling of deep economic interconnections between countries that have taken antagonistic stances towards each other. This leads to the rather curious spectacle of rivals with daggers drawn negotiating with each other for a phased dismantling of well-oiled interdependencies that serve the economic interests of all parties.

There are certain positions that are unlikely to be dismantled. The February 2022 US freeze on dollar reserves held by Russia[44] raised a red flag for other countries that might potentially face similar action in the future. There was speculation that such countries might convert their dollar denominated reserves to other currencies. However, this is an unlikely scenario in the near to middle term. More than half of dollar denominated reserves are held by allies of the US, and close to 90% of the reserves are held by countries that are allies or have at least some agreements for military cooperation with the US.[45] The large-scale migration out of dollar reserves will result in a crash in the dollar and create levels of uncertainty in international markets that no country can afford to face. Hence, despite seemingly enjoying a stranglehold on the US economy in the form of sizeable reserves, China and Russia are unlikely to be able to press their advantage in the short to medium term.

The Russia–Ukraine conflict has raised the spectre of a nuclear war with both parties engaging in a game of brinkmanship using the threat of nuclear weapons. A war even with tactical nuclear weapons would be a cataclysmic event. However, geopolitical tensions are likely to be ameliorated by the strong economic linkages between the parties involved.

The new Cold War will be characterized by economic sanctions, protectionist trade barriers, and much posturing. The real battle will be fought in the arena of technology. The stated aim of the US is to secure a decisive and long-lasting technology advantage through the aggressive use of industrial policy.[46]

In an increasingly digitalized world, the importance of computer chips for economic success is akin to the criticality of energy in the second half of the 20th century. Over 60% of the world's chips (the figure goes up to 90% in the case of the most advanced chips) are fabricated in Taiwan,[47] an outcome of the US-developed model of outsourcing chip manufacture. With neighbouring China claiming Taiwan as its own province, and the US simultaneously doubling down on its support for the island country, de-risking the semiconductor value chain represents the single most important geopolitical priority for the US, China, and countries around the world.

In August 2022, the Creating Helpful Incentives to Produce Semiconductors (CHIPS) and Science Bill was passed by the US Congress. It would provide assistance and subsidies worth $280 billion, particularly focused on the semiconductor industry.[48]

The US has also been using its good offices with Taiwan[49] and Netherlands[50] (whose company ASML has a monopoly on the machines needed to fabricate the best chips) to restrict Chinese access to semiconductors. Meanwhile, China has been ramping up its own attempts at developing indigenous manufacturing capability. In 2015, as part of its 'Made in China 2025' policy, it identified semiconductors as one of the ten high-tech sectors in which China should reduce its dependence on the west.[51] In July 2023, it announced that the export of gallium and germanium, two critical elements in semiconductor manufacturing in which China has 80% and 60% share of world production respectively, would be subject to a licensing system for national security reasons.[52]

The technology war is also being fought in the arena of clean energy technologies. As part of the CHIPS Act, the Biden administration announced a biofuel and biomanufacturing act to promote renewable technologies and manufacturing in the US. The US is also focusing on attracting the best talent in science and technology from around the world, building technology partnerships with countries such as Israel and India, and protecting existing technology advantages through aggressive controls on the inflow and outflow of investment in technology companies.[53]

In sum, a 'hot war' is unlikely. The geopolitical unravelment takes the form of an elaborate, intricate, and slow decoupling of mutually beneficial linkages, along with much sabre-rattling, and aggressive attempts to win the technology war. Given the rapid pace at which other contingencies are escalating, geopolitical tension creates the contours within which events unfold, but is not itself one of the principal protagonists.

9

THE END OF AN AGE

The playwright Arthur Miller wrote: 'An era can be said to end when its basic illusions are exhausted.'[1]

The thesis of this book is that an era is ending because its basic illusions have outlived their purpose. The era that is ending is not merely the era of the unipolar hegemon that began after the fall of the Soviet Union or the age of the ascendancy of the US which can be said to have begun around World War I. The epoch coming to a close is associated with the application of logical reasoning in all facets of life, a conviction that the rational pursuit of self-interest is consistent with social good, and that societies possessing this new religion of rationality must spread their message far and wide. This age has been variously referred to as The Enlightenment or The Age of Reason. I prefer to use the term 'The Age of Rationality' as it seems to better reflect the ubiquitous ingress of cold-blooded logic in our lives.

Central Tenets

The Age of Rationality sought to loosen the grip of three

spectres looming over human society – organized religion, the monarch who ruled by divine right, and the tyranny of nature.

These three forces were replaced by a new belief system upheld by five pillars. It asserted that:

1. Sovereign power rests in the hands of the people. The institution of democracy is an expression of that sovereign power.
2. The state must operate independently of religious authority and must not discriminate against people on the basis of religion. This gave birth of the ideal of secularism.
3. Every human being is born with certain inalienable rights, i.e., human rights, which must be protected by the state.
4. The operation of the invisible hand of the market mechanism results in an efficient allocation of resources. Markets must be allowed to function efficiently without undue interference by the government.
5. The scientific method based on reason and experimentation is the surest vehicle of human progress in all branches of human activity, including in the choice of individual ethics.

The Age of Rationality envisioned a world in which the central quest of a human being is to regain their essential transcendence, their universal identity independent of historical, cultural, social, and religious contexts. In this quest, their main ally is the power of reason. The social contract must be designed to facilitate this quest. An individual does not exist to serve society. Rather, society exists for the development of the individual. However, the development of the perfect society, i.e., utopia, is essential to create the conditions for the development of the universal human. Imagining and working toward the development of such a society is an essential task of the human race. Nature is a handmaiden of the human being, and exists for the gratification of human needs.

There are some who regard the Enlightenment discourse of universal emancipation including both men and women in its ambit as a duplicitous mask to hide the male-centred momentum of the Age of Rationality.[2] Others are more charitable and have urged that the Enlightenment be re-conceived as a dynamic and surprisingly democratic public conversation that put women's rights on the Western agenda.[3]

The writings of philosophers such as John Locke and Jean Jacque Rosseau, the Rights of Man enshrined by the French Revolution, and the American Constitution, both enacted in 1789, became scriptures of the new age.

All five pillars of the Enlightenment worked in tandem to create a worldview that spanned every facet of society. However, the pillar of science occupied a special place as it provided the most visible manifestation of the benefits of the new ideology in transforming human life.

How the Age of Rationality Played Out

The test of an ideology lies in the trajectory of its operationalization. The outcomes of the Age of Rationality comprise light and shade in equal measure.

1. Material Progress: Enlightenment philosophy led to the most dazzling phase of human material progress in recorded history. It has led to a situation in which human beings can clone certain species of life, engage in interplanetary travel and perhaps will soon build settlements on planets

other than earth. The fall of the Soviet Union, when liberal democracy was ensconced as the preeminent political system of the world, marked yet another triumph of this school of thought. Today, such is the hold exercised by democracy that even the Chinese government refers to its patently authoritarian mode of governance as a 'democracy with Chinese characteristics'.

2. Colonialism and Neo-colonialism: The Enlightenment sought to loosen the grip of the church and monarch on individuals. However, it ended up creating a new religion of sorts, where States that believed themselves to be upholders of Enlightenment values arrogated to themselves the right, indeed the duty, to spread their values to other parts of the world, by force if necessary, and by using resources garnered from the very lands they sought to 'civilize'. This 'chosen people complex' often took on the hues of racism whereby the heartless subjugation of alien economies, cultures, and ways of life were justified in the name of the 'white man's burden'. After World War II, this presumption was operationalized through economic methods including trade and foreign investment. Unexpectedly, this gave birth to a new rival – China.
3. The Debasement of the Individual: The doctrine of individualism has not created a mass of rational, evolved human beings fully capable of negotiating the thorny ethical conundrums that constitute the fabric of modern living. In fact, the reality is quite the opposite. Cut off from cultural, familial, and community contexts, and denied access to real opportunities for material progress, the average individual is a pawn at the mercy of a deluge

of content streamed at them via radios, televisions, and the internet. This content is designed to manipulate the individual and align them to the goals of the overall system, goals which mainly centre around commerce.

There is a view that emerges from the Enlightenment school that material progress is the highest ethical achievement, and material efficiency is the greatest moral good.[4] In such a world, the laggard masses are rendered into acquisitive, dissatisfied entities, shorn of every vestige of human dignity and utterly incapable of navigating the winner-takes-all worlds created by the chosen few who are able to surf the choppy waters with enviable ease. This faceless, undistinguished majority constitutes the 'deplorables' famously pilloried by Hillary Clinton in her failed US presidential bid.[5]

The valorization of human potential without an accompanying acknowledgment of the heterogeneous circumstances, obstacles, and aptitudes of individuals, and without acknowledging the reality of their many emotional scars, has created a brutal, unequal society where the underprivileged, especially those from certain races, are characterized as undeserving.[6] Or else, the philosophy has resulted in a collective that has made a certain amount of material progress but is moved by divisive doctrines that are completely at variance with the political principles that inspired the Enlightenment.[7] The electoral autocracies that constitute the standard templates of democracy today provide examples of such masses of people. Further, this mode of thought has created a mass of blue-collar workers who are staring at the only possible existential threat considered valid in a rational society – the imminent, inevitable, and immiserating loss of livelihoods on account of a galloping automation.

And, of course, it has endangered human society on account of the unsustainable exploitation of nature.

The Pinnacle of the Age of Rationality

In the previous chapter, we explored the many ways in which human civilization is unravelling. Many refer to these developments as manifestations of an Age of Unreason.[8] Others scholars argue that the age of reason ended much earlier, with the rise of the post-modern age, covered in Chapter 10 in this book.[9] However, each unravelment bears the signature of fundamental beliefs of the Age of Rationality – the faith in free markets, the pride of place accorded to technology, the use of democratic success as a justification for social outcomes, the breakdown of traditional community structures and customs, and the invocation of human rights.

For instance, in Chapter 1, we saw how banks broke free from the traditional standards of responsible lending driven by the pressures of democracy and the promise of financial engineering, the consumption levels of households became decoupled from incomes based on global trade and unfettered loan markets, businesses were unshackled from profits on account of the backing of successful entrepreneurs, the evangelists of the new age, and governments were liberated from the burden of facilitating better long term economic outcomes for the working class through a combination of unregulated credit and diversionary access to technology. Thus, society and the economy became untethered from any anchor save for the dream of technological progress.

In Chapter 2, we saw how China's growth engine stands at risk from the political compulsions of the Chinese Communist Party to retain control in an increasingly challenging economic environment. Their experience shows that the attempt to adopt the Enlightenment view on free markets while adhering to non-Enlightenment political systems was bound to run up against intractable contradictions.

In Chapter 3, we explored how the US Federal Reserve acquired the power to print trillions of dollars to navigate itself out of trouble created by its own past policies. Its compulsions highlight the risks inherent in the agenda of creating a global currency to facilitate an integrated global economic system, a key objective flowing from the ideals of the Age of Rationality.

In Chapter 4, we saw how the US in the new millennium lost face in one theatre of war after another on account of imperial overreach, an overreach that partly stemmed from its self-image as a crusader of democracy and partly from its reliance on the arms industry as an engine of democratic success.

In Chapter 5, we examined the glittering processes of urbanization and globalization of scientific cooperation that are potentially creating human catastrophes, though they were engendered from the runaway development of science and technology, the religion of the new age.

In Chapter 6, we saw how capitalism has become a totalitarian force that subjects not just natural resources to the forces of mining but also scavenges the most intimate information about human beings in search of profits. This is merely a continuation of the colonial exploitation of faraway lands, except the realms being colonized are human bodies and minds everywhere.

In Chapter 7, we observed how the relentless individualization of sex has robbed human connections of intimacy, an inevitable result of the overall process of individualization and commercialization of the Age of Rationality.

Thus, these developments are not expressions of unreason, but represent the highest degree of evolution of our age.

These phenomena have emerged as a result of a series of decisions taken to maximize self-interest, for instance the deregulation of markets, a stance actively promoted by influential strands of the Enlightenment school. On some occasions, the decisions turned awry (as in the climate crisis) because the rational pursuit of self-interest in interactive situations often leads to suboptimal outcomes. On others, unintended consequences emerged because the exercise of rationality itself becomes difficult as situations become increasingly complex, (as in the 2008 global recession).

The bloody-minded pursuit of self-interest at all costs heightened structural dualities to the point that they became unsustainable and presented the world as a series of Faustian bargains. These include mass empowerment through the internet along with mass surveillance, the emancipation of the individual from oppressive family structures along with widespread loneliness, glittering urban agglomerations along with crippling air pollution, the propagation of democracy along with the fattening of the arms industry, the presence of a stable anchor of the world economy that frequently needs to use its power to bail itself out, a state that achieves the largest, most rapid reduction of poverty in the history of mankind but ramps up its authoritarianism when faced with the challenges of economic growth, and the world's greatest democracy deeply polarized as a result of the logic of its growth trajectory.

The elites who have fashioned the world as it exists today are complicit in the unravelment we all face. Their complicity lies in the fact that to serve their narrow goals, they perpetuated the myth that greed is good, and that the pursuit of self-interest is congruent with public interest. The perpetuation of this myth takes several forms – creating the illusion of meritocracy despite the dice being loaded in favour of the rich, choosing to ignore the grave risks associated with technology, and turning a blind eye to the real interests of vast masses of people while feeding them a steady diet of shallow diversions and deep-rooted prejudices.

Or perhaps, their complicity is a result of their simple-minded gullibility, as they unquestioningly bought into the myths of the Age of Rationality.

In either case, the variety, depth and complexity of unravelment suggest the basic illusions of the era they perpetuated have served their utility and are exhausted.

10

THE AGE OF META-REASON

This book is not the first that heralds the end of the Age of Rationality. Indeed, the death knell of the Enlightenment has been rung many times before. As early as the 18th century, there arose in Germany a movement call Romanticism, which believed that the ability of humans to be inexplicably and inexpressibly moved by beauty and truth was their highest faculty, more precious than reason.[1]

However, several scholars have argued that the diffusion of enlightenment ideas took place across the world over centuries, taking on different views in different contexts.[2] Indeed, both the Communist regime and the Bretton Woods system that arose from the ruins of colonialism shared important similarities with Enlightenment thought: the belief in material progress driven by science and technology and a universalist view of utopia as a goal all societies should strive towards are two which come to mind.

However, the current juncture represents a paradigm shift in history. At no other point in time since the French Revolution has there been such a coincidence of fundamental drivers of change. These forces have been synergistically gathering momentum for close to a hundred years. Examining them will help us to appreciate that there is indeed an epochal transformation underway and that it is the foundations of the Age of Rationality that are being dislodged.

The harbingers of a new age include powerful shifts in philosophical thought, paradigm-shifting discoveries in mathematics and the natural sciences, a new consensus on academic methods of research, the rise of countries that embody a strong collectivist ethos, and the existential imperatives emanating from the twin forces of artificial intelligence and climate change. We turn to an examination of each of these.

Harbingers of the New Age

Postmodernism

If the age of rationality posits that there is an objective natural reality, which is discoverable using the method of scientific enquiry, postmodernism assets that the reality spoken of is a conceptual construct, an artefact of a certain scientific method. The postmodernists believe that several knowledge systems, those based on reason and those that are not, are equally valid and that there is no such thing as universal truth, or, indeed, a universal utopia.

Postmodernism denies that societies proceed on a linear path towards higher levels of evolution, powered by modern science and technology. It rejects meta-narratives that attempt to establish linear stages of economic growth as attempts to control societies with different value systems and force fit them into a grand framework that is aligned with the interests of those in power. It rejects the universalist world view of the Age of Rationality and brings culture to the forefront of the study of human affairs.

The influence of this mode of thought might have remained limited to academia had its currents not been turbocharged by two defining forces of the modern world, both existing before the advent of postmodern thought – psychotherapy and psychiatric medicine.

The mental health industry accords primacy to human feeling and recognizes that since humans are primarily emotional beings, their realities are determined by emotions to a far greater extent than by objective facts. Further, the self is not autonomous and separate but embedded in social, historical, and cultural contexts. Thus, modern psychoanalysis marks a definite departure from the universalism of the Age of Rationality. In parallel, medical science has shown that unregulated feelings are related to cellular pathologies.[3] A burgeoning and highly profitable pharmacopeia has arisen to address mental health challenges.

Postmodernism brings philosophical thought into alignment with the fields of psychotherapy and psychiatry. The synchronicity of philosophy, psychotherapy, and psychiatry creates mutual synergies that augur well for the good health of each element of the triad.[4]

Postmodernism is likely to play a significant role in forcing scientists to become humbler about hypotheses emerging from religious traditions, as well as alternative healing systems. In physics, when a hypothesis emerges from a mainstream scientific method, it is treated seriously no matter how outlandish it may appear to be. Empirical investigations commence to establish its veracity. For instance, in 1915, Einstein put forward his General Theory of Relativity asserting that light is bent by gravity. The first, somewhat imprecise, empirical verification only happened in 1919 and investigations continued with new demonstrations coming in as late as 1979.[5] In 1964, physicist John Bell theorized that two sub-atomic particles separated by billions of light years can be intimately linked to each other, violating the long-held belief that information cannot travel faster than the speed of light. The Bell theory was only proved in 2015,[6] fifty years after his theoretical speculations.

The assertion that bodily health is affected by mental attitudes is, on the face of it, no more peculiar than Einstein's General Theory. The claim of Eastern medicine on the role of non-physical channels of energy in the body and their role in wellness is no more implausible than quantum entanglement; and yet, such theses are generally treated with contempt because they emerge from religion or knowledge systems outside mainstream science, realms that the Enlightenment was meant to overthrow.[7] A shift has begun to take place, and it is likely to accelerate as the hegemony of modern science over knowledge is loosened.

Personally, I seek a balance between the intransigent subjectivity of postmodernists and the blithe objectivity of the rationalists. While subjectivity is a central characteristic of human experience, a complete surrender to the power of context and a wholesale denial of personal agency is unhealthy, and can even be dangerous.

Valourizing the individual testimony of emotional woundedness while at the same time characterizing efforts to examine the objective conditions attending the experience as demonstrations of insensitivity has bred a culture of victimhood where society becomes a marketplace of competing empathies.[8] This process bundles together winners and losers in the neo-liberal paradigm in a grab-bag of sympathy seekers. The winners suffering from emotional scars and the losers pre-occupied with material concerns become equal claimants of empathy. When powerful financial interests in psychotherapy, psychiatry, and medicine stand to gain from the victimhood of the winners, attention gets diverted from resolving the structural issues causing the problems in the first place.

Quantum Physics, Godel's Incompleteness Theorem, and the Qualitative Research Paradigm

The Quantum Shift

Since science is the pre-eminent pillar of Enlightenment philosophy, developments within science that throw a shadow of doubt on the fundamental principles of the enlightenment school carry special significance. The acceptance of Newton's theory of gravitation was based on observations of the precise position of planets as they revolved around the sun under the joint impacts of gravity and the centrifugal force, the force that propels them away from the attraction of the sun. It gave birth to a world view that the universe is a deterministic machine that, once set into motion, proceeds forever along predictable paths.

Quantum science strikes at the roots of the Newtonian worldview by questioning the belief that it is possible to determine the precise location of sub-atomic particles, the fundamental building blocks of life.[9] The empirical verification of the theory of gravitation was based on an understanding of the position and momentum of the planets. In contrast, Heisenberg's uncertainty principle denies the possibility of such verification in the case of sub-atomic particles. It asserts that the simultaneous determination of a fundamental particle's position and momentum is subject to a trade-off: an increase in the precision with which one dimension can be measured is always accompanied by a decrease in the precision of measurement of the other dimension.

If the Newtonian worldview was based on the belief in an objective reality that could be measured and understood, quantum science points out that the very act of measurement of the physical coordinates of a sub-atomic particle changes its fundamental properties. Thus, even if there is an objective reality, it is undiscoverable. Some would even go so far as to say that there is no objective reality.[10]

Godel's Hard Questions

The austere conceptions of Descartes postulated that every phenomenon could be doubted except the existence of the entity who doubted. This resonated in the worldview of mathematicians who pursued their lonely quest for mathematical truth in the belief that their discipline, based on pure reason, was the only reality in an ephemeral world. A core belief of the mathematical system was that any precisely expressed mathematical statement was either verifiably true or demonstrably false. Godel's Incompleteness theorem shot this comforting belief out of the water by showing that there could be true mathematical statements that could not be proved to be true.[11] Given the unverifiability of mathematical truth, the ability to 'see' truth directly through intuition began to be emphasized. This marks a perturbation, albeit slight, in the position of reason at the top of the list of human faculties.[12] And if even mathematical reality can lie beyond the reach of logical proof, the status of reason as an unfailing method to establish truths in human affairs would necessarily stand on even more shaky ground.

New Perspectives on Social Reality

The social sciences have been attempting to make the methods of physical science central to their approaches. Economics is the social science that has been most successful in achieving this assimilation. Other social sciences, such as political science or psychology, have been attempting to play catch-up. The accepted method involves the creation of hypotheses based on mathematical logic and testing of those hypotheses using statistical methods. The focus is on creating generalizable results or universal truths in the manner of natural sciences. In the process, context-specific particularities are ignored or treated as irrelevant.[13]

Even today, the discipline of economics continues to be tied to the prevalent paradigm of hypothesis testing and measurement. However, other social sciences, such as management studies, have been bolder, breaking entirely from the older method by upholding qualitative methods such as poetic representations, autobiographical ethnography, and infiltration of inaccessible sub-cultures (such as the world of drug dealers) as valid research methods.[14]

These developments in academia, cutting across disciplines, have raised fundamental questions about the role of rationality as the pre-eminent faculty capable of bringing deliverance to the human race. Once the bastion of rationality falls, all other pillars begin to crumble – individualism, the existence of a universal utopia independent of culture, the superiority of the human race as the only reasoning creature in nature – all of these begin to appear less as inexorable truths and more as illusions that have outlived their time.

The Rise of Peripheral Countries: India and China

The global establishment of a new paradigm of thought that moves beyond enlightenment must necessarily be accompanied by the rise of new powers in the realm of commerce and politics that embody new modes of viewing the world. Recall, the rise of Enlightenment thought was fuelled by the rise of the colonial powers.

Today, there exist critical players in the global economy, countries such as China and India, in which powerful currents of thought running counter to the Enlightenment ideology flourish. Indeed, such currents are even beginning to be held up as the causes for their progress. For instance, the growth of China is often ascribed to its successful balancing of economic freedom and political control.[15] It is very likely that the continued material rise of such societies will help to bring new modes of thinking to the forefront.

The hope of the Western powers was that the material rise of China, fuelled by sustained engagement with the West, would transform its political ideology and bring it within the fold of liberal democracies. Inherent in this view was the belief that democracy is the 'natural' system that prosperous nations gravitate towards and that open political systems promote economic growth. By becoming a key driver of the global economy, while retaining its single party system of governance and the communist ideology, China represents a challenge to Enlightenment thinking that cannot be ignored.

In September 2014, in a speech at an international conference held on the occasion of the 2,565th anniversary of Confucius' birth, President Xi of China claimed that 'the Chinese Communist Party is the successor to and promoter of fine traditional Chinese culture'.[16] Since then, there has been a consistent attempt to conflate Confucianism and Chinese communism to justify the political structure of China,[17] a structure that is completely at odds with the structures of liberal democracy.

While the Enlightenment philosophy accords pride of place to the individual, Confucianism gives the community the same privileged position. While the age of reason calls into question traditional customs, Confucius engaged in a quest to rediscover the vitality in ancient cultural practices. The communist movement in China initially treated Confucianism as a regressive ideology that needed to be repressed.[18] However, after acquiring power, the Chinese Communist Party sees this millennia-old culture as a source of legitimacy for its hierarchical, authoritarian structure – a useful tradition that can be invoked in an environment where its old ally, economic growth, seems to be in decline. Thus, we can expect to continue to see a materially powerful China sticking out like a sore thumb among the influential economies on account of its non-Enlightenment political and cultural practices. This continued presence is bound to affect the way the world at large thinks about the role of an individual in society, especially in an environment where societies based on individualistic beliefs seem to be falling apart.

Since its formation, India has occupied a moral high ground among nations on account of the manner in which it won its freedom and its role in the non-aligned movement.[19] Despite being the 'father' of a relatively poor nation, Gandhi became a global icon who inspired liberation movements across the world. However, had the country remained inconsequential from a material standpoint, it would have run the risk of being patronized, rather than listened to. Equally vital to India's growing influence is the fact that the country has cleaved to democracy, admittedly with varying degrees of success, despite its size and economic challenges.

After losing its way in the 1970s, the country embarked on a path of economic liberalization starting in the mid-1980s, which resulted in the creation of one of the largest middle-class markets in the world.[20] Today, with the decline in China's growth rate, India is the fastest growing large economy in the world[21] and a beacon of hope in a recessionary environment.

But purely on economic terms, India may still not have been able to make the grade as a power to reckon with. Its centrality is cemented by its geopolitical role as a neighbour and counterweight to China, with whom it has a set of longstanding border disputes. This makes it a critical player in the growing great power conflict between the US and China.

As India gains heft on the global stage, its age-old philosophy and communitarian mores will gain ground. The worldwide yoga movement already represents a vital source of India's growing soft power. This influence is bound to grow given the fact that Hinduism is a system of thought that is extraordinarily pliable. Every shade of religious predilection – from ritualistic believers, non-ritualistic believers, ritualistic non-believers, and non-ritualistic non-believers – can find room in its capacious accommodations. The ideology of rationality would constitute only one of the many hues in its bouquet of worldviews, and not necessarily the most attractive one. In that sense, it represents a challenge to the rationalist approach.

Of course, the religion is not bereft of its own perversities. For instance, the caste system has been one of the most sophisticated and large-scale systems of social exploitation the world has ever seen. Worryingly, an influential strand of the present phase of Hinduism is 'Hindutva', where the religion has acquired a political colour that seems to be having a visibly distortionary effect.

As a practising Hindu who is sceptical of all organized religion, I used to draw some comfort from the fact that Hinduism was the most disorganized of the lot. That is no longer the case. The politicization of Hinduism gives it a universalist impulse that is similar to the expansionist tendencies of the Enlightenment ideology, and equally troubling.

However, I am hopeful that a tradition that has lasted for thousands of years will outlast the insecurities of the band of worthies who currently claim to be its most ardent votaries. And that this way of thinking will fashion a new pact between the rationalists and the postmodernists. After all, a religion with a pantheon of thirty-five crore gods knows a little bit about the importance of plurality.

Existential Imperatives: AI

On 19 November 2019, Lee Sedol, the legendary champion of Go, a game of strategy regarded as far more complex than chess, announced his retirement. He was only 36 years old and was expected to enjoy several more years at the top of the game.

However, there was a problem.

In 2016, despite confident pre-game prognostications by Lee, he had been decisively defeated by a player called AlphaGo. But AlphaGo was not your everyday 'new kid on the block'. It was an artificial intelligence algorithm developed by DeepMind, a company that had been acquired by Google in 2013.[22]

Lee continued to play after his defeat. He only threw in the towel three years later when DeepMind announced that it had developed a successor to the algorithm that had played Lee. The company claimed that the successor, AlphaGo Zero, had defeated the version that Lee had played 100-0. At the time of his announcement, Lee said: 'Even if I become the number one, there is an entity that cannot be defeated.'[23]

Meanwhile, another AI tool, ChatGPT, working on the basis of its ability to scrape and process large amounts of data from the internet, and funded by Microsoft,* has been creating a sensation based on its ability to perform a variety of tasks, from collaborating on research papers for leading academic journals to writing lines of code.[24]

While ChatGPT represents a potential threat to the employability of human beings in the not-too-distant future, AlphaGo Zero presents a somewhat more serious threat to

---

* Elon Musk and Peter Thiel were early investors in both DeepMind and Open AI, the company that developed ChatGPT.

the self-image of humans as the most intelligent entities in the universe, those with the highest capacities of rationality. If machines are soon going to outpace humans in reasoning capabilities, from where will human beings derive their sense of privilege and supremacy?

The principal realm in which human beings can continue to outstrip machines in the foreseeable future is the realm of consciousness. When Rene Descartes, considered to be one of the founders of Enlightenment philosophy, wrote 'I think therefore I am',[25] he could have gone one step further, and said 'I am conscious that I think, therefore I am.' Had he done so, he would have asserted that the one incontrovertible and irreducible fact of his being was that he was conscious.

Indeed, human consciousness is a little understood phenomenon and possibly represents the last frontier for science. Some would even argue that it is an unreachable frontier since consciousness envelopes everything, including the attempt to understand it through observation and reason. This implies that to know consciousness, i.e., be conscious, we cannot ignore the methods of contemplation and meditation long espoused by the mystics and spiritual savants.

In any case, there is widespread agreement that the one quality not possessed by machines is consciousness.[26] In this context, the attempt to move beyond reason to explore the uncharted realms of consciousness becomes an existential imperative for a human race struggling to preserve its self-image.

Beyond these fundamental drivers of change, the sad truth is that suffering is the most effective of all teachers. It is quite possible that repeated catastrophes – natural disasters, pandemics, and civil wars that affect wide swathes of the global population, including the elites – will have a major role to play in the formulation of the fundamental principles of the age of meta-reason.

The following are likely to be the important developments of the new age:

1. Rationality will be displaced from its unrivalled position as the highest human faculty.
2. The vacuum left by rationality will be filled by a variety of claimants ranging from the ridiculous to the sublime. These include superstition and blind faith on the one hand, and intuition, awareness and consciousness on the other.
3. There will be a new humility towards knowledge systems not based in mainstream Enlightenment thought and, in parallel, attempts to explore the underlying logic of such systems. Traditional medicine would be a prime example. In the process, both quacks and charlatans, and seers and savants will gain ascendancy.
4. There will be a renewed attempt to probe the mysteries of consciousness as the final frontier of human understanding. There will be many hits and misses as humans grapple with the most insubstantial of all things whose 'traits cannot be seen anywhere in the physical realm'.[27]
5. There will be a recognition that human survival is based on harmonious co-existence with nature and that the logic of rationality is inadequate to assess our relationship with it.
6. The crises of climate change and inequality will re-balance power between private enterprise and government, with a movement back to greater control by strong governments and illiberal leaders aided by the power of surveillance technology.
7. With a large number of people being unemployed or

underemployed, there will be an epidemic of dissatisfaction till happiness replaces success at work as the signifier of a life well lived.

8. Current education systems will undergo a dualistic transformation – one part will shift away from a focus on standardized testing and rote learning towards nurturing creativity, emotional intelligence and adaptability, as society recognizes the importance of holistic human development. Another part will become even more competitive as a way of coping with an unpredictable future.
9. The universal culture to which the proponents of rationality aspire will be supplanted by a variety of local cultures – resilient and ephemeral, all asserting their right to flourish.
10. A large number of communities will spring up, many stretching across national borders, based on common interests, needs and aspirations. These communities will span the spectrum from the toxic to the transcendental.
11. The global governance architecture will splinter into a multitude of regional architectures including trading blocs, development banks and international organizations, each catering to the specific needs and interests of their respective regions. Principles of global engagement will emerge through a process of negotiation between such regional institutions.

Obviously, an age driven by such contradictory impulses and subject to such high levels of uncertainty will be difficult to negotiate, and yet thrilling in the glimpses it provides of the new possibilities awaiting human beings.

May we deftly navigate the perilous subjectivities looming before us.

NOTES

Introduction

1. Shaziya Allarakha, 'What Are the 72 Other Genders?', MedicineNet.
2. David Satterthwaite, 'An urbanising world', International Institute for Environment and Development, 9 April 2020.
3. 'World Infant Mortality Rate 1950–2023', Macrotrends.
4. Jonathan Woetzel et al., 'The Rise and Rise of the Global Balance Sheet: How Productively Are We Using Our Wealth?', McKinsey & Company, 15 November 2021.
5. Ibid.
6. Nouriel Roubini, 'The Unavoidable Crash,' Experience Stern, 2 December 2022.
7. Drew Desilver, 'Despite Global Concerns About Democracy, More Than Half of Countries Are Democratic', Pew Research Center, 14 May 2019.
8. Ula Chrobak, 'Solar Power Got Cheap. So Why Aren't We Using It More?', *Popular Science*, 8 October 2021.
9. Richard Samuels, Stephen Stich, and Luc Faucher, 'Reason and Rationality', *Handbook of Epistemology* (2004): 131–79.
10. Adam Smith, *The Wealth of Nations* (New York: Cosimo, 2007).
11. Paul Bairoch, 'International Industrialization Levels from 1750 to 1980', *Journal of European Economic History*, 11.2 (1982): 269
12. Ibid.
13. R. Botvinik-Nezer, M. Jones, and T.D. Wager, 'A belief systems analysis of fraud beliefs following the 2020 US election', *Nature Human Behaviour* 7, 1106–1119 (2023). https://doi.org/10.1038/s41562-023-01570-4.

14. Keith Dowding, 'Collective Action Problem', Encyclopaedia Britannica.
15. 'Entanglement', Collins English Dictionary.
16. Oxford English Dictionary.
17. Arthur Miller, 'The Year it Came Apart', *New York Magazine,* 30 December 1974–6 January 1975, 8 (1): 30–44.
18. Immanuel Kant, *Critique of Pure Reason 1781*, Cambridge: Houghton Mifflin, 1908, 370–456.

1. The USA: A Union Divided

1. Hope Yen and David Klepper, 'AP FACT CHECK: On Jan. 6 Anniversary, Trump Sticks to Election Falsehoods', *PBS*, 6 January 2022.
2. Brian Naylor, 'Read Trump's Jan. 6 Speech, a Key Part of Impeachment Trial', *NPR*, 10 February 2021.
3. Alvin Y. So, ed. *China's Developmental Miracle: Origins, Transformations, and Challenges*, London and New York: Routledge, 2016, 29–57.
4. John J. Mearsheimer, 'The Inevitable Rivalry: America, China, and the Tragedy of Great-Power Politics', *Foreign Affairs,* 19 October 2021.
5. Medard Gabel and Henry Bruner, *Global Inc.: An Atlas of the Multinational Corporation*, New York: New York Press, 2003.
6. 'GDP Per Capita (Constant 2015 US$)', World Bank, 8 July 2023.
7. Miriam A. Golden, Michael Wallerstein, and Peter Lange, 'Postwar Trade-union Organization and Industrial Relations in Twelve Countries', *Continuity and Change in Contemporary Capitalism* (1999): 194–230.
8. Fatih Guvenen, Greg Kaplan, Jae Song, and Justin Weidner, *Lifetime Incomes in the United States over Six Decades* (Working Paper 23371), Cambridge: National Bureau of Economic Research, 2017.
9. National Research Council, *The New Americans: Economic, Demographic, and Fiscal Effects of Immigration*, Washington D.C.: National Academies Press, 1997, 219–28.
10. Michael J. Mauboussin, Dan Callahan, and Darius Majd, 'The Incredible Shrinking Universe of Stocks: The Causes and Consequences of Fewer U.S. Equities', Credit Suisse, 2017.
11. Adil Abdela and Marshall Steinbaum, 'The United States Has a Market Concentration Problem', Roosevelt Institute, September 2019.
12. James W. Dean, 'The Dissolution of the Keynesian Consensus', *Public Interest,* Special Issue, 1980, 19–34.

13. 'Margaret Thatcher: A Life in Quotes', *The Guardian*, 8 April 2013.
14. George Raine, 'Creating Reagan's image/S.F. ad man Riney helped secure him a second term', *SF Gate*, 9 June 2004.
15. D.T. Yang, J. Zhang, and S. Zhou, 'Why Are Saving Rates So High in China?', *Capitalizing China*, eds Joseph P.H. Fan and Randall Morck, Chicago: University of Chicago Press, 2013, 249–79.
16. Robert E. Scott, 'Heading South: US-Mexico Trade and Job Displacement after NAFTA', *Economic Policy Institute*, 3 May 2011.
17. Federal Reserve Board, 'Remarks by Governor Laurence H. Meyer', 12 May 1998.
18. 'Bringing Homeownership Rates to Historic Levels', The White House, 7 July 1999.
19. 'President Calls for Expanding Opportunities to Home Ownership', The White House, 17 June 2002.
20. Sumit Agarwal et al., 'Did the Community Reinvestment Act (CRA) Lead to Risky Lending?', no. w18609, National Bureau of Economic Research, December 2012.
21. 'The Causes and Effects of the Lehman Brothers Bankruptcy', US Government Publishing Office, 6 October 2008.
22. 'Great Recession, Great Recovery? Trends from the Current Population Survey', *Monthly Labour Review*, April 2018.
23. 'Troubled Assets Relief Program (TARP)', US Department of the Treasury.
24. Joe Light, 'Will Fannie and Freddie Need Another Bailout?', *The Wall Street Journal*, 24 May 2016.
25. CBS/AP, 'Wall Street Doled $20B in Bonuses in 2009', *CBS News*, 23 February 2010.
26. 'Minorities, Immigrants and Homeownership', Pew Research Center, 12 May 2009.
27. Jeremy Greenwood, 'The Third Industrial Revolution: Technology, Productivity, and Income Inequality', Federal Reserve Bank of Cleveland, *Economic Review* 1999 Q2.
28. Andrew Perrin and Maeve Duggan, 'American's Internet Access: 2000–2015', Pew Research Center, 26 June 2015.
29. 'Mobile Cellular Subscriptions per 100 Inhabitants in the United States from 2000 to 2020,' Statista.

30. 'Percentage of Households in the United States with a Computer at Home from 1984 to 2016', Statista.
31. 'Smartphone penetration rate as share of the population in the United States from 2010 to 2021', Statista.
32. Ambika Choudhary, 'Facebook Inc. (FB) Q3 2014 Results: Revenue from US, Users from Asia!', *Daze Info*, 3 November 2014.
33. Michael A. Cusumano, Yiorgos Mylonadis, and Richard S. Rosenbloom, 'Strategic Maneuvering and Mass-market Dynamics: The Triumph of VHS over Beta,' *Business History Review*, 66.1, 51–94, 1992.
34. YiLi Chien and Ashley Stewart, 'The Recent Rise of U.S. National Wealth', Economic Research: Federal Reserve Bank of St. Louis, 19 October 2022.
35. Anshu Siripurapu, 'The US Inequality Debate', Council on Foreign Relations, 20 April 2022.
36. 'NASDAQ Composite: 45 Year Historical Chart', Macrotrends.
37. Glen O. Robinson, 'The Titanic Remembered: AT&T and the Changing World of Telecommunications', *Yale Journal on Regulation*, Vol. 5, 1988 517.
38. Ian Bremmer, 'The US Capitol Riot Was Years in the Making. Here's Why America Is So Divided,' *Time*, 16 January 2021.
39. Dudley L. Poston, Jr., '3 Ways That the US Population Will Change Over the Next Decade', *PBS*, 2 January 2020.
40. Leo Lowenthal and Norbert Guterman, *Prophets of Deceit: A Study of the Techniques of the American agitator*, London and New York: Verso Books, 2021.
41. Panayota Gounari, 'Authoritarianism, Discourse and Social Media: Trump as the "American agitator",' *Critical Theory and Authoritarian Populism*, ed. Jeremiah Morelock (London: University of Westminster Press, 2018), 207.
42. 'Donald Trump and Twitter – 2009 / 2022 analysis', TweetBinder Blog.
43. Donald Trump@ realDonaldTrump, Twitter.
44. Donald Trump@ realDonaldTrump, Twitter.
45. Donald Trump@ realDonaldTrump, Twitter.
46. 'Two Year Update: October 2020–December 2022', The Polarization Index.
47. Judicial Watch @JudicialWatch.

48. Judicial Watch @JudicialWatch, Twitter.
49. Judicial Watch @JudicialWatch.
50. Brianna Richardson, 'Axios | Momentive Poll: January 6th Revisited', *Curiosity at Work*.
51. Ibid.

2. China: An Uncertain Glory

1. Alvin Y. So, *China's Developmental Miracle*, M.E. Sharpe, 2003, 9–10.
2. Ministry of Information Industry, People's Republic of China, 'A Historical Leap Forward in China Information Industry', 14 September 1999.
3. US–China Perception Monitor, 'Who Is Ren Zhengfei?'.
4. R. Li-Hua and W. Sun, 'China's Technology Strategy of "Market in Exchange for Technology"', *Journal of Technology Management in China*, 2009, Vol. 4 no. 3.
5. Michaela Eglin, 'China's Entry into the WTO with a Little Help from the EU,' *International Affairs*, Vol. 73, no. 3: 489–508.
6. Richard Dobbs, et al. 'The New Global Competition for Corporate Profits', McKinsey & Company, 1 September 2015.
7. 'Shares of Gross Domestic Income', FRED Economic Data, 12 October 2022.
8. Hui Feng, *The Politics of China's Accession to the World Trade Organization*, Taylor & Francis, 2006, 151–56.
9. Tian Tao and Wu Chunbo, *The Huawei Story*, New Delhi: SAGE Publications India, 2014, 101.
10. Ibid.
11. Alice D. Ba, 'Asian Financial Crisis', Britannica, 27 July 2023.
12. Matt Hamblen, 'Cisco Drops Lawsuit against Huawei,' Computerworld, 28 July 2004.
13. 'Global Economic Slowdown Impacts 2008 International Patent Filings', WIPO, 27 January 2009.
14. Tao and Chunbo, *The Huawei Story,* New Delhi: SAGE Publications India, 105, 139.
15. Ibid, 86.
16. '"Apple Is My Teacher" Why Huawei Founder Said That?', HC Newsroom, 27 May 2019.

17. Huang Shan, 'Huawei Urges Thousands of Employees to Resign', China.org.cn, 2 November 2007.
18. 'Crisis Leadership in Action: A Balancing Act between the Past and the Future', *European Financial Review*, 18 November 2020.
19. Stone Fox Capital, 'Motorola Solutions: Does This Stock Deserve to Trade at Multi-Year Highs?', *Seeking Alpha*, 31 January 2017.
20. 'Motorola Solutions – 46 Year Stock Price History | MSI', Mactrotrends.
21. 'Lucent Stock Prices Table', Historical Stock Info.
22. 'Who owns Huawei?', Huawei.
23. 'The Complete List of World's Billionaires 2007', Areppim.
24. Eleanor Pringle, 'This Chinese Billionaire Has Lost Over 90% of His Fortune and Analysts Are Worried About the Future of His 200,000 Staff', Yahoo Finance, 20 January 2023.
25. Alexandra Stevenson and Cao Li, 'What to Know About China Evergrande, the Troubled Property Giant', *New York Times*, 9 December 2021.
26. Andong Zhu and David M. Kotz, 'The Dependence of China's Economic Growth on Exports and Investment', July 2010.
27. World Integrated Trade Solution, 'China Trade Summary 2007.'
28. 'Gross Fixed Capital Formation (% of GDP) – China', World Bank.
29. Martin Wolf, 'Long Way to Go, but Happy Ending May Be in Sight for Chinese Economy', *Irish Times*, 4 April 2018.
30. 'GDP Growth (Annual %) – China', World Bank.
31. 'Gross Fixed Capital Formation (% of GDP) – China', World Bank.
32. 'Tier 3 Cities: A Hotbed of Trouble in China's Property Sector?', Standford Center on China's Economy and Institutions, 15 December 2022.
33. 'Full text of Xi Jinping's Speech on the CCP's 100th Anniversary', *Nikkei Asia*, 1 July 2021
34. 'Addition of Huawei Non-U.S. Affiliates to the Entity List, the Removal of Temporary General License, and Amendments to General Prohibition Three (Foreign-Produced Direct Product Rule)', Federal Register, 20 August 2020.
35. C. Scott Brown, 'The HUAWEI Ban Explained: A Complete Timeline and Everything You Need to Know', Android Authority, 10 April 2023.
36. Tao and Chunbo, *The Huawei Story.*

3. Financial Fault Lines

1. 'Solana Historical Data', CoinMarketCap.
2. Barry Eichengreen, *Globalizing Capital*, Princeton University Press, 2019, 86–126.
3. Sandra Kollen Ghizoni, 'Creation of the Bretton Woods System', Federal Reserve History, 22 November 2013.
4. Barry Eichengreen, *Exorbitant Privilege: The Rise and Fall of the Dollar and the Future of the International Monetary System*, Oxford: Oxford University Press, 2011, 1–8.
5. Matthew Sherman, 'A Short History of Financial Deregulation in the United States', *Center for Economic and Policy Research*, July 2009.
6. Anastasia Nesvetailova, 'A Crisis of the Overcrowded Future: Shadow Banking and the Political Economy of Financial Innovation', *New Political Economy*, 20.3, 2015, 431–53.
7. Paul McCulley, 'The Shadow Banking System and Hyman Minsky's Economic Journey', *Insights into the Global Financial Crisis*, 2009, 257–68.
8. Huw Jones, 'World's 'Shadow Banks' Continue to Expand', *Reuters*, 5 March 2018.
9. 'Remarks by Chairman Alan Greenspan', The Federal Reserve Board, 19 March 1999.
10. Sebastian Mallaby, *The Man Who Knew: The Life and Times of Alan Greenspan*, London: Bloomsbury Publishing, 2016.
11. John Williamson, 'A Short History of the Washington Consensus'. *Law and Business Review of the Americas*, Vol. 15 no. 1, 2009, 7.
12. 'NASDAQ Composite Index (COMP)', NASDAQ.
13. 'M3 for the United States', FRED, Federal Reserve Bank of St. Louis.
14. F.A. Hayek, *Denationalisation of Money: The Argument Refined—An Analysis of the Theory and Practice of Concurrent Currencies*, 3rd ed., London: The Institute of Economic Affairs.
15. Ibid.
16. Jeffrey C. Callen and Eric K. Austin, 'Deterritorializing Utopia: The Possibility of Techno-utopias in Societies of Control', *Administrative Theory & Praxis*, Vol. 38 no. 1, 2016, 19–36.
17. Nathan Crooks, 'Peter Thiel Tells Crowd Where He'd Look for Elusive Bitcoin Founder Satoshi', *Bloomberg*, 21 October 2021.

18. Ibid.
19. Luca Fantacci, 'Cryptocurrencies and the Denationalization of Money'. *International Journal of Political Economy*, Vol. 48 no. 2, 2019, 105–26.
20. 'Global Cryptocurrency Charts', CoinMarketCap.
21. Alex Herns, 'Electricity Used to Mine Bitcoin Plummets as Crypto Crisis Widens', *Guardian*, 24 June 2022.
22. Richard Trenholm, 'Dogecoin Creator Says Cryptocurrency Is a Right-Wing "Funnel of Profiteering"', *CNET*, 15 July 2021.
23. Ben Winck, 'Dogecoin Volumes Spike 683% After Viral Tiktok Challenge Urges Buying Spree', *Markets Insider*, 8 July 2020.
24. Sophie Knight, 'Mt. Gox Says It Found 200,000 Bitcoins in "Forgotten" Wallet', Reuters, 21 March 2014.
25. 'Are NFTs Going to be Most Used for Fashion in Gaming?', *Glass*, 26 November 2022.
26. Isabelle Lee, 'Luxury NFTs Could Become a $56 Billion Market by 2030 and Could See "Dramatically" Increased Demand Thanks to the Metaverse, Morgan Stanley Says', *Markets Insider*, 26 November 2021.

4. Tectonic Shifts in Geopolitics

1. Sheri Berman, 'Islamism, Revolution, and Civil Society', *Perspectives on Politics*, Vol 1. no. 2, 2003, 257–72.
2. Samuel P. Huntington, 'The Clash of Civilizations?', *The New Social Theory Reader*, (Routledge, 2020), 305–13.
3. 'The US War in Afghanistan', Council on Foreign Relations.
4. *Medal of Honor*, Season 1, Episode 2, Produced by Allentown Productions and Compari Entertainment, distributed by Netflix.
5. Michael A. Innes, 'Perceptions of Success and Failure in ISAF Operations in Marjah, Afghanistan', Jamestown Foundation, *Terrorism Monitor* Vol. 8 Issue: 24.
6. 'President Discusses Beginning of Operation Iraqi Freedom', The White House, 22 March 2003.
7. 'Iraq War Illegal, Says Annan', BBC News, 16 September 2004.
8. Julian Borger, 'Colin Powell's UN Speech: A Decisive Moment in Undermining US Credibility', *The Guardian*, 18 October 2021.
9. Deborah Amos, 'Saddam Hussein's Trial Was Meant to Be a Symbol of a New Democratic Iraq', *NPR*, 21 March 2023.

10. Sarhang Hamasaeed and Garrett Nada, 'Iraq Timeline: Since the 2003 War', United States Institute of Peace, 29 May 2020.
11. Fawaz A. Gerges, *ISIS: A History*, rev. ed. (Princeton: Princeton University Press, 2016), 1–22.
12. Marian Żuber and Samuel Sahel Moussa, 'Arab Spring As a Background of Civil War in Syria', *International Conference Knowledge-Based Organization*, Vol. 24. no. 1. 2018.
13. John M. Owen IV and Michael Poznansky, 'When Does America Drop Dictators?', *European Journal of International Relations*, Vol. 20 no. 4, 2014, 1072–99.
14. Salim Yaqub, *Imperfect Strangers: Americans, Arabs, and US–Middle East Relations in the 1970s* (Ithaca: Cornell University Press, 2018), 145–82.
15. Editors of Encyclopaedia Britannica, 'Syrian Civil War', Britannica, 29 Aug 2023.
16. Paul J. Smith, 'The China–Pakistan–United States Strategic Triangle: From Cold War to the "War on Terrorism"', *Asian Affairs: An American Review*, Vol. 38 no. 4, 2011, 197–220.
17. Griffe Witte, 'Afghanistan War: 2001–2014', Britannica, 1 September 2023.
18. Dexter Filkins, 'Pakistanis Tell of Motive in Taliban Leader's Arrest', *New York Times*, 22 August 2010.
19. 'Pakistan's Support of the Taliban', Human Rights Watch.
20. Muhammad Shahbaz, 'Revisiting Friends & Foes: US–Pak Relation's Turbulent History and Future', *Open Journal of Political Science*, Vol. 13 no. 1, 2023, 88–118.
21. Husain Haqqani, 'Pakistan's Terrorism Dilemma', *Religious Radicalism and Security in South Asia, Honolulu: Asia-Pacific Center for Security Studies*, 2004, 351–61.
22. 'Military Expenditure (% of General Government Expenditure) – Pakistan', World Bank.
23. Amir Wasim, '50 Commercial Entities Being Run by Armed Forces', *Dawn*, 21 July 2016.
24. Haqqani, 'Pakistan's Terrorism Dilemma'.
25. Shahbaz, 'Revisiting Friends & Foes'.
26. Abdul Basit, 'Why Did the Afghan Army Disintegrate So Quickly?', *Al Jazeera*, 17 August 2021.

27. Witte, 'Afghanistan War: 2001–2014'.
28. Lindsay Maizland, 'US–Taliban Peace Deal: What to Know', Council for Foreign Relations, 2 March 2020.
29. David Zucchino, 'How the Taliban Conquered Afghanistan', *New York Times*, 18 August 2021.
30. Ibid.
31. Ibid.
32. Jodi Vittori, 'Corruption and Self-Dealing in Afghanistan and Other U.S.-Backed Security Sectors', Carnagie Endowment for International Peace, 9 September 2021.
33. 'The Clinton-Yeltsin Relationship in Their Own Words', National Security Archive, 2 October 2018.
34. Becky Little, 'When a Russian President Ended Up Drunk and Disrobed Outside the White House', History, 25 July 2023.
35. 'Bill Clinton, Boris Yeltsin, and U.S.-Russian Relations', Office of the Historian.
36. John B. Allcock, 'Slobodan Miloševié', Britannica, 25 August 2023.
37. 'Summary', Human Rights Watch.
38. 'NATO Expansion: What Yeltsin Heard', National Security Archive, 16 March 2018.
39. Ibid.
40. Ibid.
41. Daniel Treisman, '"Loans for Shares" Revisited', *Post-Soviet Affairs*, Vol. 26 no. 3, 2010, 207–227.
42. Jolle Demmers, Alex E. Fernández Jilberto, and Barbara Hogenboom, *Good Governance in the Era of Global Neoliberalism: Conflict and Depolitization in Latin America, Eastern Europe, Asia and Africa*, London and New York: Routledge, 2004.
43. Tom Parfitt and Terry Macalister, 'The End Comes for Yukos as Oil Firm Declared Bankrupt and Auction Ordered', *Guardian*, 2 August 2006.
44. Giles Tremlett, 'Putin is out to get me, says media tycoon', *Guardian*, 24 April 2001.
45. Murat Sofuoglu, 'Russia Could Have Joined NATO. But Why Didn't They Do It?', *TRT World*.
46. 'BBC Breakfast with Frost: Interview—Vladimir Putin', *BBC News*, 5 March 2000.

47. Jennifer Rankin, 'Ex-Nato Head Says Putin Wanted to Join Alliance Early on in His Rule', *Guardian*, 4 November 2021.
48. 'A Speech Delivered at the MSC 2007 by the President Vladimir Putin'.
49. Ibid.
50. Ibid.
51. 'Bucharest Summit Declaration', NATO, 3 April 2008.
52. Ellen Barry, 'Medvedev Defends Plan to Trade Places with Putin', *New York Times*, 30 September 2011.
53. Andrei Ryabov, 'Tandemocracy in Today's Russia', Russian Analytical Digest.
54. Clifford G. Gaddy and Barry W. Ickes, 'Russia after the Global Financial Crisis,' *Eurasian Geography and Economics*, Vol. 51 no. 3, 2010, 281–311.
55. Natasha M. Ezrow and Erica Frantz, *Dictators and Dictatorships: Understanding Authoritarian Regimes and Their Leaders* (New York City: Bloomsbury Publishing, 2011), 81–95.
56. John J. Mearsheimer, 'Why the Ukraine Crisis Is the West's Fault: The Liberal Delusions That Provoked Putin', *Foreign Affairs*, September/October 2014.
57. Harriet Salem and Ludmila Makarova, 'Crimean Annexation Brings Dacha Prize Closer for Putin', *Guardian*, 28 March 2014.
58. Krishnadev Calamur, 'Crimea: A Gift to Ukraine Becomes a Political Flash Point', *NPR*, 27 February 2014.
59. 'The Famine of 1932–33 (Holodomor)', Britannica.
60. Ibid
61. Anna Mikulska and Eryk Kosinski, 'What's Next for Natural Gas in Ukraine?' (Working Paper), Baker Institute.
62. Ibid.
63. Rilka Dragneva-Lewers and Kataryna Wolczuk, *Ukraine between the EU and Russia: The Integration Challenge*, New York: Springer, 2015, 21.
64. Margarita M Balmaceda, *Energy Dependency, Politics and Corruption in the Former Soviet Union: Russia's Power, Oligarchs' Profits and Ukraine's Missing Energy Policy, 1995–2006*, London and New York: Routledge, 2007, 100.
65. Roman Goncharenko, 'Zelenskiy's Path to the Presidency', Deutsche Welle, 22 April 2019.
66. Balmaceda, *Energy Dependency*, 87.
67. 'EU Reaches Gas Deal with Ukraine', *BBC News*, 1 August 2009.

68. Howard J. Wiarda, 'The Politics of European Enlargement: NATO, the EU, and the New US–European Relationship', *World Affairs,* Vol. 164, 2001, 178.
69. Sergii Leshchenko, 'Yanukovych, the Luxury Residence and the Money Trail That Leads to London,' Open Democracy, 8 June 2012.
70. Ian Traynor 'US campaign behind the turmoil in Kiev', *Guardian*, 26 November 2004.
71. Dragneva-Lewers and Wolczuk, *Ukraine between the EU and Russia*, 87.
72. Reid Standish, 'Ousted Ukrainian President: "I Supported the Ostriches. What's Wrong with That?"', Foreign Policy, 23 June 2015.
73. 'Putin: Soviet Collapse a "Genuine Tragedy"', NBC News, 26 April 2005.
74. Michael Ray, 'Ukraine Crisis', Britannica, 1 September 2023.
75. 'Russia Defends Crimea Referendum, Agrees to More Observers', *Reuters*, 16 March 2014.
76. Zoltan Barany, *Democratic Breakdown and the Decline of the Russian Military*, Princeton: Princeton University Press, 2009, 1–18.

5. Man-made Disasters

1. 'Gurgaon Residents and Corporate Hit the Ground Against Air Pollution', *Let Me Breathe*, 17 November 2019.
2. 'Charter', Delhi Development Authority.
3. Alpana Sivam, 'Housing supply in Delhi,' *Cities* 20.2 (2003): 135–141.
4. Veena Talwar Oldenburg, *Gurgaon: From Mythic Village to Millennium City*, HarperCollins India, 2018.
5. 'How Golf Sharpened Business Skill of KP Singh', *Economic Times*, 19 March 2019.
6. Ajay Modi and Karan Choudhury, 'Jat stir shakes India Inc', *Business Standard*, 20 February 2016.
7. 'Air Pollution Is a Serious Issue', A-Pag.
8. The Sagar School.
9. 'IUCN WCPA Other Effective Area-based Conservation Measures Specialist Group', IUCN.
10. 'New ILO Figures Show 164 Million People Are Migrant Workers', ILO, 5 December 2018.
11. 'International Tourist Arrivals Reach 1.4 Billion Two Years Ahead of

Forecasts', UNWTO, 21 January 2019.

12. Katarina Zimmer, 'Deforestation Is Leading to More Infectious Diseases in Humans', *National Geographic*, 22 November 2019.
13. Jane Qiu, 'How China's "Bat Woman" Hunted Down Viruses from SARS to the New Coronavirus', *Scientific American*, 1 June 2020.
14. Ibid.
15. Douglas Jordan, 'The Deadliest Flu: The Complete Story of the Discovery and Reconstruction of the 1918 Pandemic Virus', Centers for Disease Control and Prevention.
16. Ibid.
17. Ibid.
18. Marc Lipsitch, 'Why Do Exceptionally Dangerous Gain-of-Function Experiments in Influenza?', *Influenza Virus*, 2018, Vol. 1836: 589–608.
19. Ibid.
20. Ibid.
21. Scientists for Science.
22. Ron A. M. Fouchier et al., 'Transmission Studies Resume for Avian Flu', *Science*, February 2013, Vol. 339 Issue 6119, 520–21.
23. Francis S. Collins, 'NIH Lifts Funding Pause on Gain-of-Function Research', National Institutes of Health, 19 December 2017.
24. David Cyranoski, 'Inside the Chinese Lab Poised to Study World's Most Dangerous Pathogens', *Nature*, Vol. 542, 399–400, 2017.
25. Nurith Aizenman, 'Why the US Government Stopped Funding a Research Project on Bats and Coronaviruses', *NPR*, 29 April 2020.
26. 'Federal Research: NIH Could Take Additional Actions to Manage Risks Involving Foreign Subrecipients', Government Accountability Office, June 2023.
27. 'WHO Team Visits Chinese Virus Lab in Wuhan', VOA, 2 February 2021.
28. 'British Scientist from WHO Team in China's Wuhan Recused from UN-backed Commission on Covid-19 Origins', *Times of India*, 24 June 2021.
29. Charles Calisher et al., 'Statement in Support of the Scientists, Public Health Professionals, and Medical Professionals of China Combatting COVID-19', *Lancet*, 2020, Vol. 395,10226, E42 E43.
30. Maanvi Singh, Helen Davidson and Julian Borger, 'Trump Claims to Have Evidence Coronavirus Started in Chinese Lab but Offers No Details', *Guardian*, 1 May 2020.
31. 'Statement by President Joe Biden on the Investigation into the Origins

of COVID-19', The White House, 26 May 2021.

32. 'Scientific Advisory Group for the Origins of Novel Pathogens (SAGO)', WHO, 9 June 2022.
33. Ibid.
34. 'Covid-19 Origin Unclear, Lab Leak Theory Needs Study: WHO', *Outlook*, 10 June 2022.
35. 'China Calls COVID "Lab Leak" Theory a Lie after WHO Report', CP24, 10 June 2022.
36. 'Global Dashboard for Vaccine Equity', UNDP.
37. Qin Xiang Ng et al., 'Yemen's Cholera Epidemic Is a One Health Issue', *Journal of Preventive Medicine and Public Health*, 2020; Vol. 53,4: 289–92.
38. Ibid

6. Surveillance Capitalism and Its Discontents

1. Sheera Frenkel, 'How Jeff Bezos' iPhone X Was Hacked', *New York Times*, 22 January 2020.
2. Elias Groll, 'The Kingdom's Hackers and Bots', Foreign Policy, 19 October 2018.
3. This is the version of events accepted by Turkey.
4. Jim Rutenberg, Kate Kelly, Jessica Silver-Greenberg and Mike McIntire , 'Wooing Saudi Business, Tabloid Mogul Had a Powerful Friend: Trump', 29 March 2018.
5. Jeff Bezos, 'No thank you, Mr. Pecker', Medium, 8 February 2019.
6. Gavin De Becker, 'Bezos Investigation Finds the Saudis Obtained His Private Data', *Daily Beast*, 31 March 2019.
7. Ibid.
8. Ibid.
9. Ibid.
10. 'WhatsApp Inc. v. NSO Group Technologies Limited', Global Freedom of Expression.
11. Bill Marczak, John Scott-Railton, Bahr Abdul Razzak, and Ron Deibert, 'Triple Threat: NSO Group's Pegasus Spyware Returns in 2022 with a Trio of iOS 15 and iOS 16 Zero-Click Exploit Chains', Citizen Lab, 18 April 2023.
12. Ronen Bergman and Mark Mazzetti, 'The Battle for the World's Most

Powerful Cyberweapon', *New York Times Magazine*, 28 January 2002.

13. Rød-Larsen, Terje, Nur Laiq, and Fabrice Aidan, eds. *The Search for Peace in the Arab-Israeli Conflict: A Compendium of Documents and Analysis*, New York: Oxford University Press, 2014, 484.
14. Bergman and Mazzetti, 'The Battle for the World's Most Powerful Cyberweapon'.
15. Bill Marczak, John Scott-Railton, Sarah McKune, Bahr Abdul Razzak, and Ron Deibert, 'Hide and Seek: Tracking NSO Group's Pegasus Spyware to Operations in 45 Countries', Citizen Lab, 18 September 2018.
16. Joseph Cox, 'NSO Group Pitched Phone Hacking Tech to American Police', *Vice*, 12 May 2020.
17. 'Team', Genesis Partners.
18. Amitai Ziv, 'Israeli Cyberattack Firm NSO Bought Back by Founders at $1b Company Value', *Haaretz*, 14 February 2019.
19. Abhijit Ahaskar, 'Activists Fighting for Release of Bhima Koregaon 11 Targeted by Spyware in 2019: Amnesty', *Mint*, 17 June 2020.
20. Pedro Tavares, 'NetWire malware: What It Is, How It Works and How to Prevent It', Infosec, 25 November 2022.
21. Anthony Boadle, 'Brazil's Rousseff Calls off State Visit to US Over Spying', *Reuters*, 18 September 2013.
22. Zack Whittaker, 'Mueller Report Sheds New Light on How the Russians Hacked the DNC and the Clinton Campaign', *Tech Crunch*, 4 April 2019.
23. 'Pegasus: India Parliament Opens Amid Furore over Pegasus "lies"', BBC.
24. 'Independent UN rights experts call for 'immediate investigation' into alleged Bezos phone hack by Saudi Arabia', UN News, 22 January 2020.
25. For an exhaustive examination of this phenomenon, read Shoshana Zuboff, *The Age of Surveillance Capitalism: The Fight for a Human Future at the New Frontier of Power*, New York: PublicAffairs, 2020.
26. Andrew Hilts, Christopher Parsons, and Jeffrey Knockel, 'Every Step You Fake: A Comparative Analysis of Fitness Tracker Privacy and Security', Open Effect, 2 February 2016.
27. Latanya Sweeney, 'Simple Demographics Often Identify People Uniquely', Carnegie Mellon University, Data Privacy Working Paper 3, Pittsburgh 2000.

28. Eileen Guo, 'A Roomba Recorded a Woman on the Toilet. How Did Screenshots End up on Facebook?', *MIT Technology Review*, 19 December 2022.
29. Aron Darmody and Detlev Zwick, 'Manipulate to Empower: Hyper-relevance and the Contradictions of Marketing in the Age of Surveillance Capitalism', *Big Data & Society*, 7.1, 2020, 2053951720904112.
30. Subrat Patnaik, Lewis Krauskopf and Paresh Dave, 'Analysis: For Google, Plenty of Cash with Nowhere to Go', *Reuters*, 29 April 2021.
31. Chun Siong Soon, et al., 'Unconscious Determinants of Free Decisions in the Human Brain', *Nature Neuroscience*, Vol. 11, 543–45, 2008.
32. Annabelle Lever, 'Privacy Rights and Democracy: A Contradiction in Terms?', *Contemporary Political Theory*, 5.2, 2006, 142–62.
33. 'Privacy Online: Fair Information Practices in the Electronic Marketplace—A Report to Congress', Federal Trade Commission, May 2000.
34. Zuboff, *The Age of Surveillance Capitalism*, New York: PublicAffairs, 2019.
35. Sarah Krouse, 'How Google Spies on Its Employees', The Information, 23 September 2021.
36. 'Letter from Larry Page and Sergey Brin', US Securities and Exchange Commission, Exhibit 99.3.
37. Denyse O'Leary, 'Is Google a Cult? Or Does It Just Act That Way?', Mind Matters, 14 August 2019.
38. Francesca Giuliani-Hoffman, 'How the Washington Post has changed under Jeff Bezos', *CNN Business*, 16 August 2019.
39. Amy Chozick and David Gelles, 'Time Magazine Is Bought by Marc Benioff, Salesforce Billionaire', *New York Times*, 16 September 2018.
40. Gian M. Volpicelli, 'Jeff Bezos Has Given a Masterclass in How to Respond to Blackmail', *Wired*, 8 February 2019.
41. Theo Zenou, 'A novel predicted the metaverse (and hyperinflation) 30 years ago', *Washington Post*, 30 June 2022.
42. Daniel Ruby, 'Roblox Statistics 2023 — (Users, Revenue & Trends)', Demand Sage, 31 July 2023.
43. Eric Schmidt and Jared Cohen, *The New Digital Age: Transforming Nations, Businesses, and Our Lives*, London: Vintage, 2014.
44. 'Share of Desktop Search Traffic Originating from Google in Selected Countries as of April 2023', Statista.

45. 'Google Agrees to Change Its Business Practices to Resolve FTC Competition Concerns in the Markets for Devices Like Smart Phones, Games and Tablets, and in Online Search', Federal Trade Commission, 3 January 2013.
46. Billy Perrigo, '"The Capabilities Are Still There." Why Cambridge Analytica Whistleblower Christopher Wylie Is Still Worried', *Time*, 8 October 2019.
47. 'Hearing Before the United States Senate Committee on the Judiciary: Testimony of Mark Zuckerberg, Facebook, Inc.', US Senate Committee on the Judiciary, 17 November 2020.
48. Arya Hodjat, 'Facebook Faces First Fine in Data Scandal Involving Cambridge Analytica', VOA, 11 July 2018.
49. 'FTC Imposes $5 Billion Penalty and Sweeping New Privacy Restrictions on Facebook', Federal Trade Commission, 24 July 2019.
50. 'Facebook to Pay $100 Million for Misleading Investors About the Risks It Faced from Misuse of User Data', US Securities and Exchange Commission, 24 July 2019
51. Patricia Zengerle and Richard Cowan, 'Trump watched Jan. 6 US Capitol Riot Unfold on TV, Ignored Pleas to Call for Peace', Reuters, 22 July 2022.
52. Hannah Mia, 'Trump tweets Amid Violent Capitol Hill Insurrection as Leaders Beg Him to Address the Nation', CNBC, 6 January 2021.
53. 'Transcript: "Go Home"—Trump Tells Supporters Who Mobbed Capitol to Leave, Again Falsely Claiming Election Victory', WBUR, 6 January 2021.
54. Ibid.
55. Donald Trump. @TheRealDonaldTrump. Twitter.
56. Donald Trump. @TheRealDonaldTrump. Twitter.
57. 'Permanent suspension of @realDonaldTrump', Twitter Blog, 8 January 2021.
58. Bobby Allyn, 'Facebook Bans President Trump from Posting for the Rest of His Presidency', *NPR*, 7 January 2021.
59. Ibid.
60. Nick Clegg, 'In Response to Oversight Board, Trump Suspended for Two Years; Will Only Be Reinstated if Conditions Permit', Meta, 4 June 2021.
61. Sarah Kopit, 'Why Big Tech and Conservatives Are Clashing on Free

Speech', *Bloomberg*, 12 January 2021.

62. 'US House lawmakers introduce bipartisan bills to target Big Tech', *The Hindu*, 12 June 2021.
63. Rachel Myrow, 'Senate Antitrust Panel Appears Ready to Tussle with Big Tech', KQED, 22 September 2021.
64. Lina M. Khan, 'The Separation of Platforms and Commerce', *Columbia Law Review*, 119.4, 2019, 973–1098.
65. David McCabe, 'Amazon Says the New FTC Chair, Lina Khan, Should Recuse Herself from Investigations', *New York Times*, 30 June 2021
66. 'Countries with the largest digital populations in the world as of January 2023', Statista.
67. Timothy Philips, 'Five Charts That Explain the Rise of China's Technology Giants', Schroders, 27 September 2017.
68. Mario Glowik, 'Case study: Alibaba Group', in *Global Strategy in the Service Industries*, London: Routledge, 2017, 96–105.
69. Laura He, 'Tencent Is First Asian Company to Top US$500 Billion in Value, Joining Apple and Facebook', *South China Morning Post*, 20 November 2017.
70. Norihiko Shirouzu and Paul Lienert, 'China Ride-hailing Giant Didi Eyes Purpose-built Fleet as Auto Market Shifts', Reuters, 24 April 2018.
71. Scott Murdoch, Samuel Shen and Selena Li, 'China's New Rules for Offshore Listings Spark Concern about Lengthy Approval Process', Reuters, 21 February 2023.
72. George Calhoun. 'What Really Happened to Jack Ma?', *Forbes*, 24 June 2021.
73. Ibid.
74. 'Document 32016R0679', EUR-Lex, 4 May 2016.
75. 'Everything Is Stupid—The Metaverse', The Daily Show, 17 March 2022.
76. Matt Krantz, '13 Firms Hoard $1 Trillion In Cash (We're Looking at You Big Tech)', *Investor's Business Daily*, 2 March 2022.
77. Samuel Stolton, 'Elon Musk's Dream Ideas', *Guardian*, 18 February 2018.
78. Isaac Chotiner, 'Why Elon Musk Bought Twitter', *New Yorker*, 26 April 2022.
79. Vlad Savov, 'Musk's Grand Vision for "Free Speech" On Twitter Faces Reality Check in Asia', *Japan Times*, 3 May 2022.
80. 'Bill Gates doubts Musk's Twitter buy', CTV News, 5 May 2022.

81. Vlad Savov, Jeff Bezos Takes Aim at Musk's Twitter Deal with China Jibe', *Bloomberg*, 26 April 2022.

7. The Eroding Human Connect

1. 'Pillow Talk', Little Riot.
2. Ashley Carman, 'The Kissenger Simulates Kissing Your Long-distance Lover', *The Verge*, 29 December 2016.
3. 'Get You', Genius, 18 April 2018.
4. 'And I Love Her', Mojim.
5. 'Papa Loves Mama Lyrics', JioSaavn.
6. F. Lehmann, A. Pedro, Antonio Bolivar G, and Rodolfo Quintero R, 'Russell E. Marker. Pioneer of the Mexican Steroid Industry', *Journal of Chemical Education*, Vol. 50, 3, 1973, 195.
7. 'The Birth Control Pill: A History', Planned Parenthood.
8. Sarah Bridge, 'A History of the Pill', *Guardian*, 12 September 2007.
9. 'The Birth Control Pill: A History', Planned Parenthood.
10. Claudia Goldin and Lawrence F. Katz, 'The Power of the Pill: Oral Contraceptives and Women's Career and Marriage Decisions', *Journal of Political Economy*, Vol. 110,4, 2002, 730–70.
11. Leila Hessini, 'Abortion and Islam: Policies and Practice in the Middle East and North Africa', *Reproductive Health Matters*, Vol. 15(29), 2007: 75–84.
12. Hamoun Rozati, Thomas Handley, and Channa Jayasena, 'Process and Pitfalls of Sperm Cryopreservation', *Journal of Clinical Medicine*, 2017, Vol. 6(9), 89.
13. 'Fertility & Reproductive Health: Egg Freezing', UCLA Health.
14. Anthony Giddens, *The Transformation of Intimacy: Sexuality, Love and Eroticism in Modern Societies*, New Jersey: John Wiley & Sons, 2013.
15. Ibid.
16. Eva Illouz, *Cold Intimacies: The Making of Emotional Capitalism*, Cambridge: Polity, 2007.
17. Anna Brown, 'A Profile of Single Americans', Pew Research Center, 20 August 2020.
18. Amanda Barroso, 'Key Takeaways on Americans' Views of and Experiences with Dating and Relationships', Pew Research Center, 20 August 2020.

19. S. Kennedy and S. Ruggles, 'Breaking Up Is Hard to Count: The Rise of Divorce in the United States, 1980–2010', *Demography*, 51, 587–98, 2014.
20. Ibid.
21. Ibid.
22. Ibid.
23. Ibid.
24. Juliana Menasce Horowitz, Nikki Graf, and Gretchen Livingston, 'Marriage and Cohabitation in the US', Pew Research Center, 6 November 2019.
25. Ibid.
26. Luce Irigaray, *An Ethics of Sexual Difference*, Ithaca: Cornell University Press, 1993.
27. Myisha Battle, 'Sex Coaching is the New Frontier of Sexology', Medium, 24 August 2016.
28. Melissa Lin, 'Online Dating Industry: The Business of Love', Toptal.
29. Ibid.
30. Second Life, https://secondlife.com/.
31. Mitch Wagner, 'Sex in Second Life', InformationWeek, 26 May 2007.
32. Ross Benes, 'Porn Could Have a Bigger Economic Influence on the US than Netflix', Quartz, 20 June 2018.
33. Sam Horton, 'The Porn Industry Leads Streaming Services in User Data Mining', My Tech Decisions, 2 January 2019.
34. Surbhi Gupta, 'Top 10 Most Porn Watching Countries in the World, Pakistan on the First Position', *Daily News Post*, 21 July 2021,.
35. Stephen Maddison, '"Make Love Not Porn": Entrepreneurial Voyeurism, Agency and Affect', in *Networked Affect*, eds. Susanna Paasonen, Ken Hillis, and Michael Petit, (Cambridge: MIT Press, 2014).
36. Esther Perel, *Mating in Captivity: Reconciling the Erotic and the Domestic* (HarperCollins, 2006).
37. Juliana Horowitz, Nikki Graf and Gretchen Livingston, 'Marriage and Cohabitation in the US', Pew Research Center 6 November 2019.
38. 'Our Epidemic of Loneliness and Isolation: The US Surgeon General's Advisory on the Healing Effects of Social Connection and Community', US Department of Health and Human Services.
39. Bianca DiJulio, Liz Hamel, Cailey Muñana, and Mollyann Brodie, 'Loneliness and Social Isolation in the United States, the United Kingdom, and Japan: An International Survey', KFF, 30 August 2018.

40. National Academies, *Social Isolation and Loneliness in Older Adults: Opportunities for the Health Care System*, 2020.
41. Vivek H. Murthy, *Together: Loneliness, Health and What Happens When We Find Connection*, London: Profile Books, 2020.
42. Ibid.
43. 'Loneliness in America: How the Pandemic Has Deepened an Epidemic of Loneliness and What We Can Do About It', Making Caring Common Project, February 2021.
44. Colleen Walsh, 'Young Adults Hardest Hit by Loneliness During Pandemic', *The Harvard Gazette*, 17 February 2021.
45. Bonnie Berkowitz and Chris Alcantara, 'The Terrible Numbers That Grow with Each Mass Shooting', *Washington Post*, 9 May 2021.
46. Aili herself is in a polyamorous relationship with 5 men, of which 2 relationships are platonic.
47. V. Kumar, 'Causes of Divorce in India: An Analysis', *NLUA Law & Policy Review*, Vol. 1 no. 1, 2015, 48–60.
48. A. Dutt, 'How and Why Number of Young Indian Couples Getting Divorced Has Risen Sharply', *Hindustan Times*, 4 January 2015, New Delhi.
49. 'The Essential Clayton Christensen Articles', *Harvard Business Review*, 24 January 2020.
50. Nida Fazli, 'Kaumi Yak Jehati', Rekhta.

8. The Seven Unravelments

1. Michael Bennon and Francis Fukuyama, 'China's Road to Ruin: The Real Toll of Beijing's Belt and Road', *Foreign Affairs*, 22 August 2023.
2. Vitor Gaspar, Paulo Medas, and Roberto Perrelli, 'Global Debt Reaches a Record $226 Trillion', *IMF Blog*, 15 December 2021.
3. Michael Pettis, 'How Does Excessive Debt Hurt an Economy?', Carnegie Endowment for International Peace, 8 February 2022.
4. Ibid.
5. Rana Mitter and Elsbeth Johnson, 'What the West Gets Wrong About China: Three Fundamental Misconceptions', *Harvard Business Review*, May–June 2021.

6. Steven Pressman, 'The Decline of the Middle Class: An International Perspective'', *Journal of Economic Issues*, Vol.41 no.1, 2007: 181–200.
7. Kellie Woodhouse, 'Health Care and Higher Ed', Inside Higher Ed, 19 July 2015.
8. Ibid
9. Daniel Vaughan-Whitehead, ed. *Europe's Disappearing Middle Class?: Evidence from the World of Work* (Cheltenham: Edward Elgar Publishing, 2016).
10. Jake Frankenfield, 'What Is Middle Class Income? The Latest Numbers Available', Investopedia, 14 March 2023.
11. Study by the National Council of Applied Economic Research quoted in Anirudh Krishna and Devendra Bajpai, 'Layers in Globalising Society and the New Middle Class in India: Trends, Distribution and Prospects', *Economic and Political Weekly*, Vol. 50, no. 5, 2015, 69–77.
12. Jonathan Ablett et al., 'The "Bird of Gold": The Rise of India's Consumer Market', McKinsey & Company, 1 May 2007.
13. Amitav Ghosh, 'The Great Uprooting: Migration and Displacement in an Age of Planetary Crisis', *The Massachusetts Review*.
14. Sukriti Vats, '35% Senior Citizens in India Suffer Abuse by Sons, 21% by Daughters-in-law, Finds Survey', *The Print*, 15 June 2022.
15. '"Depressed" Shraddha Had Red-Flagged Aftab's Anger Issues, Reveals Doc Who Advised Mehrauli Murder Victim', *News 18*, 18 November 2022.
16. Ibid.
17. Leo Sands, 'Pakistan Floods: One Third of Country Is Under Water – Minister', *BBC News*, 30 August 2022.
18. 'East Africa Hit by Drought, Yet Kenya's Lake Turkana Is Flooding', *BBC News*, 18 October 2022.
19. Yuen Meikeng, 'Flooded with Haunting Memories, *The Star*, 18 December 2022, 18 December 2022.
20. Louise Boyle, 'Europe Was Blighted by Unprecedented Heat, Drought and Fires in 2022 – And More Is on the Way', *The Independent*, 20 April 2023.
21. 'Thousands Evacuate, Several Homes Destroyed After Large Fire Erupts in Northern California', CBS News, 2 September 2022.
22. 'Weather-related Disasters Increase Over Past 50 Years, Causing More Damage but Fewer Deaths', World Meteorological Organization, 31 August 2012.

23. 'The Paris Agreement', United Nations Climate Change.
24. 'Emissions Gap Report 2022', UNEP, 27 October 2022.
25. 'Inadequate Progress on Climate Action Makes Rapid Transformation of Societies Only Option – UNEP', UNEP, 27 October 2022.
26. Ula Chrobak, 'Solar Power Got Cheap. So Why Aren't We Using It More?', *Popular Science*, 8 October 2021.
27. 'The World Needs More Diverse Solar Panel Supply Chains to Ensure a Secure Transition to Net Zero Emissions', IEA, 7 July 2022.
28. 'Clean Energy Supply Chains Vulnerabilities', IEA.
29. Servet Yanatma, 'Europe's "Energy War" in Data: How Have EU Imports Changed Since Russia's Invasion of Ukraine?', Euronews.green, 24 February 2023.
30. 'Energy Fact Sheet: Why Does Russian Oil and Gas Matter?', IEA, 21 March 2022.
31. Maria Shagina, 'Russia's Demise as an Energy Superpower, *Survival*, 64:4, 2022, 105–10.
32. Daniel Yergin, *The New Map: Energy, Climate, and the Clash of Nations*, London: Penguin Books, 2020.
33. 'Climate Adaptation', United Nations.
34. Ibid.
35. 'Security Council Fails to Adopt Draft Resolution on Ending Ukraine Crisis, as Russian Federation Wields Veto', United Nations, 25 February 2022.
36. 'Yuval Harari Warns Humans Will Be "Hacked" If Artificial Intelligence Is Not Globally Regulated', CBS News, 29 October 2021.
37. Sean Dodson, 'Was Software Responsible for the Financial Crisis?', *Guardian*, 16 October 2008.
38. Yuval Noah Harari, *Homo Deus: A Brief History of Tomorrow*, London: Vintage, 2016.
39. Murray Shanahan, *The Technological Singularity*, Cambridge: MIT press, 2015.
40. 'China Foreign Exchange Reserves', Trading Economics.
41. James Dobbins, Howard J. Shatz, and Ali Wyne, 'Russia Is a Rogue, Not a Peer; China Is a Peer, Not a Rogue', *Rand*.
42. 'Energy Fact Sheet: Why does Russian oil and gas matter?', IEA, 21 March 2022.
43. Gustavo Ferreira and Jamie Critelli, 'China's Global Monopoly on Rare-Earth Elements', Parameters Vol. 52, no. 1, 2022: 57-72.

44. 'US Treasury Announces Unprecedented & Expansive Sanctions Against Russia, Imposing Swift and Severe Economic Costs', US Department of the Treasury, 24 February 2022.
45. Colin Weiss, 'Geopolitics and the US Dollar's Future as a Reserve Currency', *International Finance Discussion Paper* 1359, Washington: Board of Governors of the Federal Reserve System.
46. 'Global China: US–China Relations Through the Lens of Technology Competition—A Conversation with Tarun Chhabra' Brooking Institution, 30 September 2022.
47. 'Taiwan's Dominance of the Chip Industry Makes It More Important', *The Economist*, 6 March 2023.
48. 'Fact Sheet: Chips and Science Act Will Lower Costs, Create Jobs, Strengthen Supply Chains, and Counter China', The White House, 9 August 2022.
49. Alan Crawford, Jarrell Dillard, Helene Fouquet, and Isabel Reynolds, 'The World Is Dangerously Dependent on Taiwan for Semiconductors', *Bloomberg*, 26 January 2021.
50. Pieter Haeck, 'The Dutch Get Ensnared in US–China Chips Fight', *Politico*, 5 January 2023.
51. Maria Demertzis, 'The Critical Importance of Chips – And Having a Plan for Them', *Bruegel*, 17 October 2022.
52. Zeyi Yang, 'China just fought back in the semiconductor exports war. Here's what you need to know', *MIT Technology Review*, 10 July 2023.
53. Ibid.

9. The End of an Age

1. 'Arthur Miller: "An era can be said to end when its basic illusions are exhausted"', Economic Sociology & Political Economy.
2. Barbara Taylor, 'Feminism and the Enlightenment 1650-1850', *History Workshop Journal*, no. 47, 1999, 261–72, *JSTOR*.
3. Margaret C Jacob, 'The Mental Landscape of the Public Sphere: A European Perspective', *Eighteenth-century Studies*, 28.1, 1994: 95–113.
4. Benjamin M. Friedman, 'The Moral Case for Growth', *International Economy*, 19.4, 2005: 40.
5. Katie Reilly, 'Read Hillary Clinton's "Basket of Deplorables" Remarks About Donald Trump Supporters', *Time*.

6. Khiara M. Bridges, 'The Deserving Poor, the Undeserving Poor, and Class-Based Affirmative Action', *Emory LJ*, 66, 2016: 1049.
7. Richard Snyder, 'Beyond Electoral Authoritarianism: The Spectrum of Nondemocratic Regimes', In *Electoral Authoritarianism: The Dynamics of Unfree Competition*, Lynne Rienner, 2006, ed. Andreas Schedler, 219–31.
8. Susan Jacoby, *The Age of American Unreason*, Vintage, 2009.
9. Jörn Rüsen and Bill Templer, 'Historical Enlightenment in the Light of Postmodernism: History in the Age of the "New Unintelligibility"', *History and Memory*, Vol. 1, no. 1, 1989, 109–31. *JSTOR*.

10. The Age of Meta-Reason

1. Tim Blanning, *The Romantic Revolution*, London: Hachette, 2012.
2. Sebastian Conrad, 'Enlightenment in Global History: A Historiographical Critique', *The American Historical Review*, Vol. 117, Issue 4, October 2012, 999–1027.
3. Šimić, Goran, Mladenka Tkalčić, Vana Vukić, Damir Mulc, Ena Španić, Marina Šagud, Francisco E. Olucha-Bordonau, Mario Vukšić, and Patrick R. Hof, 'Understanding Emotions: Origins and Roles of the Amygdala,' *Biomolecules* Vol. 11, no. 6, 2021: 823.
4. Roger A. Frie, ed., *Understanding Experience: Psychotherapy and Postmodernism*, Oxfordshire: Routledge, 2004.
5. 'Experimental Evidence for General Relativity', Britannica.
6. Zeeya Merali, 'Quantum "Spookiness" Passes Toughest Test Yet', *Nature*, 525, 14–15, 2015.
7. See introduction of Hubert Cheung, et al., 'Understanding Traditional Chinese Medicine to Strengthen Conservation Outcomes', *People and Nature*, Vol. 3 no. 1, 2021: 115–123.
8. Lilie Chouliaraki, 'Victimhood: The Affective Politics of Vulnerability', *European Journal of Cultural Studies*, Vol. 24 no. 1, 2021: 10–27.
9. Kathryn Schaffer and Gabriela Barreto Lemos, 'Obliterating Thingness: An Introduction to the "What" and the "So What" of Quantum Physics', *Foundational Science*, 26, 7–26, 2021.
10. 'A Quantum Experiment Suggests There's No Such Thing as Objective Reality', *MIT Technology Review*, 12 March 2019.
11. 'Gödel's Incompleteness Theorems', Stanford Encyclopedia of Philosophy.

12. Alfred Driessen, 'Philosophical Consequences of the Gödel theorem', 2005.
13. Tom Burns, and Ewa Roszkowska, 'Rational Choice Theory: Toward a Psychological, Social, and Material Contextualization of Human Choice Behavior', *Theoretical Economics Letters*, 6.2, 2016: 195–207.
14. Willem J. Schurink, 'Qualitative Research in Management and Organisational Studies with Reference to Recent South African Research', *SA Journal of Human Resource Management*, 1.3, 2003: 2–14.
15. So, *China's Developmental Miracle*.
16. Jin Kai, 'The Chinese Communist Party's Confucian Revival', *The Diplomat*, 13 September 2014.
17. Ibid.
18. 'How Did Confucianism Win Back the Chinese Communist Party?', *The Economist*, 23 June 2021.
19. Itty Abraham, 'From Bandung to NAM: Non-alignment and Indian foreign policy, 1947–65', *Commonwealth & Comparative Politics*, Vol. 46 no. 2(2008): 195–219.
20. Study by the National Council of Applied Economic Research quoted in Anirudh Krishna and Devendra Bajpai, 'Layers in Globalising Society and the New Middle Class in India: Trends, Distribution and Prospects', *Economic and Political Weekly*, Vol. 50, no. 5, 2015, 69–77.
21. 'India to Remain Fastest-Growing Major Economy: World Bank', *The Economic Times*, 7 June 2023.
22. Billy Perrigo, 'DeepMind's CEO Helped Take AI Mainstream. Now He's Urging Caution', *Time*, 12 January 2023.
23. Agence France-Presse, 'Go Game Master Quits Saying Machines "Cannot Be Defeated"', *Guardian*, 27 November 2019.
24. Abid Haleem, Mohd Javaid, and Ravi Pratap Singh, 'An Era of ChatGPT as a Significant Futuristic Support Tool: A Study on Features, Abilities, and Challenges', *BenchCouncil Transactions on Benchmarks, Standards and Evaluations*, Vol. 2 no. 4, (2022): 100089.
25. 'Cogito, Ergo Sum', Britannica.
26. Christof Koch, 'Will Machines Ever Become Conscious?', *Scientific American*, 1 December 2019.
27. Bhagavad Gita, Chapter 13, verses 13–15

ACKNOWLEDGEMENTS

This book didn't take very long to write but its conceptualization and research seemed to take ages. Professor Rajen Gupta was by my side through much of that uncertain process with invaluable feedback and encouragement.

Given that the contents of the book span a wide array of topics, I needed a reliable set of readers to check if I was on the right track. Nikash Pandey, Chandrika Mago, Gautam Kumar, Abeer Kapoor, Ranjit Shastri, Vinay Singh, KT Ravindran, Dunu Roy, Latika Thukral, Neelam Ahluwalia, Rajat Gururaj, Ozair Ansari, Madhushree Nanda, Puneet Bindlish, Rajnish Wadehra, Reema Bhatia, Professor Sanil V., Prof. Satish Jain and Gurbachan Singh provided key inputs at various stages of the writing process.

My father, P.S. Prasad, was one of the small set of readers I had in mind when writing this book. His validation of the first draft was a shot in the arm. My mother-in-law, Geeta Mathur, the mistress of spices of the Konarika kitchen, ensured I remained as far as possible from the image of the famished writer with her sumptuous home deliveries.

Several batches of students at the Management Development Institute-Gurgaon were the 'guinea pigs' for a lot of the material covered in this book. My appreciation goes to them for their insights and feedback.

Thanks to Alka Gauri Ma'am for the music, Amanda Besyedin for the dancing, and Shifra Arwas for the laughter. And gratitude to Paramahansa Yogananda for bringing meditation into my life.

My editor at Hachette India, Sonali Jindal, and the copy editor, Ananya Bhatia, made this book better with their gentle nudges. My thanks to them.

The late Samir Mathur ('Sam Cha') loved to dance and enjoyed railing against the ideology of rationality. I think he would have got a kick from this book and its title.

The late John Mason was a most inspiring and generous principal for generations of school students, including me. I had hoped to re-establish contact with him after many years with this book. In my mind, the first copy goes to him.

INDEX